This is the textbook, now in a considerably revised and upd[ated form, that I first used] many years ago as a new Bible translator and then later as a t[ranslation consultant in Africa.] The book is a veritable *multum in parvo*, covering in the space of some 300 pages the vast field of Bible translation methodology (principles) and application (practice) – from initial research and project planning, to final draft testing and revision. I made frequent use of this text in many different aspects of teaching and fieldwork, with translators on various levels of academic education and actual experience.

Bible Translation is comprehensive in terms of content, yet also admirably clear, pedagogically sound, and demonstrably effective in getting the job done over the years. Indeed, it was written by the teacher who taught me. I can therefore recommend this text to serve as a primary resource in worldwide translator-training programs just as enthusiastically today as I did over three decades ago!

Ernst R. Wendland, PhD
Professor, Stellenbosch University
Former UBS Translation Consultant
Author of biblical, scholarly titles at UBS and SIL International

I warmly welcome the appearance of the fourth edition of Katharine Barnwell's seminal training manual, *Bible Translation: An Introductory Course in Translation Principles*. From its inception, this book was crafted to equip speakers of the world's lesser known languages to translate Scripture into the languages of their hearts. It is relentlessly practical and reflects a sound, measured, methodical pedagogy. Practical exercises are liberally interspersed in the text, which guide the student to apply theoretical lessons in specific, practical situations.

This fourth edition has updated content reflecting recent advances in Bible translation methodology, including the innovative Luke Partnership workshops. Weblinks are included for ancillary content such as PowerPoint presentations for use in group training sessions. Earlier editions were published in a form which allowed for translation and adaptation into French and other languages of wider communication, and I am grateful to see that this tradition continues in the fourth edition. I give this book my warmest endorsement as a sharp tool to equip saints around the world for fruitful works of service in the Bible translation cause.

Larry Jones, PhD
Senior Vice President Emeritus
Seed Company, a Wycliffe Bible Translators Affiliate

Katy Barnwell delivered the gold standard in introductory translation training with earlier editions of this ground-breaking training manual. And the gold standard keeps getting better! In addition to the basic concepts that we expect, this fourth edition takes advantage of continued advancement in related fields, such as communication theory and software tools. In addition, the user is given access to professionally produced PowerPoint slides to supplement the teaching. Many translators remain in Katy's debt!

Freddy Boswell, PhD
Former SIL Executive Director
Former SIL International Translation Coordinator
SIL Senior Translation Consultant
Linguist and Translation Advisor among the Cheke Holo people, Solomon Islands

I used an early draft of Katy Barnwell's book, *Bible Translation: An Introductory Course in Translation Principles*, third edition, translated into French, to train a Bible translator. With the *Manuel de traduction biblique* (1991), that translator was able to understand the translation process, and then explain it clearly to others. He now applies the manual as a consultant, training other Bible translators. In West Africa, in both Anglophone and Francophone areas, *Bible Translation* quickly became the basis of many translation principles courses. Without a doubt many of the translators and consultants working in these areas today began their journey with training based on Katy's book.

This fourth edition continues the tradition as a practical manual that teaches by guiding participants through the applied, interactive use of the many examples. It is suitable for one-on-one training, for teaching a group, and even for self-teaching. I would highly recommend it to anyone seeking to introduce translators to the principles of translation. In this fourth edition, PowerPoint presentations are linked electronically to each chapter for teaching the principles, which makes it even more valuable, making it a good resource for any translator or trainer of translators.

Ann White, MA Linguistics
Linguist and Translation Advisor among the Dogon people of Mali
Translation Consultant serving in West Africa
Seed Company, a Wycliffe Bible Translators Affiliate

Having been in the Bible translation ministry since 1978 and having used earlier editions of this book to train translators at many Introductory Courses in Translation Principles and at the Luke Partnership Programmes, I consider this manual the best manual ever made available for the training of translators, be they mother tongue speakers or otherwise.

The rearrangement of the subject matter in this version, in which the translation principles are taught first then followed by the procedures, is excellent. The revised table of contents makes it easy to reference a topic quickly and to search for a topic. Also helpful in this revised version is the content organisation, in which each chapter begins with an introduction of the topic followed by common English examples, then introduces other-language examples.

The fact that difficult topics like Unknown Ideas, Key Biblical Terms and the Meaning of Words are introduced at a later stage in the manual is helpful, especially for participants who are in the process of learning to translate for the first time.

I therefore endorse this revised version as a must-have manual for all Bible translators.

Danjuma Nanbol Gambo, MA Linguistics
Administrator, Luke Initiative for Scripture Translation
Instructor of Applied Linguistics and Translation Principles courses
Former Project Advisor to the Mumuye Language and Translation Project
Translation Consultant for the Mumuye NT Revision Project and the Etkwen (Ichen) Project

This is to me still the definitive Bible translator training manual, though published originally more than forty years ago. Born of the functional equivalence teachings of Nida and others in the 1960–70s, it is used today across the globe in all the major Bible translation organisations. I have used it for twenty years with the United Bible Societies, SIL International, the Seed Company, and with National Bible Translation Organization (NBTO) translators in Africa and Asia; trainees have ranged from those who had not completed primary-school to highly educated bishops and professors.

This edition has been updated with insights from Gutt, Wendland, Nord, and others. It includes additional Old Testament references, provides much on Paratext and gives many links to online resources. There are, of course, more sophisticated translation theories and critical approaches, but I have found those to be useless without the foundation which this book provides. Anyone with a basic knowledge of biblical languages and exegesis, and ability to use Paratext, who has worked through this book is fundamentally equipped to start translating the Bible.

Andy Warren-Rothlin, PhD
Global Translation Advisor, United Bible Societies
Former Professor of Hebrew, PhD Programme Director, Theological College of Northern Nigeria
Translation Consultant under GILLBT, Bible Society of Nigeria, UBS-Africa, UBS Global Mission Team

For more than four decades Katharine Barnwell's *Bible Translation* has been a primary resource for training Bible translators. But a revision was long overdue, and in my view, there is only one person who could do it properly. Dr Katy, as many of us like to call her, has done it for us. Several years of work have gone into this new edition. This is not just an update but a thorough revision that includes Old Testament examples and concerns, recent strategies and theoretical approaches, and advances in computing that contribute to our task. I commend Katy for undertaking such a large task, and I highly recommend this fourth edition of *Bible Translation* for the continuing task of training translators.

Robert "Bob" Carter, MA Linguistics, MA Hebrew Bible Translation
Former Linguist-Translator and Translation Advisor
Former International Translation Consultant, SIL International
Senior Translation Consultant, Seed Company

Bible Translation
An Introductory Course in Translation Principles

SIL International®

Series Editor
Susan McQuay

Managing Editor
Eric Kindberg

Editorial Staff
Gene Burnham, Volume Editor
James Weaver, Proofreader

Production Staff
Lois Gourley, Composition Director
Judy Benjamin, Compositor
Barbara Alber, Graphic Designer, author photo, and cover design

Bible Translation
An Introductory Course in Translation Principles

Fourth Edition

Katharine Barnwell

SIL International®
Dallas, TX USA

© 2020 by SIL International®
LCCN: 2020936476
ISBN: 978-1-55671-407-8

All rights reserved

No part of this publication may be reproduced, stored in a retrieval system, or transmitted in any form or by any means—electronic, mechanical, photocopy, recording, or otherwise—without the express permission of SIL International®. However, short passages, generally understood to be within the limits of fair use, may be quoted without permission.

First edition 1975
Second edition 1978
Third edition 1986
Reprinted 1992, 1994, 1998
Reformatted 2002, 2017
Fourth edition 2020

Data and materials collected by researchers in an era before documentation of permission was standardized may be included in this publication. SIL makes diligent efforts to identify and acknowledge sources and to obtain appropriate permissions wherever possible, acting in good faith and on the best information available at the time of publication.

Copies of this and other publications of SIL International® may be obtained through distributors such as Amazon, Barnes & Noble, other worldwide distributors and, for select volumes, publications.sil.org:

SIL International Publications
7500 W. Camp Wisdom Road
Dallas, TX 75236-5629 USA

General inquiry: publications_intl@sil.org
Pending order inquiry: sales_intl@sil.org

Scripture quotations identified as *ESV* or that are not identified as a specific Bible version are from the *ESV® Bible* (*The Holy Bible, English Standard Version®*), © 2001 by Crossway, a publishing ministry of Good News Publishers. All rights reserved. Used by permission.

Scripture quotations identified as *CEV* are taken from the *Contemporary English Version*, © 1991, 1992, 1995 by American Bible Society. Used by permission.

Scripture quotations identified as *GNT* are from the *Good News Translation in Today's English Version*, Second edition, © 1992 by American Bible Society. Used by permission.

Scripture quotations identified as *JBP* are taken from *The New Testament in Modern English*, © 1960, 1972 by J. B. Phillips. Administered by The Archbishops' Council of the Church of England. Used by permission.

Scripture quotations identified as *KJV* are from *The Authorized (King James) Version*. Rights in the *Authorized Version* in the United Kingdom are vested in the Crown. Reproduced by permission of the Crown's patentee, Cambridge University Press.

Scripture quotations identified as *NET* are from the *NET Bible®* © 1996–2016 by Biblical Studies Press, LLC. http://netbible.com. All rights reserved. Used by permission.

Scripture quotations identified as *NIV* are from the *Holy Bible, New International Version®*, *NIV®*, © 1973, 1978, 1984, 2011 by Biblica, Inc.® All rights reserved worldwide. Used by permission.

Scripture quotations identified as *NJB* are taken from the *New Jerusalem Bible*, © 1985 by Darton, Longman and Todd, Ltd., and Éditions du Cerf.

Scripture quotations identified as *NLT* are taken from the *Holy Bible, New Living Translation*, © 1996, 2004, 2015 by Tyndale House Foundation. All rights reserved. Used by permission of Tyndale House Publishers, Inc.

Scripture quotations identified as *REB* are taken from the *Revised English Bible*, © 1989 by Cambridge University Press and Oxford University Press. All rights reserved.

Scripture quotations identified as *RSV* are from the *Revised Standard Version of the Bible*, © 1946, 1952, 1971 by the National Council of Churches of Christ in the USA. All rights reserved. Used by permission.

Contents

Figures ix
Introduction xi
Abbreviations xv

Part 1: Translation Principles 1
   1. What Is Translation? 3
   2. Different Styles of Translation 9
   3. Some English Translations of the Bible 17
   4. More about Meaning-Based Translation 25
   5. Qualities of a Good Translation 29
   6. Towards Naturalness – Beginning to Explore the Receptor Language 39
   7. How We Communicate with One Another 47
   8. Communicating across Cultures and across Time 53
   9. More about Cross-Cultural Communication 59

Part 2: Translation Procedures 69
  10. A Ten-Step Procedure in Translation 71
  11. Step 1: Exegesis – Discovering the Meaning of the Source Text 77
  12. Step 2: Making the First Draft 83
  13. Keyboarding the Translation – An Introduction to the Paratext Program 87
  14. Step 3: Supplementary Helps – Book Introductions and Section Headings 91
  15. Step 3, *continued*: Supplementary Helps – Footnotes, Cross-References,
       Parallel Passages, Glossary, Illustrations, Maps, and More 97
  16. Step 4: The Team Check 101
  17. Step 5: Testing the Translation with the Receptor Community 105
  18. Step 6: Preparing for the Consultant Check – How to Make a Back Translation ... 113
  19. Step 7: Checking the Translation with a Consultant 119
  20. Steps 8 to 10: The Later Stages of the Translation Process 123
      Step 8: Reviewing and more testing – focus on reviewing 123
      Step 9: Final editing and consistency checking – preparing for publication 124
      Step 10: Final reading for approval by receptor-language church and
              community representatives 125

Part 3: Studying Words and How They Are Used (Lexical Meaning) 127
  21. Exploring the Meanings of Words 129

22. Translating Unknown Concepts 141
23. More on Translating Unknown Concepts 155
24. Translating Key Biblical Terms 161
25. Exploring Terms Referring to the Supernatural World 173

Part 4: More on Discovering the Meaning 177
26. Discovering the Meaning – Event Ideas 179
27. Discovering the Meaning – "Of" Phrases in English (Genitive Constructions) 185
28. Discovering the Meaning – Active and Passive Voice 193
29. Discovering the Meaning – Shortcuts 199
30. Discovering the Meaning – Complex Passages 201
31. Discovering the Meaning – Order of Events 207
32. Discovering the Meaning – Long and Short Sentences 211

Part 5: Figures of Speech and Other Challenges 213
33. Figures of Speech – Comparisons 215
34. Other Figures of Speech 229
35. Rhetorical Questions 241
36. Translation Challenges – A Review 251

Part 6: Discovering Your Language 255
37. Principles of Consistent Spelling 257
38. Different Kinds of Texts – Speech Genres 265
39. Discovering Your Language – How to Chart a Text 271
40. Pronoun Reference 277
41. Looking at the Big Picture – Discourse Perspective 285

Part 7: Planning and Organising a Bible Translation Project 299
42. The Role of the Churches and Community in a Translation Project – Translation Is Teamwork! 301
43. Preparing a Translation Brief 307
44. Planning and Organising a Translation Project – Discussion Topics 315

Appendix: The Cultural and Geographical Background of the Bible 319

References 321

Figures

Figure 1. A ten-step translation procedure 71
Figure 2. Display of a Paratext translation screen in the Malagasy-Bara language of Madagascar 88
Figure 3. Team check in progress 103
Figure 4. This screenshot illustrates the display for showing a back translation and the "interlinearizer" window, in the Malagasy-Bara language of Madagascar ... 116
Figure 5. Translation checking in progress 122
Figure 6. Local Bible translation project 304

Introduction

This training manual is addressed to those who are translating, or preparing to translate, the Bible into a language that they speak fluently, usually the language that they speak as their first language, also commonly referred to as their mother tongue. It can be used as a textbook during formal courses or in less formal training situations. The aim of the training is fourfold. Those who follow the course will

1. gain an in-depth understanding of the principles of Bible translation;
2. develop skills and learn procedures for using these principles to achieve meaningful translations that communicate the original author's message accurately and effectively to the new audience;
3. discover the beauty of their own language and develop a vision for communicating the Scriptures faithfully, using the rich resources of that language; and
4. experience the benefits of cooperation and teamwork in the translation process, adapting the procedures to fit the local situation.

Recognising the increasing focus on the translation of the Old Testament in recent years, this fourth edition of the manual includes more examples from the Old Testament and more exercises with Old Testament texts.

This edition also addresses issues relating to oral communication, both in drafting translations and in distributing the translated Scriptures. Audio transmission of the Scriptures has been an increased focus in recent years and distribution on mobile phones or other electronic devices, in addition to in printed form, will be discussed.

Another topic addressed in more detail in this new edition is the importance of identifying (a) the specific audience for whom a proposed translation is intended, (b) the situation in which that translation will be used, and (c) the purpose it is intended to achieve. The term *skopos* is used to refer to the "intended purpose and use" of a translation. This issue will be discussed in Part 7 of this manual, including a review of how to develop a "translation brief" that records the agreed goals and procedures for a project, taking into account the expectations and preferences of the receptor community concerned.

Translation theory

Theories of translation have been extensively discussed by others. This manual aims to help translators apply insights from these theories in their translation work.

The translation principles presented in the first edition, published in 1975, were developed from *The Theory and Practice of Translation*, by E. A. Nida and C. R. Taber, 1969, and from *Translating the Word of God*, by J. Beekman and J. C. Callow, 1974. The goal of a translation is to communicate to a new audience the meaning equivalent to that which is communicated in the source text, focusing on the message that is being communicated rather than on its form, using the natural, idiomatic form of the receptor language. "Equivalent meaning" includes both the content of the message and the intended impact of the message, reflecting the attitude and emotions of the original author. This approach to translation was further developed by de Waard and Nida in *From One Language to Another: Functional Equivalence in Bible Translating*, 1986, and by others. (See chapter 2.)

While these principles are still foundational, this edition also aims to help translators apply insights on the nature of communication, especially cross-cultural communication, developed by Ernst-August Gutt (*Translation and Relevance: Cognition and Context*, second edition 2000) and others. A good communicator has in mind the person or people to whom he is communicating and adjusts the form of his message accordingly. The situation of the person receiving the message and interpreting its meaning must also be considered. The biblical authors wrote their messages for people living at a very different time in history, having a very different cultural background, bringing different knowledge and assumptions to their understanding of the text. These issues are discussed and illustrated in chapters 7, 8, and 9.

It is not the purpose of this manual to promote any single theory of translation, but to demonstrate how different insights and approaches can help translators find effective solutions to translation challenges.

Translation practice

Translation practice is an important part of the training program. The best way to learn to translate is by translating. Practice in translation is an integral part of the training process. It is suggested that translators-in-training choose an initial translation goal with consideration of the long-term plans for the project in which they are, or will be, involved as translators. The section headed "Translation practice" at the end of chapter 9 lists some suggestions for initial translation practice. As trainee translators study the principles and procedures presented, they will apply these to the translation of the passages they have chosen as their initial goal, as well as to the translation practice exercises included in each chapter.

Additional resources

At the end of many chapters, and occasionally in the text, information is provided that enables users of this book to access PowerPoint presentations and other presentations and documents on the topics being taught. These materials are referred to as "*BT4* online materials," and are available from SIL International via the internet at **publications.sil.org/bibletranslation_additionalmaterials**. Each resource link has a number preceding the title which corresponds to the textbook chapter number.

To access these materials, copy the bolded URL above into your web browser, then scroll down to select the item from the index provided, and click to open. These resources can also be downloaded.

Introduction

Also listed at the end of some chapters are (a) links to websites that are relevant to the topic concerned, and (b) suggestions for further reading on this topic, sometimes including links (URLS) providing direct access to the item concerned.[1]

Acknowledgement and appreciation

I deeply appreciate the help of all those who have contributed to the development of these training materials, as we have worked together internationally, developing and using the materials in introductory courses in Bible translation, Luke Partnership workshops, and in other ways, over many years. I want to mention specifically the contribution of Stephen Payne for developing selected PowerPoints, incorporating graphics, of Ernst-August Gutt for sharing recent insights on cross-cultural communication, and of Tony Pope for sharing his perception on exegetical issues. Examples from many different languages have been contributed by translators and other colleagues, including Lee Ballard, Daniel Gya, Yaluna Yiljep, and Bev Erasmus. Janet Stahl and Margaret Hill have shared insights on audio and visual productions and on crafting stories, and Helen Abbot has been quick to help resolve software challenges. Sincere thanks also to those translators, translation teams, and other individuals who have graciously allowed their photographs to be used to illustrate different aspects of translation work. And special thanks to the Global Publishing team for their patience and skill in their roles as editors, and to Gayle Sheehan for processing the online materials.

> It is widely recognised in the world today that both men and women have responsible roles as Bible translators, as translation consultants, and in other tasks relating to Bible translation. Regrettably, the English language does not have a third person singular pronoun that covers both men and women. Please understand that, in this manual, when making general statements about translation personnel, the pronoun "he" is used generically, to include both men and women. This is to avoid the tedium of repeating "he or she," or the use of the unpronounceable form "s/he." Thank you for your forbearance!

> In this manual, Scripture quotations in English that are not identified as a specific Bible version are from the *ESV® Bible* (*The Holy Bible, English Standard Version®*). ESV has been chosen for this purpose because it aims to retain transparency with the form of the original language Hebrew or Greek text, keeping the original sentence structure and idioms as closely as possible.

A note on terminology

In earlier editions of this training manual the term "mother tongue translator" was used, to refer to translators who speak the receptor language as their first language. This group of translators was thus distinguished from translators who learned the language as adults and, while working closely with first-language speakers of the language, were primarily responsible for the translation.

---

[1] In this textbook, *Bible Translation: An Introductory Course in Translation Principles*, 4th ed., will be abbreviated to *Bible Translation*. In cross references it is further abbreviated to "*BT4*."

Nowadays in the great majority of Bible translation projects, the translators speak the receptor language as their first language, often still referred to as their "mother tongue."

It has been pointed out that the language a person learns from his mother or primary care giver is not always the same as the language that he knows best or uses most extensively, or which he identifies as his own language. In this manual, therefore, the term "first language" is used to refer to any of the following situations:

1) the language that the speaker has learned from early childhood through contact with parents or primary caregivers, or
2) the language that he has learned fluently through growing up in a bilingual or multilingual context, or
3) the language that, for other reasons, he knows best or identifies with as his own language. This may apply in situations where several languages are widely used, or where a people group has shifted their location, or where immigration has taken place.

In this textbook, the trainee translator is frequently addressed directly. The term "your language" is therefore also used to refer to the translator's first language.

See further the extensive discussion of the term "mother tongue" and related terms in collected papers in the forthcoming volume, *Language and Identity in a Multilingual, Migrating World*, edited by J. Steven Quakenbush and Gary F. Simons, 2020, SIL International. See especially the following papers:

Sangsok Son. "Translanguaging, identity and education in our multilingual world."

Simons, Gary F. "'Heart language' as a technical term: A critical review."

Abbreviations

Bible versions referred to:

CEV	*Contemporary English Version*
ESV	*English Standard Version*
GNT	*Good News Translation,* also known as the *Good News Bible* and *Today's English Version*
JBP	*The New Testament in Modern English* (J. B. Phillips' translation)
JB	*Jerusalem Bible*
KJV	*King James Version*
NET	*NET Bible*
NASB	*New American Standard Bible*
NEB	*New English Bible*
NIV	*New International Version*
NJB	*New Jerusalem Bible*
NLT	*New Living Translation*
REB	*Revised English Bible*
RNJB	*Revised New Jerusalem Bible*
RSV	*Revised Standard Version*

Other abbreviations:

BT4	*Bible Translation: An Introductory Course in Translation Principles* (4th edition)

Part 1

Translation Principles

Chapter 1

What Is Translation?

Welcome to the study of Bible translation! This course is designed to train those who are involved in translating Scripture into their own language, or who are preparing for this task.

In this first chapter, we begin by looking at some examples of translation, seeking to discover what happens when translation takes place.

1.1 Some examples of translation

Read the following story (adapted from Fox 1959:175), which was first told in the K'iche' (Quiché) language of Guatemala:

> It is said that being one man not from here, not known where the his or the he comes where. One day these things he walks in a finca or in them the coast-lands, he saw his appearance one little necklace, or he thought that a little necklace the very pretty thrown on the ground in the road. He took the necklace this he threw in his mouth for its cause that coming the one person another to his behindness, for his that not he encounters the one the following this way in his behindness, not he knows and that the necklace the he threw in his mouth this one snake and the man this one died right now because not he knows his appearance the snake or that the he ate this not this a necklace only probably this snake.

In this first version, each K'iche' word in the original story is replaced by the nearest English word.

Now compare this with another version of the same story:

> There is a story about a certain man. He didn't come from this part of the world, and indeed, I don't know where he came from. One day this man was walking in the coastlands (in a "finca" as they say), when he saw a little necklace, or rather, what he thought was a very pretty little necklace, lying in the road. There was someone coming along behind him, so he grabbed this necklace and threw it into his mouth, because he didn't want that other person to see it. Well, he did not know that the necklace that he threw in his mouth was really a snake. And the man died there and then because he did not recognise that

particular kind of snake, and did not know that the thing he put in his mouth was not a necklace at all, but a snake.

For discussion

☐ Why is the first version difficult to understand?
☐ Does the first version communicate the meaning of the story?
☐ Note some of the changes that have been made in the second version.
☐ In your opinion, which of the two versions is the most faithful translation of the K'iche' story?
☐ In your own words, give a definition of a good translation.

> **What is translation? A definition for discussion**
>
> Translation is retelling, as exactly as possible, the *meaning* of the original message in a way that will be understood by the speakers of the language into which the translation is being made.

1.2 Some exercises: Practice in applying the definition of translation

Exercise 1

(1) Take a short passage written in your own language. Two or three sentences are enough. First, word-by-word, underneath each word in the language, write the English for that word. Does this make a translation that an English speaker will understand?

(2) Then make a clear translation, expressing the meaning of the passage in a natural way in English.

(3) Discuss your translation with someone who speaks English as their first language.

Exercise 2: Mark 2:19

Compare the different versions of Mark 2:19 that are given below and answer the questions that follow.

Greek text with word-for-word key in English

(Here and elsewhere, the Hebrew or Greek text has been written in English letters so that a person who does not know the Hebrew or Greek alphabet can read it.)

kai	eipen	autois	ho	Iēsous:	mē	dunantai
And	he-said	to-them	the	Jesus	not	they-are-able

hoi	huioi	tou	numphōnos,	en	hō	ho	numphios
the	sons	of-the	bridechamber,	in	which	the	bridegroom

met'	autōn	estin,	nēsteuein?	hoson	chronon	echousin	ton
with	them	he-is,	to-fast?	What	time	they-have	the

numphion	met'	autōn	ou	dunantai	nēsteuein.
bridegroom	with	them,	not	they-are-able	to-fast.

English version A (the word-for-word English key repeated)

And he-said to-them the Jesus, Not they-are-able the sons of-the bridechamber, in which the bridegroom with them he-is, to-fast? What time they-have the bridegroom with them, not they-are-able to-fast.

English version B (King James Version)

And Jesus said unto them, Can the children of the bridechamber fast, while the bridegroom is with them? As long as they have the bridegroom with them, they cannot fast.

English version C (New International Version)

Jesus answered, "How can the guests of the bridegroom fast while he is with them? They cannot, so long as they have him with them."

English version D (Good News Translation)

Jesus answered, "Do you expect the guests at a wedding party to go without food? Of course not! As long as the bridegroom is with them, they will not do that."

> *The expression "children of the bridechamber" is an idiom in the Greek language referring to the guests at a wedding, particularly the friends of the bridegroom. In one language where the expression "children of the bridechamber" was translated word-for-word, the people thought that it meant "the children who the bride has borne before her marriage." This fitted well with the custom of the area where it was considered a good thing for a woman to have borne children before her marriage as proof of her fertility! So beware! A translation that follows the words of the original message, word-for-word, may sometimes give a wrong meaning.*

Questions for exercise 2

(1) Comparing versions A and B, write down some ways in which the translator of version B has followed very closely the original Greek form. Is there anything in version B that readers might find hard to understand?

(2) Comparing versions B, C, and D, write down ways in which translators of versions C and D have re-expressed the meaning to help readers understand.

Remember

The words and expressions of each language are different. The way that words are arranged in sentences in each language is different. If the translator keeps too closely to the grammar and words of the original language, the translation may be
unnatural,
confusing, and
it may even give the wrong meaning.

Exercise 3: Mark 2:3–5

Compare the following versions of Mark 2:3–5 and answer the following questions:

A literal, word-for-word key to the original Greek text

And they-come carrying to him paralytic, being-carried by four. ⁴And not being-able to-bring to-him, because-of the crowd, they-removed the roof where he-was, and having-made-opening, they-lowered the mattress/stretcher where the paralytic was-lying. ⁵And having-seen the Jesus the faith of-them, he-says to-the paralytic, "Child, they-are-forgiven of-you the sins."

English version A (English Standard Version)

And they came, bringing to him a paralytic carried by four men. ⁴And when they could not get near him because of the crowd, they removed the roof above him, and when they had made an opening, they let down the bed on which the paralytic lay. ⁵And when Jesus saw their faith, he said to the paralytic, "Son, your sins are forgiven."

English version B (New International Version)

Some men came, bringing to him a paralyzed man, carried by four of them. ⁴Since they could not get him to Jesus because of the crowd, they made an opening in the roof above Jesus by digging through it, and then lowered the mat the man was lying on. ⁵When Jesus saw their faith, he said to the paralyzed man, "Son, your sins are forgiven."

English version C (New Living Translation)

Four men arrived, carrying a paralyzed man on a mat. ⁴They couldn't bring him to Jesus because of the crowd, so they dug a hole through the roof above his head. Then they lowered the man on his mat, right down in front of Jesus. ⁵Seeing their faith, Jesus said to the paralyzed man, "My child, your sins are forgiven."

Questions for exercise 3

(1) Discuss the versions given above. Do they all express the same meaning, as far as you are able to judge?

(2) Compare the different ways in which the meaning is expressed in these versions. List some of the specific differences of form that you notice.

(3) Make a translation of these verses into your own language. Think of someone in your home community and make a translation that you believe will communicate the meaning clearly to that person.

> **Terms to remember**
>
> *Original language*: The language in which a specific text of Scripture was originally written, either Hebrew (most of the Old Testament), Aramaic (a few parts of the Old Testament), or Greek (the New Testament).
>
> *Receptor language*: The language into which the translation is being made. The term "receptor audience" refers to those who speak the receptor language, those for whom the translation is being made. The term "target language" is sometimes used as an alternative to receptor language.
>
> *Source language*: The language or languages from which a translator is translating. The ultimate source languages from which the Bible is translated are the languages in which the text was originally written, namely, Hebrew, Aramaic, and Greek. It would be ideal if every Bible translator had sufficient knowledge of the original languages to be able to translate directly from the original texts. In practice, many translators refer to reliable translations in an intermediary source language. This may be a major international language, such as English or French, or another language of wider communication (LWC). The original Hebrew, Aramaic, or Greek text is always the final authority. See further discussion in sections 3.4 and 3.5.
>
> *Source text*: The Bible text that is being translated.

> **Remember**
>
> - *The Bible is the Word of God*, inspired by the Holy Spirit. The translator has a very serious responsibility not to change the meaning in any way. He must be careful not to add anything to the message of the original author, or to leave any part of that message untranslated.
> - *The Scriptures are intended to be understood.* The original author of each book of Scripture wrote in a language that he believed would be well understood by those for whom the message was intended.
> - Each language has its own grammar, its own words and expressions, its own unique ways of expressing meaning. In order to express the meaning of the message he is translating, a translator must use grammatical forms and words that are different from those of the language he is translating from. That is to be expected. The important thing is that the meaning of the message is unchanged.
> - The task of a translator is to translate the *meaning* of the message, rather than the individual words.

Additional resources on "What Is Translation?"

BT4 online materials

1_Quiche_story.pptx
1_Comparing_versions-Mark_2_19.pptx

Chapter 2

Different Styles of Translation

2.1 The difference between "literal" and "meaning-based" translations

Example: Matthew 3:8

Greek text with word-for-word key in English:

poiēsate	*oun*	*karpon*	*axion*	*tēs*	*metanoias*
do/make/produce	therefore	fruit	fit/appropriate	of-the	repentance

English versions: (See chapter 3, section 3.2, for a discussion of the various Bible versions.)

    a. Bring forth therefore fruits meet for repentance. (*KJV*)
    b. Bear fruit that befits repentance. (*RSV*)
    c. Produce fruit in keeping with repentance. (*NIV*)
    d. Prove your repentance by the fruit you bear. (*REB*)
    e. Do those things that will show that you have turned from your sins. (*GNT*)
    f. Go and do something to show that your hearts are really changed. (*JBP*)
    g. Prove by the way you live that you have repented of your sins and turned to God. (*NLT*)

Translations a, b, c, and d are all *fairly literal*. In other words, they follow the *form* of the Greek quite closely.

- They all keep the word "fruit" - an idiom or figure of speech in the Greek text.
- They all keep the abstract noun "repentance" as a noun, following the grammar of the Greek text.
- Except for d, they follow the same order of words and clauses as the Greek text.

Translations e, f, and g all re-express the *meaning* of the original message in a way that is more understandable and more natural in English. They are more *meaning-based*.

Literal and *meaning-based* are terms used to describe a continuous range of styles of translation varying from *very literal*, through *fairly literal*, to *fairly meaning-based*, and *very meaning-based* -

and points in between. There are no fixed categories. Bible versions can be compared in terms of being generally "more literal" or "more meaning-based."

English versions that tend to be more meaning-based most of the time may have some passages that are very literal. Similarly, versions that tend to be more literal, may be very meaning-based at times.

> ### Remember
> - A *literal* translation is one that aims to communicate the original message while also following closely the form of the language used in the source text. A literal translation has a high level of formal correspondence (similarity in form).
> - A *meaning-based* translation is one that aims to communicate the meaning of the original message in a way that will be understood well by the intended hearers, using the natural form of the receptor language.

Changes of form that commonly occur in meaning-based translations

- Change in the order of the words: A meaning-based translation uses the order of words that is natural in the receptor language. A more literal translation attempts to follow the order of words in the source text.
- Change in idiomatic expressions: A meaning-based translation uses words and expressions that communicate the meaning of the original text to the receptor audience. These forms may be different from those of the original text.
- Change in the connecting words or phrases: A meaning-based translation uses ways that are natural in the receptor language to indicate how larger units of text are connected together.

Exercise

For each of the following passages, for each English version, do the following:

(1) Underline any places in the translation where the translator has used grammatical forms that are different from those of the Hebrew or Greek text, or where a different idiom or expression has been used.

(2) For each English version, note whether you feel the translation is literal or meaning-based. You may qualify your answers as very literal, fairly literal, meaning-based, or very meaning-based.

(3) If there is a translation of any of these verses in your own language, or in a national language that you know, look up the translation of each verse to see whether it is literal or meaning-based.

Look at each verse in its context.

Job 38:3

Hebrew text with word-for-word key in English:

ʾĕzār-nāʾ	kəgeber	ḥălāṣệkā	wəʾešʾāləkā	wəhôdîʿēnî
gird	like-a-man	your-loins	and-I-will-ask-you	and-(you)-declare-to-me

English versions:
   a. Gird up your loins like a man, I will question you, and you shall declare to me. (*RSV*)
   b. Gird up now thy loins like a man; for I will demand of thee, and answer thou me. (*KJV*)
   c. Dress for action like a man; I will question you, and you make it known to me. (*ESV*)
   d. Brace yourself like a man; I will question you, and you shall answer me. (*NIV*)
   e. Now stand up straight and answer the questions I ask you. (*GNT*)
   f. Pull yourself together, Job! Up on your feet! Stand tall! I have some questions for you, and I want some straight answers. (*The Message*)

Psalm 1:6

Hebrew text with word-for-word key in English:

kî	yōḏēaʿ	yhwh	dereḵ	ṣaddîqîm
because	knows	Yahweh	way	of righteous-men

wəḏereḵ	rəšaʿîm	tōʾḇēḏ
and-way	of evil-men	will-perish

English versions:
   a. The righteous are guided and protected by the LORD, but the evil are on the way to their doom. (*GNT*)
   b. For the LORD knoweth the way of the righteous; but the way of the ungodly shall perish. (*KJV*)
   c. ...for the LORD knows the way of the righteous, but the way of the wicked will perish. (*ESV*)
   d. For the LORD watches over the way of the righteous, but the way of the wicked leads to destruction. (*NIV*)
   e. The LORD protects everyone who follows him, but the wicked follow a road that leads to ruin. (*CEV*)
   f. For the LORD watches over the path of the godly, but the path of the wicked leads to destruction. (*NLT*)

Romans 15:12

Greek text with word-for-word key in English:

kai	palin	Esaias	legei,	estai	hē	rhiza	tou	Iessai,
and	again	Isaiah	says,	there-will-be	the	root	of-the	Jesse

kai	ho	anistamenos	archein	ethnōn,	ep	autō	ethnē	elpiousin
and	the	one-rising	to-rule	nations,	in	him	nations	will-hope

English versions:
   a. And further Isaiah says, "The root of Jesse shall come, he who rises to rule the Gentiles; in him shall the Gentiles hope." (*RSV*)

b. And again, Esaias saith, There shall be a root of Jesse, And he that shall rise to reign over the Gentiles; In him shall the Gentiles trust. (*KJV*)

c. And again, Isaiah says, "The Root of Jesse will spring up, one who will arise to rule over the nations; in him the Gentiles will hope." (*NIV*)

d. And in Isaiah, it says: The root of Jesse will appear, he who rises up to rule the nations, and in him the nations will put their hope. (*NJB*)

e. Once again, Isaiah says, "The Scion of Jesse shall come, a ruler who rises to govern the Gentiles; on him shall they set their hope." (*REB*)

f. And in another place Isaiah said, "The heir to David's throne will come, and he will rule over the Gentiles. They will place their hope on him." (*NLT*)

g. And again, Isaiah says, "A descendant of Jesse will appear; he will come to rule the Gentiles, and they will put their hope in him." (*GNT*)

h. And again Isaiah says, "The root of Jesse will come, and the one who rises to rule over the Gentiles, in him will the Gentiles hope." (*NET*)

2 Corinthians 6:11

Greek text with word-for-word key in English:

to	*stoma*	*hēmōn*	*aneōgen*	*pros*	*humas,*	*Korinthioi,*
the	mouth	of-us	is-open	towards	you,	Corinthians,

hē	*kardia*	*hēmōn*	*peplatuntai*
the	heart	of-us	is-wide/enlarged

English versions:

a. Our mouth is open to you, Corinthians; our heart is wide. (*RSV*)

b. O ye Corinthians, our mouth is open unto you, our heart is enlarged. (*KJV*)

c. People of Corinth, we have spoken frankly and opened our heart to you. (*NJB*)

d. We have spoken very frankly to you, friends in Corinth; we have opened our heart to you. (*REB*)

e. Oh, dear Corinthian friends! We have spoken honestly to you, and our hearts are open to you. (*NLT*)

f. Friends in Corinth, we are telling the truth when we say there is room in our hearts for you. (*CEV*)

g. Dear friends in Corinth! We have spoken frankly to you; we have opened our hearts wide. (*GNT*)

2.2 "Functional equivalence" translation, earlier known as "dynamic equivalence"

Dr Eugene Nida, a leader in the development of Bible translation theory, described the goal of translation as "reproducing in the receptor language the closest natural equivalent of the source language message, first in terms of meaning, and secondly in terms of style" (Nida and Taber 1969:12). In other words, the translator's priority is that the new audience, those who receive the translation, will understand the message that the original author was aiming to communicate to the original audience, in terms both of its content and of its impact.

The term "dynamic equivalence" has sometimes been misunderstood to imply that the translation focuses particularly on the equivalence of *emotive* impact. While comparison of the emotive or emotional response is included, Nida's intended ideal is equivalence in all areas of meaning. For that reason, in his later writings, Nida used the term "functional equivalence" in preference to "dynamic equivalence."

Nida maintains concern for equivalence of style as a secondary goal, while stressing that communicating the meaning of the original message accurately and clearly must have priority. In studying English versions (see chapter 3, section 3.2), it will be observed that for versions listed in groups 3.2.1 and 3.2.2, it is possible to trace correspondence to the form of the original language text. Versions in group 3.2.3, however, like the *Contemporary English Version*, although based on careful study of the original text, do not attempt to keep correspondence in form.

In *From One Language to Another: Functional Equivalence in Bible Translating*, co-authored with Jan de Waard in 1986, Nida affirmed that the Bible translator's task is "to faithfully reproduce the meaning of the text in a form that will effectively meet the needs and expectations of receptors whose background and experience are very different from those who were the original receptors of the biblical documents" (1986:14).

Nida also advised translators to consider the circumstances in which a translation will be used, recognising that public reading is an important way of communicating Scripture. Translations should be in a form that can be read aloud without ambiguity, using a level of language that "can be readily grasped when heard" (1986:17).

The *Good News Translation*, 2nd edition (1992), is an example of a translation that aimed to put these principles into practice.

Idiomatic

In *Translating the Word of God*, published in 1974, John Beekman and John Callow introduced the term *idiomatic*, summarising as follows: "If the form (of a translation) corresponds more to the form of the original text, it is classed as literal; if its form corresponds more to the form of the receptor language, then it is classed as idiomatic" (Beekman and Callow 1974:21).

2.3 More on principles of functional equivalence: The importance of context

In an article published in 1997, "Redefining a functional theory of translation," Edward R. Hope, a translation consultant with the United Bible Societies, further stressed the need for translators to study the full context of the message they are translating. The basic unit of translation is not the word, or even the sentence, but the whole text.

In addition to studying the written text (the linguistic context), translators need to study the historical and cultural context in which the text was written and the purpose for which it was written. Having immersed themselves in the original situation, translators then aim to retell the message in a way that the receptor audience can understand.

Translators need to identify the essential background information that the new audience needs in order to understand the text, and to consider how to make this available to the new audience. The development of software programs such as Paratext have made it possible to include section headings, footnotes, and other helps with a translation and to test these with other speakers along with the translated text. See further chapters 14 and 15.

Principles of how to communicate a message to an audience in a different historical and cultural situation are also discussed in the translation approach termed "relevance theory." This approach is explained and illustrated in chapters 7, 8, and 9.

2.4 "Literary-rhetorical" or "Literary functional" approach to translation

Ernst Wendland draws attention to the fact that "verbal beauty and power were and are an integral part of the message of Scripture" (2004:33). He suggests there is room for a style of translation that aims to reproduce the literary quality of the Scriptures, focusing particularly on "a discourse-centred, genre-based perspective" (2002:228). In a short summary of this approach, Wendland writes,

> "*Literary* functional equivalence" translation (*LiFE* for short) is a methodological extension, or practical application of de Waard and Nida's "functional equivalence" approach (1986). This translation procedure is based upon the assumption (supported by various types of discourse and esthetic analyses, e.g., Wendland 2004, 2013, 2014; Wilt 2005a, 2005b) that the Hebrew and Greek Scriptures, by and large, exemplify literary texts of comparatively high quality, and therefore any interlingual rendition should manifest a corresponding level of excellence (to the degree possible under the prevailing circumstances of text production). (2018:1)

There are many different kinds (genres) of text in the Bible, ranging from books of the law to worship songs. To achieve this goal, translators need to study the features that characterise each genre in the original texts. More "helps for translators" are being produced that highlight these features, and there are increasing opportunities for translators to study the biblical languages and appreciate the forms of the original.

Translators also need to explore the resources of the receptor language, studying different kinds of indigenous texts. In preparing to translate psalms, for example, consider whether there are features of appropriate indigenous songs that could be used effectively in translations.

It seems that many "common language" translations could be improved if translators give attention to appreciating the beauty and impact of the original text and to exploring ways in which this can be effectively reproduced in translations, looking especially at larger units of text. Translation is not a mechanical process, following rules, but a creative art! More could be done to identify members of the translation team and reviewers who are gifted in expressing themselves well. They should be encouraged to develop and use their skills. This issue is discussed and illustrated further in chapter 38.

Additional resources on "Different Styles of Translation"

BT4 online materials

2_Comparing_two_kinds_of_translation.pptx
2_On_different_kinds_of_translation.pdf
2_The_goal_of_translation.pptx

For further reading

Beekman, John, and John Callow. 1974. *Translating the Word of God: With Scripture and topical indexes*. Grand Rapids: Zondervan. Also accessible *on Translator's Workplace*.

de Waard, Jan, and Eugene A. Nida. 1986. *From one language to another: Functional equivalence in Bible translating.* Nashville: Thomas Nelson Publishers.

Hope, Edward R. 1997. Redefining a functional theory of translation. *Current Trends in Scripture Translation,* UBS Bulletin 182/183:7–19.

Nida, Eugene A., and Charles R. Taber. 1969. *The theory and practice of translation.* Leiden: E. J. Brill for the United Bible Societies. Originally published in the series, *Helps for Translators* 8. Reprinted 1974 and 1982. Fourth impression 2003.

Nida, Eugene A. 1979. Translating means communicating: A sociolinguistic theory of translation, parts 1 and 2. *The Bible Translator* 30(1):101–107 and 30(3):318–325. Accessible at http://www.ubs-translations.org/tbt/1979/01/TBT197901.html?num=101&x=6&y=15&num1=.

Wendland, Ernst R. 2002. A literary-rhetorical approach to biblical text analysis and translation. In Timothy Wilt (ed.), *Bible translation: Frames of reference,* 179–230. Manchester: St. Jerome Publishing.

Wendland, Ernst R. 2004. *Translating the literature of Scripture: A literary-rhetorical approach to Bible translation.* Publications in Translation and Textlinguistics 1. Dallas: SIL International.

Wendland, Ernst R. 2018. Literary functional equivalence translation. For those who have registered with Academia.edu, this is accessible at https://www.academia.edu/3168198/_Literary_Functional_Equivalence_LiFE_Translation--A_Brief_Description.

Wilt, Timothy, ed. (2002) 2014. *Bible translation: Frames of reference.* Manchester: St. Jerome Publishing. Republished, London: Routledge.

Zogbo, Lynell, and Ernst R. Wendland. 2000. *Hebrew poetry in the Bible: A guide for understanding and for translating.* Helps for Translators. New York: United Bible Societies.

Chapter 3

Some English Translations of the Bible

3.1 Early English translations of the Bible

The first English translation was made by John Wycliffe, based on the Vulgate, the Latin translation of the original texts. Wycliffe's translation was completed about AD 1382.

The first English translation to be based on the original Hebrew, Aramaic, and Greek texts was prepared by William Tyndale. Tyndale completed the translation of the New Testament and part of the Old Testament. Accused of heresy, he was burned to death in AD 1536. Watch the following video titles, available on Amazon:

John Wycliffe – The Morning Star

God's Outlaw – The Story of William Tyndale

Martin Luther – The Idea That Changed the World (Luther's translation into German, and the translation principles he applied, influenced Tyndale in his translation into English.)

At the end of this chapter, there are links provided to websites that give further information about both historical and modern versions of the Bible. The *King James Version (KJV)*, also called the "Authorized Version," contained a high percentage of Tyndale's translation. The *KJV* was published in AD 1611; subsequent editions became the standard version of the Bible in English for more than 350 years.

Because the English language has changed over the last 400 years, the *KJV* is now difficult for most speakers of modern English to understand. Also, since the time this translation was made, further discoveries of early biblical manuscripts have made it possible for scholars to be more sure of the original reading of the Hebrew and Greek texts at certain points.

3.2 Modern English translations of the Bible

In recent years, many new translations of the Bible have been made in English. The versions listed below are some of the most widely used. For the Old Testament, all the translations listed are based on the Masoretic Hebrew text. For the New Testament, translations are based on the Greek text researched by biblical scholars, as compiled in the Nestle-Aland Greek text, 27th or 28th edition.

3.2.1 English versions that maintain a fairly high level of correspondence to the form of the original Hebrew, Aramaic, or Greek texts

Revised Standard Version (RSV)

First published in 1952, revised edition 1971, the *RSV* was widely accepted at the time of its publication. For many years it was used as the accepted version in many churches and schools.

English Standard Version (ESV)

The *ESV*, first published in 2001, is a revision of the 1971 edition of the *RSV*. Like the *RSV*, it is an "essentially literal" translation.

New American Standard Bible (NASB)

The *NASB*, published in 1971, updated 1995, has sought to render the grammar and terminology of the original text in contemporary English. Special attention has been given to translating verb tenses in order to give the English reader a rendering as close as possible to the sense of the original Greek and Hebrew texts.

3.2.2 Other reliable, widely accepted English translations, also maintaining some correspondence with the form of the original language texts

New International Version (NIV)

The *NIV* is a careful version in modern English, less literal than the *RSV* and *ESV*, while still enabling the reader to relate to the form of the original language texts. A reliable guide to follow where there are possible differences of interpretation.

The *NIV* was first published in 1984. The latest update, published in 2011, reflects changes in the English language, also recent discoveries about biblical languages and the historical cultural backgrounds of the Bible. The *NIV Study Bible* is very helpful for translators; it includes many helpful articles, notes, glossary items, maps, and illustrations.

The *NIV* has become popular for use in churches and schools. Currently (2019) it is probably the most widely used of all modern English versions.

NET Bible (NET)

The *NET Bible* is a new translation of the Bible, prepared by twenty-five experts in the biblical languages. They worked directly from the best currently available Hebrew, Aramaic, and Greek texts.

As the abbreviated name, *NET*, suggests, this was the first Bible prepared primarily for use online. See it online at https://lumina.bible.org/bible. It has many exegetical notes, available as jump links in the digital text or displayed in a parallel column. The notes cover the following issues: (a) variant forms in the original text, (b) translation issues, and (c) study notes including comments on the historical and cultural background of the passage and other information to help the reader understand the text.

Good News Translation (GNT), widely known as the Good News Bible, also known as Today's English Version

The *Good News Translation* (*GNT*) is described as a "common language" Bible. It is a clear and simple modern translation aiming to express the meaning of the original language texts, in a way that people can understand.

The New Testament appeared in 1966 as *Good News for Modern Man: The New Testament in Today's English Version*, translated by Dr Robert G. Bratcher in consultation with a committee appointed by the American Bible Society. The full Bible was published in 1976; the second edition was published in 1992.

New Living Translation (NLT)

Kenneth Taylor began translating for his family of ten children. *Living Letters* was published in 1962 and the whole Bible in 1971. That translation was published as the *Living Bible*, a lively paraphrase in everyday English, based on the *American Standard Bible* (1901). Dr Taylor worked from an English version, re-expressing to make the meaning clearer, rather than directly translating the original Hebrew and Greek texts. Ken Taylor's son, Mark D. Taylor, working with a team of highly qualified scholars, revised this work. The *New Living Translation* has been widely used, respected both for its exegetical accuracy and its clarity. The full Bible was first published in 1996, a second edition in 2004, and further editions with minor revisions in 2007 and 2015.

New English Bible (NEB) and Revised English Bible (REB)

The *New English Bible* (1970) is an accurate translation made by careful scholars, in a rather literary style of British English. The *Revised English Bible* (1989) is an updated version, commissioned by a committee representing several church denominations.

Jerusalem Bible (JB), the New Jerusalem Bible (NJB), and the Revised New Jerusalem Bible (RNJB)

The first edition of the *Jerusalem Bible* was prepared in French, published in 1956. In 1966 an English version was published, translated with reference to the original language texts while being much influenced by the French version. A careful revision by a team of scholars, the *New Jerusalem Bible*, was published in 1985. This is a translation in a fairly literary style by scholars of the Roman Catholic tradition. A further revised version of Psalms and the New Testament was published in February 2018 as the *Revised New Jerusalem Bible*, described as a "thoroughly reworked translation" giving priority to accuracy of translation and suitability for being read aloud. The full Bible was released in a study edition in 2019.

3.2.3 Versions in colloquial, everyday modern English

J. B. Phillips (JBP)

Letters to Young churches, a translation of the epistles, was originally prepared for the benefit of the youth group of the church in south-east London where J.B. Phillips was vicar during the Second World War. In response to demand, Phillips then translated other parts of the New Testament, working from the Greek text. *The New Testament in Modern English* was published in 1958. A revised edition was published in 1972. The translation may rightly be described as idiomatic and dynamic. Perhaps because of its use of a British dialect of English, it has been more popular in the UK than in the USA, but has become widely respected, as the first of the "modern English" translations.

Contemporary English Version (CEV)

The *Contemporary English Version*, published by the American Bible Society in 1995, is a translation that aims to be easily understood by all, avoiding "Bible" language. It was prepared by a team of Bible scholars, with input from a wide range of reviewers.

The Message

Translated by Eugene Peterson and published in 2002, *The Message* is an idiomatic, rather explicit, translation (perhaps better described as a paraphrase) in a very colloquial form of everyday English, with particular focus on communicating the emotive impact of the original Bible text. With the goal of making the meaning of the text as relevant as possible to the intended audience, the meaning is sometimes retold/reapplied as if in a modern western cultural context. For example, Matthew 6:11 "Give us each day our daily bread" (*ESV*), is translated in *The Message* as "Keep us alive with three square meals." Used with discretion, *The Message* can be a source of good ideas for expressing the meaning in English, but is not recommended as a source text for translators.

3.3 Finding out more about Bible versions

The principles that have been followed in making a specific translation of the Bible are usually explained in a "Preface" or "Introduction," which can be found in its first pages.

From the "Preface" to the English Standard Version:

"The *ESV* is an 'essentially literal' translation that seeks as far as possible to reproduce the precise wording of the original text and the personal style of each Bible writer. As such, its emphasis is on 'word-for-word' correspondence, at the same time taking full account of differences of grammar, syntax, and idiom between current literary English and the original languages. Thus it seeks to be transparent to the original text, letting the reader see as directly as possible the structure and meaning of the original."

From the "Introduction to the New Testament" in the New English Bible:

"We have conceived our task to be that of understanding the original as precisely as we could (using all available aids), and then saying again in our own native idiom what we believed the author to be saying in his."

From the "Introduction" to the translation by J. B. Phillips:

"For, as I see it, the translator's function is to understand as fully and deeply as possible what the New Testament writers had to say and then, after a process of what might be called reflective digestion, to write it down in the language of the people today."

From the "Preface" to the New International Version:

"We have sought to recreate as far as possible the experience of the original audience – blending transparency to the original text with accessibility for the millions of English speakers around the world."

3.4 From which English, or other language, versions should we translate?

It would be ideal if every Bible translator had a fluent knowledge of the original biblical languages. In practice, many translators are working from reliable translations in English, French, or other major languages of wider communication.[1]

Translators should use at least two versions of the Bible for constant reference when translating. One should be a version that maintains some transparency with the form of the original text. For translators for whom English is their intermediary source language, the *New International Version* (*NIV*) is suggested. A 2016 interaction on MAP (a website where translation consultants interact), responding to the question, "What are the most popular English 'model' translations?", indicates that many translation projects are choosing the *New International Version* as a source text. This reflects the fact that, in recent years, the *NIV* has gained wide acceptance as a careful and well-balanced translation.

Responses in this interaction indicate that either *Good News Translation* or the *New Living Translation* is commonly chosen as the second reference text.

This decision on which English (or other language) versions should be used as the source texts needs to be discussed with church leaders of all denominations in the receptor language area. Make sure that those who are making the decision are fully informed of the issues to be considered.

Major English Bible versions can be easily viewed and compared in the Paratext and *Translator's Workplace* software programs that have been designed specifically for Bible translators. See the illustration in chapter 13. Further information about these important resources is accessible at http://paratext.org/about/pt (for Paratext) and https://www.sil.org/resources/publications/tw (for *Translator's Workplace*).

Translators also need to refer to translations in languages of wider communication that are spoken in the region concerned. For example, for projects in languages spoken in northern Nigeria, versions in Hausa will be referred to; for projects in the Solomon Islands, the Solomon Islands Pijin Bible will be consulted. (See the note about YouVersion at the end of chapter 11.)

---

[1] A "language of wider communication," often referred to as a LWC, is a language used as a medium of communication between those who may speak other languages as their first language. It may be a language that is spoken internationally, such as English, French, or Arabic. Or it may be an officially recognised national language in a country where many languages are spoken – examples are Indonesian, spoken as the official national language in Indonesia, a country where more than 700 different languages are spoken, or Tok Pisin, an English-based creole language, officially recognised as a national language of Papua New Guinea. Or it may be a language that is spoken widely across a region, including several countries, such as Hausa spoken in Northern Nigeria and neighbouring regions of west Africa, or Swahili spoken widely in Tanzania, Kenya, Uganda, and neighbouring areas. A language spoken less widely but used by speakers of several neighbouring languages to communicate with each other may also be referred to as a LWC.

3.5 The authority of the original text

There will be times when a translator needs to discover the exact form and/or meaning of the original Hebrew, Aramaic, or Greek text in order to achieve accuracy. *UBS Translator's Handbooks* (United Bible Societies) and *Translator's Notes* (SIL International) provide helpful information and are readily available in Paratext. *UBS Translator's Handbooks* and *Translator's Notes* can also be found, with other biblical commentaries, in *Translator's Workplace*. Translation consultants and exegetical advisors will also be able to help, responding to the translator's questions.

If a translator has opportunity to study Hebrew and/or Greek, this is very desirable and will enable him or her to make the best use of the available translation helps and commentaries. There are excellent courses, whether in a seminary or Bible college, or online for individual personal study.

Particularly recommended are courses offered by the Jerusalem Center for Bible Translators. See the website www.bibletranslators.org for further information. See also the websites iblt.ac (Institute for Biblical Languages and Translation), www.biblicallanguagecenter.com (Biblical Language Center), and https://www.polisjerusalem.org/biblical-hebrew-language-course (Jerusalem Institute of Languages and Humanities).

In situations where a New Testament has been completed and the team is about to begin work on the Old Testament, serious consideration should be given to enabling the key translator(s) to take one of the excellent training programs for learning Hebrew.

The "source language text" in Paratext provides access to the original language text, with facility to view the transliterated text, grammatical analysis, and lemma forms with jump links to lexicons and other geographical and cross-cultural information. See also the computer program BART, standing for *Biblical Analysis and Research Tool*. For further information see http://software.sil.org/bart/.

For discussion

Which Bible version do you use for personal study? What are the reasons you chose that version?

Additional resources on "English Translations of the Bible"

Websites

Gray, David. 2018. A history of Bible translation.
 https://www.sil.org/system/files/reapdata/12/42/68/124268508927339898977716740725691923975/A_History_of_Bible_Translation.docx.pdf.
Jeffcoat III, John L. 2013. English Bible history.
 http://www.greatsite.com/timeline-english-bible-history/index.html.
 There is a summary timeline at the end of the paper.

Videos

Brake, Donald. History of Bible translation. This can be viewed at
 https://www.youtube.com/watch?v=Af4Q_PGYTd0.

Brunn, Dave. 2013. *One Bible, many versions: Are all translations created equal?* Downers Grove, IL: Inter-Varsity Press. This can be viewed at https://www.youtube.com/watch?v=MxwYK2duyPg.

How the Bible came to us, subtitled *The Bible: Mankind's Oldest Modern Book.* This can be viewed at https://www.youtube.com/watch?v=RnBqhyQklU0.

The following videos are available for purchase on Amazon.com:
John Wycliffe – The Morning Star
God's Outlaw – The Story of William Tyndale
Martin Luther – The Idea That Changed the World

For further reading

Bascom, Robert A. 2017. Bases and models revisited: The importance of using different types of reference translations. *The Bible Translator* 68(1):3-10.

Brunn, Dave. 2015. Form and function in Bible translation: Where theory meets practice. *Journal for Baptist Theology and Ministry* 12(1):3–19. http://www.baptistcenter.net/journals/JBTM_12-1_Spring_2015.pdf.

Metzger, Bruce. 2001. *The Bible in translation: Ancient and English versions.* Grand Rapids: Baker Academic.

Wendland, Paul. 2018. *Bible translations for the 21st century: Formal and functional equivalence in Bible translation.* Bjarne Wollan Teigen Reformation Lectures: Lecture II. (For those who have registered with Academia.edu, this is accessible at https://www.academia.edu/3782915/Bible_Translations_for_the_21st_Century_Formal_and_Functional_Equivalence_in_Bible_Translation.)

Chapter 4

More about Meaning-Based Translation

In this chapter we study examples where the meaning of certain combinations of words is different from the meaning of those words when taken separately. The term *idiom* is used to describe expressions of this kind. The forms used to translate such expressions may be very different in different languages.

For a discussion comparing idioms and figures of speech, see PowerPoint 33_Figures_of_speech_1-Introduction.pptx.

4.1 What is an "idiom"?

An *idiom* is an expression where the words taken together mean something different from the individual meaning of the words. Idioms are often unique to a certain culture.

Thus, an *idiomatic expression* is a phrase that is natural and meaningful in a specific language, although not necessarily in other languages.

English has many idioms. For example,

   a. to break the silence
   b. to be caught red-handed
   c. to be scatter-brained
   d. to have a feather in your cap
   e. It's raining cats and dogs!
   f. How do you do?

4.2 How to translate idioms

Usually idioms cannot be translated literally into another language. Think about translating the idiom as a unit rather than translating its individual words. The meaning of the idiom must be expressed in a way that gives the right meaning in the other language.

Sometimes the meaning of an idiom in the source text is best translated by words that give the intended meaning in a direct way:

Luke 2:51	His mother kept all these things in her heart. (*RSV*)

In translating this verse into the Kilba language of Nigeria, the translator expressed the true meaning directly: "his mother went on thinking about these things." In Kilba, "to keep something in your heart," translated literally, means, "to bear a grudge about something."

Isaiah 13:18	They will have no mercy on the fruit of the womb; their eyes will not pity children.
NLT	They will have no mercy on helpless babies and will show no compassion for children.
CEV	No pity will be shown to babies and children.

The ESV follows the original Hebrew idiom "fruit of the womb." The meaning may not be clear to the modern English reader. NLT and CEV translate the meaning directly.

Sometimes an idiom in the source text may be translated by an idiom in the receptor language; usually this is an idiom that is different from the original one:

Genesis 35:29	(Isaac was)...old and full of days. (*ESV*, following the Hebrew text)
NIV	old and full of years
NLT	at a ripe old age
NET	an old man who had lived a full life
Acts 18:6	"Your blood be on your own heads! I am innocent."
GNT	"If you are lost, you yourselves must take the blame for it! I am not responsible."

Igede, Nigeria, literally translated: "Your heads are not in the palms of my hands! My hand and foot are not there!

The ESV follows the original Greek idiom closely. GNT uses an idiom that is more natural in modern English. Igede uses an idiom that expresses the intended meaning naturally in Igede. All three translations have the same meaning.

4.3 Using idioms to make a translation lively and natural

Sometimes there may be an idiom in the receptor language that expresses effectively the emotive impact of the source text, even where the source text does not use an idiomatic form:

Mark 5:43	He strictly charged them.
GNT	Jesus gave them strict orders.

Mbembe, Nigeria, literally translated: "Jesus pulled their ears."

Luke 22:56	She looked straight at him. (*GNT*)

Igede, Nigeria, literally translated: "She bit him with her eye."

Exercise 1

Translate the following passage into your own language, using natural idioms or non-idiomatic forms, as appropriate in each case. Try to keep the same lively conversational style.

"There is no point in getting hot and bothered about it," said his brother-in-law. "Just be patient and bide your time a little. The whole thing will blow over before you can say 'Jack Robinson.'" "It's all very well for you to talk," grumbled the other.

Exercise 2: For discussion

Many languages have idiomatic ways of talking about emotions or feelings. Write down and discuss several different ways in which you could express each of the following concepts in your language:

   a. He is very hungry.
   b. He is happy.
   c. He is angry.
   d. He is afraid.
   e. He is amazed.

Remember

- Keep alert to recognise idioms in the source text.
- Translate idioms in a way that communicates their true meaning. Either translate the meaning directly or use an idiom that has the same meaning.
- Check carefully to see whether the idiom you are proposing to use has any additional implications that do not fit in the context.
- Keep in mind the nature of the text you are translating. Some idioms may be appropriate in everyday conversation, but not appropriate in more formal speech.
- Using natural idioms in a translation makes the style of the translation lively and interesting.

Exercise 3

For each of the following passages, translate the passage into either your own language or a language of wider communication in the region where you live. Discuss any places in your translation where either (a) the idiom or (b) the grammar of the receptor language is different from that of the source text.

Passage A:

The child lay on the ground, crying bitterly. He had broken his bottle of kerosene and cut himself badly in the fall, and he was afraid his mother would read him the riot act.

Passage B:

"Good heavens," exclaimed the driver, "We shall hit that lorry if it doesn't move over." He slammed on the brakes and pulled his car sharply to the right. By the skin of their teeth they avoided a collision.

Exercise 4

For each of the following references, looking at the text in its context, do the following:

(1) Underline every example of an idiom. Compare with other English versions where this seems helpful.

(2) Re-express the meaning of the idiom in English in a way that makes the meaning clear.

(3) Express the meaning in your own language in a way that gives a similar impact, either by a direct translation or by using an idiom that gives this meaning in your language.

Luke 16:20	And at his gate lay a poor man named Lazarus, full of sores. (*RSV*)
Luke 17:12-13	And as he entered a village, he was met by ten lepers, who stood at a distance and lifted up their voices, saying, "Jesus, Master, have mercy on us."
John 2:3	When the wine ran out, the mother of Jesus said to him, "They have no wine."
Acts 2:37	Now when they heard this, they were cut to the heart.
Acts 11:21	And the hand of the Lord was with them.
Acts 11:22	The report of this came to the ears of the church in Jerusalem.
Acts 13:22	I have found in David the son of Jesse a man after my heart, who will do all my will.
Acts 17:8	With these words they threw the crowd and the city authorities in an uproar. (*GNT*)

> **A reminder:** In this manual, Scripture quotations in English that are not identified as a specific Bible version are from the *English Standard Version* (*ESV*). *ESV* has been chosen for this purpose because it aims to retain transparency with the **form** of the original Hebrew or Greek text, keeping the original sentence structure and idioms as closely as possible.

Additional resources on "Meaning-Based Translation"

BT4 online materials

4_Recognizing_idioms-Examples_and_exercises.pptx

Chapter 5

Qualities of a Good Translation

When deciding whether a translation is a faithful rendering of the original text, there are four basic questions to ask.

5.1 Is the translation accurate?

Does it communicate the *meaning* of the original message as closely as possible, that is, in a way the audience for whom it is intended will understand? Has the meaning been changed in any way?

- A translation is *inaccurate* if the meaning of the translation is different in any way from the original message. For example,

    Omission: The translation is inaccurate if part of the meaning is missing.

    Addition: The translation is inaccurate if anything has been added to the meaning.

    Change: The translation is inaccurate if the meaning has been changed in any way.

- An *accurate* translation is not one that is as near to the form of the original message as possible, but one that expresses the same meaning as the original message, as exactly as possible.

This is the goal for which translators strive.

5.2 Is the translation clear?

Does the translation communicate the meaning in a way that the receptor audience will readily understand? Do the people for whom the translation is being made understand what it means? Is what they understand equivalent to the meaning that the original author intended to communicate to his audience?

It is recognised that there are some parts of the Bible where teaching and background knowledge is needed before the message can be fully understood. There are also some parts that may be difficult to understand because of the content of the message. Spiritual insight, given by the Holy Spirit, is needed.

For the translator, the important thing is that there is nothing in the wording of the translation that makes the message difficult to understand. The translator should translate in a way that makes the message as clear as possible.

5.3 Is the translation natural?

Does the translation flow fluently? Is it the kind of language that the people of the intended audience speak every day? Does it sound good when read aloud? It is clear from references in both the Old and New Testament that, historically, the Scriptures were intended to be read aloud.

> With the development of many easily accessible audio and video devices in recent years, more people than ever are *listening* to the Scriptures. Translators should read their translations aloud and listen to how the translation sounds. They should ask colleagues and others to read the translations aloud too, to see how they sound, seeking to maintain the fluency and emotional impact of the original.

5.4 Is the translation acceptable to the intended audience?

Is there anything in the form of the language that might cause church leaders or others to reject the translation? Is there anything that could cause offense? Consider the following:

- ☐ The style of the translation – are they happy with the kind of language that is being used? Is it too conversational? Or is it too formal?
- ☐ The dialect chosen – often a very sensitive issue; resolution involves careful study of dialect differences and of attitudes.
- ☐ The choice of specific key terms, especially if these differ from those in a major language version that is used in the area concerned. (One published New Testament in Nigeria was almost rejected by the church because of the term used to translate "wine.")
- ☐ Issues related to the members of the translation team and the denominations they represent.

In order to achieve a translation that is acceptable to the churches and community, be sure to follow these procedures:

- **Involve representatives of the church and community of the receptor language area in planning, supporting and carrying out the translation project.** This includes working with the leadership to develop a translation brief at the beginning of the project. A translation brief is an agreement recording decisions reached on such issues as the goals of the project, the style of the translation, and the dialect to be used. See part 7 of this manual, "Planning and Organising a Bible Translation Project."
- Throughout the project, **share draft translations with typical members of the intended audience, observe reactions and give opportunity for comments.** Have groups of representative reviewers appointed to read and/or listen to the translation and give feedback. For further suggestions, see chapters 17 and 20.

Exercise 1

For each pair of sentences, state whether (1) the two sentences are the same in meaning (in other words, they are different ways of saying the same thing), or (2) they are different in meaning.

1) a. It rained all night.
   b. Rain fell all night.
2) a. John was very surprised when he heard the news.
   b. The news very much amazed John when he heard it.
3) a. It was a hot day.
   b. The day was hot.
4) a. Peter's house
   b. The house that belongs to Peter
5) a. I bought cloth to make a new dress for Mary.
   b. I bought a new dress for Mary.
6) a. I bought vegetables in the market.
   b. I bought tomatoes and onions in the market.
7) a. My parents are well.
   b. My mother and father are well.
8) a. John is ill; he has malaria very badly.
   b. John is very ill indeed.
9) a. There are four rooms in the house.
   b. The house has four rooms and a kitchen at the back.
10) a. In my opinion the government is doing well and making many improvements in the country. But there are many people who do not agree that this is so.
    b. Opinions are divided concerning the government. Some say they are doing well and making many improvements in the country. Others do not agree.

Exercise 2: Acts 5:1–6

This is an exercise in evaluating the accuracy of a draft translation. Study these verses carefully in *NIV* and *GNT* and compare with the draft translation.

For each verse, evaluate whether the draft translation is accurate or inaccurate. If the draft translation is inaccurate at any point, state why it is inaccurate – noting any omissions, additions, or changes that have been made.

NIV	*GNT*	Draft translation
¹ Now a man named Ananias, together with his wife Sapphira, also sold a piece of property. ² With his wife's full knowledge he kept back part of the money for himself, but brought the rest and put it at the apostles' feet.	¹ But there was a man named Ananias, who with his wife Sapphira sold some property that belonged to them. ² But with his wife's agreement he kept part of the money for himself and turned the rest over to the apostles.	¹ But a man named Ananias and a woman called Sapphira sold a piece of property; ² he kept some of the money that he had got from the sale of the property, and his wife knew about this.

NIV	GNT	Draft translation
³ Then Peter said, "Ananias, how is it that Satan has so filled your heart that you have lied to the Holy Spirit and have kept for yourself some of the money you received for the land? ⁴ Didn't it belong to you before it was sold? And after it was sold, wasn't the money at your disposal? What made you think of doing such a thing? You have not lied just to human beings but to God."	³ Peter said to him, "Ananias, why did you let Satan take control of you and make you lie to the Holy Spirit by keeping part of the money you received for the property? ⁴ Before you sold the property, it belonged to you; and after you sold it, the money was yours. Why, then, did you decide to do such a thing? You have not lied to people—you have lied to God!"	³ But Peter said, "Ananias, why has Satan made you tell this lie? ⁴ The land, belonged to you, you were free to do what you liked with it. When you sold it, you were free to do whatever you liked with the money. So what made you decide to do what you have done?"
⁵ When Ananias heard this, he fell down and died. And great fear seized all who heard what had happened. ⁶ Then some young men came forward, wrapped up his body, and carried him out and buried him.	⁵ As soon as Ananias heard this, he fell down dead; and all who heard about it were terrified. ⁶ The young men came in, wrapped up his body, carried him out, and buried him.	⁵ When Ananias heard what Peter said, he fell down dead. Everyone who heard what had happened was very afraid. ⁶ Some people wrapped his body in a blanket and carried it out and buried it in the graveyard.

5.5 Looking for the clearest way to express the meaning, with a specific audience in mind

In any language, there will be different ways of expressing the same concepts. Your aim as a translator is to express the meaning of the source text, the meaning that the original author intended to communicate, in a way that those receiving the translation will easily understand.

Exercise 3

Quoted below are verses of the Bible in different versions. These examples illustrate how the same meaning can be expressed in different ways, all of which are accurate to the original text. For each passage, do the following:

(1) Compare the translations and put a mark beside the one that you think would be understood best by a reader who has had limited opportunity for schooling. Look at the verse in its context, where this seems helpful.

(2) For any versions that seem to you to be less clear to someone with this background, note any reasons why they are more difficult to understand.

Matthew 1:1

> ESV   The book of the genealogy of Jesus Christ, the son of David, the son of Abraham.

5.5 Looking for the clearest way to express the meaning, with a specific audience in mind

NLT	This is a record of the ancestors of Jesus the Messiah, a descendant of David and of Abraham.
GNT	This is the list of the ancestors of Jesus Christ, a descendant of David, who was a descendant of Abraham.

Matthew 2:1–2a

NIV	After Jesus was born in Bethlehem in Judea, during the time of King Herod, Magi from the east came to Jerusalem and asked, "Where is the one who has been born king of the Jews?"
REB	Jesus was born at Bethlehem in Judaea during the reign of Herod. After his birth astrologers from the east arrived in Jerusalem, asking, "Where is the new-born king of the Jews?"
GNT	Jesus was born in the town of Bethlehem in Judea, during the time when Herod was king. Soon afterward, some men who studied the stars came from the East to Jerusalem and asked, "Where is the baby born to be the king of the Jews?"

Matthew 3:14–15a

KJV	But John forbad him, saying, I have need to be baptized of thee, and comest thou to me? And Jesus answering said unto him, Suffer it to be so now: for thus it becometh us to fulfil all righteousness. Then he suffered him.
NLT	But John tried to talk him out of it. "I am the one who needs to be baptized by you," he said, "so why are you coming to me?" But Jesus said, "It should be done, for we must carry out all that God requires." So John agreed to baptize him.
REB	John tried to dissuade him. "Do you come to me?" he said. "It is I who need to be baptized by you." Jesus replied, "Let it be so for the present; it is right for us to do all that God requires." Then John allowed him to come.

Matthew 4:4

NIV	Jesus answered, "It is written, 'Man shall not live on bread alone, but on every word that comes from the mouth of God.'"
GNT	But Jesus answered, "The scripture says, 'Human beings cannot live on bread alone, but need every word that God speaks.'"

Matthew 4:6b

KJV	For it is written, He shall give his angels charge concerning thee: and in their hands they shall bear thee up, lest at any time thou dash thy foot against a stone.
NIV	For it is written, "He will command his angels concerning you, and they will lift you up in their hands, so that you will not strike your foot against a stone."

NLT	For the Scriptures say, "He will order his angels to protect you. And they will hold you up with their hands so you won't even hurt your foot on a stone."

Matthew 6:7

ESV	And when you pray, do not heap up empty phrases as the Gentiles do; for they think that they will be heard for their many words.
CEV	When you pray, don't talk on and on as people do who don't know God. They think God likes to hear long prayers.
NET	When you pray, do not babble repetitiously like the Gentiles, because they think that by their many words they will be heard.

Mark 10:46

NLT	Then they reached Jericho, and as Jesus and his disciples left town, a large crowd followed him. A blind beggar named Bartimaeus (son of Timaeus) was sitting beside the road.
NET	They came to Jericho. As Jesus and his disciples and a large crowd were leaving Jericho, Bartimaeus the son of Timaeus, a blind beggar, was sitting by the road.
ESV	And they came to Jericho. And as he was leaving Jericho with his disciples and a great crowd, Bartimaeus, a blind beggar, the son of Timaeus, was sitting by the roadside.
NIV	Then they came to Jericho. As Jesus and his disciples, together with a large crowd, were leaving the city, a blind man, Bartimaeus (which means, "son of Timaeus"), was sitting by the roadside begging.

Exercise 4

Compare the following translations and indicate which expresses the meaning most clearly. Discuss the reasons why.

1 Samuel 2:18

RSV	Samuel was ministering before the LORD, a boy girded with a linen ephod.
ESV	Samuel was ministering before the LORD, a boy clothed with a linen ephod.
GNT	In the meantime the boy Samuel continued to serve the LORD, wearing a sacred linen apron.
NLT	But Samuel, though he was only a boy, served the LORD. He wore a linen garment like that of a priest.

1 Samuel 2:21a

ESV	Indeed the LORD visited Hannah, and she conceived and bore three sons and two daughters.
GNT	The LORD did bless Hannah, and she had three more sons and two daughters.

5.5 Looking for the clearest way to express the meaning, with a specific audience in mind

Psalm 45:6

- RSV — Your divine throne endures for ever and ever. Your royal scepter is a scepter of equity.
- ESV — Your throne, O God, is forever and ever. The scepter of your kingdom is a scepter of uprightness.
- GNT — The kingdom that God has given you will last forever and ever. You rule over your people with justice.

Exercise 5: Genesis 3:8–10

For each verse, compare the draft translation with the *RSV* and *GNT*. Note examples of any points in the draft translation that are *not accurate,* or *not clear,* or *not natural English.*

RSV	GNT	Draft translation
8 And they heard the sound of the LORD God walking in the garden in the cool of the day, and the man and his wife hid themselves from the presence of the LORD God among the trees of the garden. 9 But the LORD God called to the man, and said to him, "Where are you?" 10 And he said, "I heard the sound of thee in the garden, and I was afraid, because I was naked; and I hid myself."	8 That evening they heard the LORD God walking in the garden, and they hid from him among the trees. 9 But the LORD God called out to the man, "Where are you?" 10 He answered, "I heard you in the garden; I was afraid and hid from you, because I was naked."	8 The man and his wife saw the Lord God walking in the garden in the evening, and the man and his wife hid themselves so that God should see them not 9 and the Lord God called the man, he said, "Are you where?" 10 The man said, "I heard the Lord God in the garden and I hid from you and I was naked."

> **Remember**
>
> A good translation is
>
> *Accurate* – The translation re-expresses the *meaning* of the original message as exactly as possible in the receptor language.
>
> *Clear* – The translation is *understandable*; the message is communicated in such a way that the intended audience can easily understand the meaning that the original author intended his audience to understand.
>
> *Natural* – The translation does not sound foreign. It does not sound like a translation at all, but like someone speaking fluently in a natural way.
>
> Thus, the three most important qualities of a good translation are
>
> *Accuracy*
>
> *Clarity*
>
> *Naturalness*
>
> These have been described as the "ABCs of Bible translation: Accurate, Beautiful, and Clear."
>
> A fourth very important quality to consider is
>
> *Acceptable* – The form of the translation is *acceptable* to the intended audience. A translation that for some reason is not accepted by the intended audience will not achieve its purpose, even though it is accurate, clear, and natural.

Additional resources on "Qualities of a Good Translation"

BT4 online materials

5_Qualities_of_a_good_translation.pptx
5_Qualities_of_good_translation-Poster.pptx

Website

(Forum of Bible Agencies International: https://forum-intl.org/.

The Forum of Bible Agencies International is a partnership of international organisations involved in Bible translation. Their website opens with the following statement:

> The Forum of Bible Agencies International…exists to promote collaboration and cooperation amongst Bible Agencies with a shared vision of working together to maximise the access and impact of God's word.

A joint statement, titled "Basic Principles and Procedures for Bible Translation," was agreed to and approved by member agencies in 1999, updated in 2006, and again in April 2017. The April 2017 version includes principles to be observed in sign language translations.

This statement can be viewed at https://forum-intl.org/resources/ under the "Translation Standards" option, and is also available on *Translator's Workplace*.)

For further reading

Barnwell, Katharine. 1983. Towards acceptable translations. *Notes on Translation* 95:19–25.

Dooley, Robert A. 1989. Style and acceptability. The Guaraní New Testament. *Notes on Translation* 3(1):49–57.

Gross, Carl. 2003. Acceptability—The supreme translation principle? *The Bible Translator* 54(4):424–434. http://www.ubs-translations.org/bt/archives_1950_2012/.

> *The Bible Translator* is the quarterly journal of the United Bible Societies. The complete text for vols. 1–51 (1950–2012) can be viewed at http://www.ubs-translations.org/bt/archives_1950_2012/. Recent issues (classified as "Technical Papers" and "Practical Papers") can be ordered by individual subscription through Sage journals at https://journals.sagepub.com/home/tbt.
>
> *Notes on Translation* was published by SIL International until 2005. Articles can be viewed on *Translator's Workplace*.
>
> In 2005, SIL International began to publish the *Journal of Translation* (online only). The website https://www.sil.org/resources/publications/jot gives further information on this journal. Currently the *Journal of Translation* is published without subscription one or more times per year by SIL International. Articles are published in the form of PDF files that may be freely downloaded.
>
> Another website of interest, recently developed under the auspices of the United Bible Societies, is the *Translation Insights and Perspectives* tool accessible at https://tips.translation.bible. The tool collects and presents stories about specific translations of the biblical text. An introduction to the program can be viewed at https://vimeo.com/359167436/acb88959ed.

Chapter 6

Towards Naturalness – Beginning to Explore the Receptor Language

A translator at work on translating into his own language needs to be deeply conscious of the rich resources of that language, including

- ☐ the sounds (phonology) of the language – its unique inventory of consonants, vowels, and other features such as tones and intonation;
- ☐ the grammar of the language, reflecting sets of distinctive features relating to issues such as tense, plurality, gender, and many more, with a unique pattern (structure) of arranging these; and
- ☐ a wealth of vocabulary developed over many, many years to enable users to communicate and relate to each other in their own cultural environment.

A translator, as he translates, focuses on the source text, and is conscious of the grammatical and vocabulary distinctives of the source language. An experienced translator develops the skill of also keeping the richness of his own language in focus, avoiding the temptation to carry over the patterns and structure of the source language.

Here are some suggestions on how a translator can develop an explicit awareness of the unique features of his own language and keep this in focus as he translates. These exercises will also help translators develop their writing skills.

6.1 Practise writing freely in your own language

If your language has only recently been written down, then you may not have had much opportunity to write freely in the language. Practice will help you to write the language more and more fluently and easily. It also helps you to get used to writing the language consistently. Some suggestions:

- ☐ Do your people have proverbs, well-known sayings giving a word of wisdom? Think of ten proverbs and write them down.
- ☐ Write a letter to a friend overseas and tell him about yourself – for example, where you were born, where you went to school, what you like doing, what you hope to do in your life.

☐ Write letters to friends or family members; tell them about your daily life or about special events that have happened recently. These will not be translations, but accounts that you write freely out of your head. Write to different people and consider how your style changes, depending on whom you are addressing. Consider how a letter written to a close friend from your home area may be different from a letter to someone who lives in another country, a person you have never met.

A collection of stories

(1) Think of a good story in your own language. This can be a traditional story or any kind of story. Tell the story in your own words, recording it as you speak.

(2) Replay the recorded story. Play it slowly, sentence by sentence, and write it down just as you told it.

(3) Now go over the story to see if there are ways you can polish and improve it. Read it to other speakers of your language and discuss with them whether there are ways in which it can be further improved.

Consider writing a collection of stories in your language, to publish. If there are well-known story-tellers in your area, consider asking them to tell stories while you make a recording as they speak. Then transcribe the recordings and prepare a book of stories, giving the story-tellers due credit. This material will be a valuable resource for the study of the natural forms of your own language.

A project of this kind will help you to develop your skill in writing your language. Such a book is also likely to be very popular with people in your area. The stories will be good, easy-reading material for new readers.

Writing other kinds of texts

As time goes on, make recordings of other kinds of texts in this way; for example, songs, texts about the history of your people, descriptions of customs and local activities, speeches given on special occasions, teaching, and conversations. As you write these down and study them, you will observe the different styles and characteristics of each kind of text.

The Bible includes stories, history, songs, poems, prophecies, exhortations, speeches, conversations, letters, and more. Practice in writing different kinds of text in your own language will prepare you for translating these different kinds of texts in the Bible. See further discussion on different kinds of writing (genres) in chapter 38.

When you are translating, you are influenced by the way that the message is expressed in the source language. But when you are writing freely in your own language, you are thinking only in your own language, so your writing will be more natural and expressive. In this way, you will develop a good style of writing, and this will improve your skill in translating too.

6.2 Practise telling Bible stories in your language

Bible stories are always popular with children and with adults too. Much of the Bible text was told orally at first and then written down. The stories Jesus told, now written down in the Gospels, are a wonderful example of this.

Telling Bible stories orally is a valuable skill in itself, and it is also good preparation for Bible translation. See chapter 12, section 12.2, for discussion of a method for drafting a translation starting with an oral version.

Much has been written in recent years on telling Bible stories. See the articles and presentations listed at the end of this chapter for suggestions on developing this skill.

6.3 Study your language and find out about its grammar and style

Every language has its own unique grammar and pattern. Even though you have spoken your language fluently almost all your life, you may not have studied the grammar yet. Begin to study texts written in your own language. Look especially for ways in which the grammar is different from English. You will discover the beautiful patterns of the language!

Part 6 of this manual gives some detailed guidance on how to study the structure of your language and how to observe the features of the language that maintain fluent, well-connected discourse. This is something you will continue to explore.

> **Remember**
>
> Take time to discover the resources of your own language, the rich pattern of its grammatical features, and the wealth of its vocabulary.

Below are some examples of the kind of adjustments that may be necessary in a translation. These will vary greatly from language to language, depending on the grammar and style of each language. Some of these features are typical of certain families of languages, that is, languages that are related to each other.

6.3.1 In English, it is possible to have several prepositional phrases expressing time or place in one clause, all dependent on one verb

In some languages, however, it is necessary to state the implied verbs and to break one long clause down into several shorter clauses, each having its own verb. In many languages, ideas of direction and position are expressed by verbs rather than by prepositions. Experiment to see whether or not this is true of the language into which you are translating.

In these examples, prepositional phrases are underlined. (The symbol ⇒ means, "This could be re-expressed as.")

And Joseph also went up <u>from Galilee, from the town of Nazareth, to Judea.</u> (Luke 2:4)
⇒ Joseph *rose/got-up* from the town of Nazareth in Galilee, and *went to* Judea.

Silas and Timothy arrived <u>from Macedonia.</u> (Acts 18:5)
⇒ Silas and Timothy *came* from Macedonia, and arrived here.

We came by a straight course <u>to Cos,</u> and the next day <u>to Rhodes,</u> and <u>from there to Patara.</u> (Acts 21:1)
⇒ We went straight, and *came/reached* to Cos. On the next day we *travelled/reached* to Rhodes. Then *we left* Rhodes, *travelled* again, *reached* to Patara.

Fill the jars <u>with water</u>. (John 2:7)

> ⇒ *Bring/fetch* water, *take/use* it to fill the jars.

But I was let down <u>in a basket</u> <u>through a window</u> <u>in the wall</u>, and escaped his hands. (2 Corinthians 11:33)

This verse was translated in one language as follows:

> ⇒ Then people took me, put me in basket, which they tied to ropes; *they opened window/opening in wall which surrounded town, they lowered me to ground*; then I ran, escaped from him.

In English there are three prepositional phrases in one clause. In the translation, each is linked with a separate verb. Some background information is also supplied to make the reference to a window in the wall meaningful as the idea of a wall surrounding a town was quite unknown in the receptor area.

Remember

Many languages use more verbs than English does.

6.3.2 Different languages have different ways of linking sentences and clauses

As you study the grammar of your own language you will become aware of ways in which connections between sentences are different from those of English.

Even in English versions, there are differences in the use of connecting words. In the *King James Version*, for example, sentences in a narrative text often begin with the connecting word "and." This reflects the fact that in the original Greek text, the connecting word *kai* frequently occurs at the beginning of a sentence. In modern English, however, "and" is not commonly used at the beginning of a sentence. "And" is used to connect clauses within a sentence, or to connect a sequence of nouns, but much less often at the beginning of a sentence. For example, in Matthew 2:4–8, compare the occurrence of the connecting word "and" in *King James Version* with its non-occurrence in *NIV* or *GNT*. *NIV* and *GNT* reflect natural sentence connection in modern English. The use of connecting words will be discussed further in chapters 39 and 41.

6.3.3 Many languages use expressive exclamations that can be used in translating quotations of direct speech to express the feelings of the speaker meaningfully

Acts 23:4   Those who stood by said, "Would you revile God's high priest?"
In English this is a rhetorical question. It is not a request for information, but an expression of surprise and indignation. In oral speech, this would be indicated by the intonation or tone of the voice. In some languages, an exclamation may be needed to indicate these feelings:

> ⇒ Those who stood by said, "*Tcha*! You abuse like that the high priest who does the work of God!"

Some examples of exclamations in the Hausa language are "*Haba!*" "*Ashe!*" "*To!*" What exclamations are used in your language? What emotions do they express? Think of contexts in the Bible in which they would be appropriately used.

> **Translate in a way that will make people feel and react naturally**
>
> - Aim to make the readers feel what the original hearers felt.
> - Where there is deep emotional feeling in the message, this should be communicated – it is part of the message.
> - Where there is strong emphasis in the message, try to retain this in the translation.

6.4 Translation practice with non-Scripture exercises

Exercise 1

(1) Retell the following story in your own language. Begin by reading the story through, then retell the story orally, recording it as you speak. Transcribe the recording.

(2) Then compare the transcription with the original text and make any improvements needed to make the story more accurate to the original text in terms of meaning.

(3) Compare your translation of the story with the original English text to find ways where you have used expressions or grammar that are different from the source language. Discuss these with your advisor or staff-tutor. If possible, discuss your translation with other speakers of the language.

One day a poor man took a pot of milk to market. "I shall get a good price for this milk," he thought. "I will buy some eggs with the money. One of our hens will sit on them and then I shall have a dozen little chicks. Soon the chicks will become hens. They will all lay eggs. Then I shall buy a calf with the money. The calf will grow into a cow too. Soon I shall have a dozen cows. I shall be a rich man."

The man was very happy. He clapped his hands with joy. The pot of milk fell off his head. And that was the end of all his dreams.

Exercise 2

Instructions, as for exercise 1.

Once upon a time, a long, long time ago, Tortoise wanted to be the wisest animal in the world. So one day he collected up all his knowledge and put it in a calabash, thinking that he would tie the calabash to the top of a tall tree; then he would be able to keep all that knowledge for himself.

When he had put all his knowledge in the calabash, he tied it round his middle and started to climb the tree. He tried and he tried and he tried, but his legs were so short that he could not reach round the calabash and round the tree.

Along came his friend Rabbit. "What are you trying to do, Friend Tortoise?" he asked. Tortoise replied, "I am trying to climb to the top of this tree so that I can fasten all my knowledge there and keep it for myself. Then I will be the wisest animal in the world." "Why don't you tie it on your back? Then you will be able to climb the tree," suggested Rabbit.

So Tortoise tied the calabash on his back and started to climb the tree. But he had only climbed a little way when he stopped. "I thought I had all the knowledge in the world in my calabash," he said, "but I see that there is some which I left out. Let me go down and put it in the calabash. Maybe there is some more knowledge which I have left out."

And that is why nowadays Tortoise always carries the calabash on his back. He is looking for all the knowledge he has left out, so that one day he will be the wisest animal in the world.

Exercise 3

Translate a text recorded or written in your own language into another language.

(1) Take any short story or other text in your own language. It could be a story you have written in writing practice sessions, or any story. Make a translation of this story or text into English (or into any other language of wider communication of your choice).

(2) Underline places in your English translation where the grammar or idiomatic expressions you have used are different from those of the version in your own language. Discuss these with someone who speaks English as their first language.

This exercise helps you become more aware of ways in which the grammar of your own language is different from English or other languages.

Exercise 4

Translate a story from a language of wider communication (if applicable).

(1) Take any short story or other text in any language of wider communication in your country (for example, Indonesian, Amharic, Hausa, Arabic, Fulani, Swahili) and translate it into your own language.

(2) As in previous exercises above, underline places in your translation where you have used an idiomatic expression or grammatical construction that is different from that of the source language. Discuss these with your consultant or staff-tutor.

Additional resources on "Towards Naturalness – Beginning to Explore the Receptor Language"

BT4 online materials

6_Audio_and_visual_productions.pptx
6_How_to_craft_stories.pptx

For further reading

Brown, Rick. 2004. Communicating God's Message in an oral culture. *International Journal of Frontier Missions* 21(3):122–128. Available online at https://www.ijfm.org/PDFs_IJFM/21_4_PDFs/Oral%20Comm%20Brown-2.pdf.

Cohen Ioannides, Mara W. 2013. Translator as storyteller: A study of the book of Esther. *Journal of Translation* 9(1):23–29. https://www.sil.org/resources/publications/jot/9.1.

de Vries, Lourens. 2000. Bible Translation and Primary Orality. *The Bible Translator* 51(1):101–113.

Franklin, Karl. 2018. Comparing the processes of Bible translation and Bible storytelling. *GIALens* 12(1). http://www.gial.edu/documents/gialens/Vol12-1/Franklin-Comparing-BT-and-Storytelling.pdf.

Kelly, Brian. 2018. Preliminary questions to consider when looking at an oral translation approach. *GIALens* 12(1). http://www.gial.edu/documents/gialens/Vol12-1/Kelly-Preliminary- Questions.pdf.

Sim, R. J., and E. Korhonen. 1984. Frequency of verbs: Is our translation natural? *The Bible Translator* 35(2):224–229. http://www.ubs-translations.org/bt/archives_1950_2012/.

Thomas, Elaine. 1984. How to increase naturalness in translation by mother-tongue translators. *Notes on Translation* 106:6–9.

Maxey, James A. 2009. *From orality to orality: A new paradigm for contextual translation of the Bible.* Biblical Performance Criticism 2. Eugene, OR: Cascade Books.

Wendland, Ernst R. 2013. *Orality and the Scriptures: Composition, translation, and transmission.* Publications in Translation and Textlinguistics 6. Dallas: SIL International.

Chapter 7

How We Communicate with One Another

When we translate, we become part of the process of communicating a message from the original author to a new audience. Translation is a special kind of communication. In this chapter we consider what is involved in the process of communication.

7.1 The nature of communication

Communication typically involves the following parts:

(1) *A communicator,* someone who is communicating the message: He (or she) speaks or writes with a specific audience in mind. The communicator expresses his message in a way that he believes his audience will understand.

(2) *The audience,* the person or people receiving the message: When the audience receives the message, they expect the message to make sense; they expect to be able to understand it. So they make assumptions, using what they know already, in order to find the meaning of the message they are receiving.

Example 1

A shopkeeper, selling bread, asks the customer: "How many loaves do you need?" The buyer replies, "Three."

The shopkeeper does not need to say, "How many loaves of bread do you need?" He might even say just, "How many do you need?" The buyer does not need to say in full, "I want three loaves," because it is clear from the situation and the form of the question that he is referring to loaves of bread.

In speaking, we usually avoid redundancy. We say the words that are necessary to communicate what we want the audience to understand. We do not put into words information that already seems to be clear from the context.

The receiver of a message anticipates that the message will make sense. He assumes that the speaker is trying to communicate a meaningful message. So he interprets the message in a way that makes sense to him in that situation.

Example 2

A mother, seeing her child about to put his hand in the fire, cries out, "No!"

The message that the child understands is, "Don't put your hand in the fire!" Another person, hearing, "No!" in a different situation would understand something quite different.

In spoken communication where both speaker and hearer are interacting in the same situation, sentences are often short and may be grammatically incomplete.

This is also true in situations where the audience is waiting expectantly for certain information, as in the following newspaper headlines referring to an event that is already in the minds of the audience.

Example 3

   a. "THEY'VE LANDED!" ~ This was a newspaper headline at a time when people were waiting anxiously for news of astronauts on their way to the moon. It was not necessary to say in full, "Three men in a space ship have landed on the moon."
   b. "BORG WINS!" ~ For those of a certain background and living in a certain part of the world at a certain period of time, there was no need to say more. The audience knew that this meant, "Björn Borg, a very well-known tennis star, has won the Wimbledon tennis tournament this year."

We do not have to think consciously about taking the context into account. We learned to do this automatically as we learned to speak.

For discussion

   (1) Listen to conversations that you hear around you. Write down three examples of a short interchange where you observe that a speaker expresses only a part of his meaning in words, because he assumes that the context will enable the hearer to understand what he means.
   (2) Think of an example where there was some misunderstanding. What was the reason? Did the person who misunderstood what the speaker was trying to say make some assumptions that were not in fact correct?

7.2 Successful communication

Successful communication happens when the meaning that the audience understands is the same as the meaning the communicator intended to communicate.

The author of the message expresses his message in a way that he expects his intended audience will be able to understand correctly, both what he says in words and what he intends to imply. Knowing his audience, the author says what he believes is needed for them to understand the whole of his message. How you express what you want to say depends largely on whom you are addressing and what that person knows already.

Spoken communications between people who know each other well and who are in the same situation may be very brief!

7.3 Wider context

The context of a message is not limited to the immediate physical environment or to what has just been said. It may include other factors. Context is anything outside of the utterance itself that is relevant for its production or interpretation. This could include such things as

- ☐ previous communications, the memory of what has been said on an earlier occasion;
- ☐ information that is already known to both the speaker and the hearer, because of shared experience or shared cultural background – the speaker knows the hearer already has this information;
- ☐ recognition of the attitude or mood of the speaker – for example, whether he is happy, angry, or has a strong motivation for what he is trying to say. Is he sincere in what he is saying, or is he perhaps joking?
- ☐ what the hearer knows about the speaker will also influence his understanding. Rightly or wrongly, he may make assumptions about the reliability or truthfulness of the message that he is hearing; and
- ☐ what makes sense in the situation. For example, consider the following questions:
  - "Have you seen my wife?" said to a friend you meet as he is knocking on your front door, is likely to be understood as "Have you seen my wife within the last few minutes?"
  - "Have you been to Australia?" spoken in a friendly conversation is likely to be understood as "Have you ever been to Australia, anytime during your lifetime?"

7.4 Recognising the implications (inferences)

As we have seen in the examples above, for an utterance to make sense to the hearer, it needs to relate to the context in some way. The hearer uses his knowledge of the situation to make a connection with what has just been said and to draw some *inference* that he believes the speaker, the communicator, by *implication*, wants him to understand.

Example 4

If someone says, "It is four o'clock," the hearers assume he had a purpose in saying this. In other words, he is saying something that is relevant to their situation. Depending on their knowledge of the situation, their response might be, "Yes, it is time to stop work and go home." Or it might be, "We need to hurry up with what we are doing, we have not got much time left." Or it might be, "Time for a cup of tea!" The original speaker's next words will indicate whether or not the intended implication of his statement was correctly understood.

In normal conversation, what is said next indicates either that the hearer(s) understood the implication of the speaker correctly, OR that there was some misunderstanding and the hearers did not understand what the speaker intended to communicate. In the latter case, the speaker will usually explain what he really meant.

Example 5

In a village in South Sudan, a speaker once remarked, "I didn't go to church because of the birds." His hearers understood well his reason for not going to church. They knew that, as harvest time approaches, farmers in that area have to chase the birds away from their farms constantly, otherwise they will lose all their crops.

The speaker's reason for not going to church was understood by the original hearers; they understood it because they belonged to the same culture as the speaker.

The message might be translated for people who are not familiar with this culture, "I didn't go to church because I had to keep the birds away from my farm." This is the meaning that the original speaker intended (implied) and that the original hearers understood (inferred).

Example 6

> A Frenchman, speaking French, described an incident as follows: "He drove straight down the left-hand side of the road."

In France, as in many countries, vehicles travel on the right-hand side of the road. The implication of the speaker's message was, therefore, that the man was driving on the *wrong* side of the road. In the United Kingdom, however, it is correct to drive on the left-hand side of the road. If the message is translated literally for people in the United Kingdom, the point that he was on the wrong side would not be understood. A good translation of the statement intended for people in the United Kingdom would be: "He drove straight down the wrong side of the road."

Such a translation is accurate to the historical situation, it expresses what the speaker means, and the speaker's meaning is likely to be correctly understood by the hearers.

Example 7: A biblical example – John 2:1–11

Regina Blass, an experienced translation consultant, writes about this passage as follows:

> In the wedding report of Cana (John 2:2), it is obvious that more was intended to be communicated than what was said. When Mary says: "They have no more wine" she did not only want to inform Jesus about this, but to make Jesus do something about it. This becomes obvious when Jesus says: "Mother, what do I have to do with you. My time has not come yet." In order to understand why Jesus responds the way he does we cannot just deal with the written utterances, we need to enter into deduction using specific background knowledge. Modern communication theorists, Grice (1978), Sperber and Wilson (1986, 1995), claim that what is communicated is not so much what is said but what is implicated. (2001:50–52)

All that Mary said was, that the wine was finished. Why did she tell Jesus this? Jesus understood the implication of what she was saying. She wanted him to take some action to help those who were in an embarrassing situation because they had underestimated the amount of wine that would be needed for their guests. He understood this *implication* and acted accordingly.

7.5 Summary

As we have seen, the communication of a message involves both

- information that is stated *explicitly*, that is, it is stated in words; and
- information that is assumed by the author; he knows that the audience already has access to that information. This is sometimes referred to as *implicit* information.

It may also involve an inference or implication, some new aspect of meaning that the communicator wants and expects the hearer to deduce from the message. The hearer will only understand the message if he has access to both the explicit information and the implicit information. In spoken conversation, this may be what has just been said. Or it may be some fact that both the speaker and the hearer already know, so it does not need to be restated.

7.6 Communication in the context of the receptor culture

In normal communication, the communicator makes explicit as much information as he believes the audience needs to understand what he wants to communicate. However, when a message is translated for someone of a different cultural background, the receiver of the message may not have all the necessary "clues" that he needs to interpret it correctly.

In Bible translation, the original message was given for people of a different cultural background, at a period of time at least nearly 2000 years ago, and in a specific situation. The translator has the challenge of trying to reframe that message in a way that enables the new hearers to understand the implications of the original message. This issue will be discussed further in the next chapter.

Additional resources on "How We Communicate with One Another"

BT4 online materials

7_How_we_communicate.pptx

Websites

Dooley, Robert A. 2008. Relevance theory and discourse analysis: Complementary approaches for translator training. *GIALens* 2(3). https://www.diu.edu/documents/gialens/Vol2-3/Dooley-Relevance-theory.pdf.
Pattemore, Stephen. Translation is communication. https://www.youtube.com/watch?v=GbLPzNmyZVI.
Pattemore, Stephen. A quick guide to relevance theory – Introducing some technical terms. https://www.youtube.com/watch?v=VAwro8BPPbM.

For further reading

The following publications explain the principles of *Relevance Theory*, a perception of communication that focuses on the understanding of the receptor audience.

Blass, Regina. 2001. A response to Cahill. Notes on Translation 15(3):50–52.
Gutt, Ernst-August. 2000. *Translation and relevance: Cognition and context*. Second edition. Manchester: St. Jerome Publishing. Reprint, London: Routledge, 2014.
Hill, Harriet, Ernst-August Gutt, Margaret Hill, Christoph Unger, and Rick Floyd. 2011. *Bible translation basics: Communicating Scripture in a relevant way*. Dallas: SIL International.
Kerr, Glenn J. 2011. Dynamic equivalence and its daughters: Placing Bible translation theories in their historical context. *Journal of Translation* 7(1):1–19. See https://www.sil.org/resources/publications/entry/43391.
Sperber, Dan, and Deirdre Wilson. 1995. *Relevance: Communication and cognition*. Second edition. Oxford/Cambridge: Blackwell Publishers.
Wendland, Ernst R. 2014. *Contextual frames of reference in translation: A coursebook for Bible translators and teachers*. London: Routledge.

Chapter 8

Communicating across Cultures and across Time

The following example is contributed by Lee Ballard (personal communication), a translation consultant who worked for many years in the Philippines. The text below is a fairly literal translation of a story originally told in the Ibaloi language, spoken in the Philippines. It aims to put you in the position of someone who is reading about events that happened in a country and culture quite unknown to him.

8.1 An Ibaloi story

One of those who found (some of the buried money) was Juan Bejar.... They arrived with it at night at his house, and he did-"*kapi*"-for-it that night at his house at Salakoban. Yes, it was at his house where he did-"*kapi*"-for-it.

The next morning, as they were eating the head, the new jawbone fell down. And it was not tilted when it fell but rather it was upright and it was pointing east. When the old women saw it, they said, "Do-it-a-second-time. Perhaps they have regarded-it-as-insufficient." And yes, Juan did-"*kapi*"-for-it a second time.

The following questions are intended to test whether or not this English translation is meaningful to you. Answer these questions as best you can:

a. What is "*kapi*"?
b. Why did they do "*kapi*"?
c. Who were eating the head?
d. The head of what?
e. What fell down?
f. The jawbone of what?
g. Where did it fall from?
h. What is the significance of the jawbone's being upright and pointing east?
i. What was the old women's reaction to what happened?
j. Why did they react in this way?
k. How do you understand the sentence, "Perhaps they have regarded it as insufficient"?

There are many things that are not clear to us. This is because the writer of the story was writing for fellow Ibaloi people. There are things from the Ibaloi culture that he assumed his audience already knew, and so he did not explain them.

Now read another translation of the same story:

> One of those who found some of the buried money was Juan Bejar.... They brought it to his house at night, and he <u>celebrated the feast of "*kapi*" with a pig as payment to the ancestral spirits</u>. Yes, it was at his house there in Salakoban that he celebrated the <u>feast of</u> "kapi" for it.
>
> The next morning, <u>as they were having the traditional community breakfast following feasts, the jawbone of the pig that had been sacrificed the previous evening</u> fell down from the eaves of the house where it is traditionally hung. And it was not tilted when it fell but rather it was upright, and it was pointing east <u>where the ancestral spirits are said to live</u>. When the old women saw it, they regarded it all as a bad omen and said, "Celebrate 'kapi' a second time. Perhaps <u>the ancestral spirits</u> have regarded the pig you sacrificed as insufficient payment." And yes, Juan celebrated "kapi" for it a second time.

For non-Ibaloi people, this second version of the story is more meaningful. Why? Because cultural information that is essential for understanding the point of the story has been provided for the reader. (This information has been underlined in the second version of the story.) The hearers of the original story were themselves Ibaloi people, so they already knew these facts. But hearers from a different cultural background need to have that information made available to them.

8.2 The translator's challenge

Every message arises out of a specific context. The speaker (or writer) has a certain audience in mind as he gives his message. This will affect the form of his message. It will affect his decision on what information to include or leave out.

The audience who are receiving the translated Scriptures are in a different situation from the hearers of the original message. The geographical and political setting in which they live is very different, their customs and way of life are different. Sometimes objects or concepts are mentioned that are unfamiliar to them. They may interpret the message in the light of their own culture, and so sometimes come to conclusions that are incorrect because they are not what the original author intended.

The audience of the translation can only understand the original author's message if they have access to both the explicit information that the author stated in words, and the implicit information that the author assumed the audience would know.

8.3 Historical faithfulness

The Bible is a historical document. The books of the Bible were written at specific times in history for people of a certain cultural background. Even the most recent of the books of the Bible were written almost 2000 years ago.

In studying the meaning of the source texts, the translator must consider carefully the historical situation in which each book of the Bible was written, and the specific audience to whom it was addressed. The meaning of the original message that the author intended to communicate can only be fully understood in the light of that original situation.

8.4 The translator's aim

The translator must balance two goals:

- faithfulness to the historical situation – he must not change the message; he must not change the historical situation or the cultural background; and
- communication effectiveness – at the same time, he aims to express the message in a way that hearers from the receptor language and culture will be able to understand, as accurately as possible, the meaning that the original author intended to communicate.

8.5 Explicit information and implicit (assumed) information

The author's message can only be understood if the hearer has access to both the *explicit* information, and the *implicit* information needed to interpret correctly the meaning that the author intended to communicate.

The speaker (or writer) has only succeeded in communicating his message if the receiver of the message has correctly understood the whole message, both what was explicit and what was implicit.

Remember

The aim of the translator is to enable the audience of the translation to understand the same message that the hearers of the original message understood.

8.6 Making necessary background information available to the receptor audience

It is your goal as a translator to communicate the original message in such a way that the hearers of the translation will understand what the author intended to say.

This does not mean that all the implicit information should be made explicit in the translation. That might lead to the main point of the message being obscured by background details. The implicit information that should be made explicit is only what the receptor audience needs in order to understand the main point of the message.

Sometimes the necessary historical and cultural information can be supplied outside the text, for example, by a footnote or an illustration. Chapters 14 and 15 suggest some ways in which essential background information can be made available to the reader in ways that are supplementary to the text.

> **Guidelines**
> - Only information that is already assumed by the author in the original text may be made explicit. No new information may be added.
> - Implicit information may be made explicit under the following conditions:
>   a. If it is essential in order to communicate the main point of the message
>   b. If without the implicit information, no meaning or wrong meaning would be communicated
>   c. If it can be done without distorting the main focus or theme of the message
>   d. If it is appropriate to the original situation in which the message was given
> - Evaluate your translation by asking yourself the question, "Will the receivers of this translation understand accurately what the original author was saying?"

8.7 Faithfulness to Scripture

Sometimes people fear that a meaning-based translation is betraying the inspiration of the Scriptures. Such a fear arises out of a deep reverence for the Scriptures and an understanding that God inspired the very words of the text in their original language. It should be remembered, however, that the form of the Bible's message (the words and the grammar of the Greek, Hebrew, and Aramaic text) is just the means of expressing the message in those languages. It is the meaning of that message that is universal and that is inspired by God. The translator must share the same deep reverence for the Scriptures, and do his utmost, with God's help, to be faithful in expressing the true meaning of the Scriptures. It is his goal to express this message in such a way that its meaning will be understood and not hidden by bad translation.

It is also important for the translator to pay careful attention to the details of the original message, and to the precise meaning of the grammar and words in which it is expressed. Details of the grammar and words express important distinctions of meaning. Although the translator will not keep the same grammatical forms, he must re-express accurately those same distinctions of meaning as closely as possible.

8.8 Making *explicit* information *implicit*

It may sometimes be necessary to leave implicit in the translation information that is explicit in the source text. Usually, this is to avoid unnatural redundancy in the receptor language. The important point is always to make sure that there is no loss of information in the translation, and that the same emphasis and emotional impact are maintained.

8.9 An exercise: Luke 2:1–2

In Luke 2:1–2 there is some assumed information that may need to be made explicit in a translation. Look up the verse in its context and look at different English versions. Restate the passage in English, making the assumed information explicit.

Luke 2:1–2   In those days a decree went out from Caesar Augustus that all the world should be registered. ²This was the first registration when Quirinius was governor of Syria.

Note: There are two possible interpretations of verse 2. The first interpretation is that this was the first census that was taken in the Roman world; it happened when Quirinius was governor of Syria. The second interpretation is that this was the first census that happened when Quirinius was governor, implying there could have been a previous census and that there was at least one more census during the time when Quirinius was governing. The UBS Translator's Handbook recommends following the first interpretation.

Points to ponder

Translation is a form of communication, not just a linguistic activity.

The translator "is cautioned not to confuse linguistic translation with 'cultural translation,' transforming the Pharisees and Sadducees, for instance, into present-day religious parties. In other words, the historical particularity of the text is to be respected" (Carson 1987:3).

"Dynamic equivalence is therefore to be defined in terms of the degree to which the receptors of the message in the receptor language respond to it in substantially the same manner as the receptors in the source language. This response can never be identical, for the cultural and historical settings are too different, but there should be a high degree of equivalence of response, or the translation will have failed to accomplish its purpose" (Nida and Taber 1969:24).

"The central claim of relevance theory is that human communication crucially creates an expectation of *optimal relevance*, that is, an expectation on the part of the hearer that his attempt at interpretation will yield *adequate contextual effects at minimal processing cost*" (Gutt 2000:31–32).

Additional resources on "Communicating across Cultures and across Time"

BT4 online materials

8_Communicating_full_meaning-Ibaloi.pptx

For further reading

Carson, D. A. 1987. The limits of dynamic equivalence in Bible translation. *Notes on Translation* 121:1–15.

Carson, D. A. 2003. The limits of functional equivalence in Bible translation – and other limits too. In Glen G. Scorgie, Mark L. Strauss, and Steven M. Voth (eds.), *The challenge of Bible translation: Communicating God's word to the world*, 65-113. Grand Rapids, MI: Zondervan.

Gutt, Ernst-August. (2000) 2014. *Translation and relevance: Cognition and context.* Second edition. Manchester: St. Jerome Publishing. Reprint, London: Routledge.

Hill, Harriet. 2006. *The Bible at cultural crossroads: From translation to communication.* Manchester: St. Jerome Publishing.

Nida, Eugene A., and Charles R. Taber. 1969. *The theory and practice of translation.* Leiden: E. J. Brill for the United Bible Societies. Originally published in the series *Helps for Translators* 8. Reprinted 1974 and 1982. Fourth impression 2003.

Wendland, Ernst R. 1987. *The cultural factor in Bible translation: A study of communicating the Word of God in a central African cultural context.* UBS Monograph Series 2. London: United Bible Societies.

Chapter 9

More about Cross-Cultural Communication

In the previous chapter, we saw that a message originally written for one audience may be difficult for a different audience to understand. There are several possible reasons for this: it may be because the message includes

- information that the author assumes his audience already knows because they come from the same cultural background as himself;
- references to historical events that the author assumes his audience will know about, especially events that are recorded in the Old Testament; and
- actions that are symbolic and have a special significance for people of the original culture.

In this chapter we will look at examples of each of these situations in turn and consider ways to achieve successful communication in these cross-cultural contexts.

9.1 Information that the author assumes the audience already knows

As we have seen, if the author and his readers or hearers come from the same cultural background, the author may not explicitly mention background information that he assumes his audience already knows. To the audience of a translation, however, this information may be unknown and because of this they may misunderstand the author's main message.

The biblical examples below illustrate that it is often possible to provide some help for the reader in the text of the translation itself.

Mark 7:26   Now the woman was a Greek, a Syrophoenician by birth. (*RSV*)

    GNT   The woman was a Gentile, born in the region of Phoenicia in Syria.

The word that is translated in RSV and NIV as "Greek" was also used more generally to refer to "a Gentile, any non-Jewish person." In this context, the major point of the story is that, even though she was not a Jew, the woman is asking Jesus to help her.

Mark 12:14   Is it lawful to pay taxes to Caesar or not?

    REB   Are we or are we not permitted to pay taxes to the Roman emperor?

The word "Caesar" is not a personal name; it is a title given to the Emperor of Rome. The point of this incident is that Jesus is being asked whether it is according to Jewish law to pay taxes to the supreme ruler of the Romans, who were enemies and oppressors of the people of Israel. Although the REB translation does not explain all the implications of the original situation, it provides the reader with the correct information as to who "Caesar" was. For full understanding, the reader would also need to know about the political situation at that time. He would need to know that the Romans were ruling Israel and how patriotic Jews felt about this. This fuller background information can be provided in other ways (see chapter 14).

Luke 7:44   You gave me no water for my feet.

The original author assumed that the hearer would know that it was the custom for people to give a visitor water in order that he could wash his feet. This was the normal thing to do in Palestine when a visitor arrived. To the audience in another culture, however, this custom may be unfamiliar. If the translator is thinking of the new readers, he might translate: "You did not give me water to wash my feet."

NLT translates: "When I entered your home, you didn't offer me water to wash the dust from my feet." The message has not been changed. The idea of washing, which was originally assumed, has been made explicit.

Colossians 4:11   These are the only men of the circumcision among my fellow workers.

Circumcision is known in many cultures. But its function within each culture may be very different. In some cultures (for example, USA) it has no religious significance but is done purely for medical and hygienic reasons. In some societies, it is done to teenage boys and is associated with attaining manhood. In others, it may symbolise joining a certain religious group or being recognised as part of a certain family group. But the correct understanding of biblical references depends on the fact that circumcision signified being a Jew. For this reason, the GNT translates Colossians 4:11, "These three are the only Jewish believers who work with me."

Philippians 3:5   circumcised on the eighth day

Because of their knowledge of Jewish custom, the original readers would have understood that "the eighth day" meant the eighth day from birth. In a translation for hearers from another culture, it may be necessary to make the information "from birth" explicit. NLT translates: "I was circumcised when I was eight days old." The original meaning of the message is not changed. See Genesis 17:9–14.

Exercise 1

In each of the following passages, there is some assumed information. This may need to be made explicit in a translation. Look up the verse in its context and look at different English versions. Restate each passage in English, making the assumed information explicit.

Matthew 12:1–2   At that time Jesus went through the grainfields on the Sabbath. His disciples were hungry, and they began to pluck heads of grain and to eat. ² But when the Pharisees saw it, they said to him, "Look, your disciples are doing what is not lawful to do on the Sabbath."

Matthew 18:17   If he refuses to listen even to the church, let him be to you as a Gentile and a tax collector.

Mark 4:35   Let us go across to the other side.

Acts 22:2   And when they heard that he was addressing them in the Hebrew language, they became even more quiet.

Hebrews 11:30   By faith the walls of Jericho fell down after they had been encircled for seven days.

9.2 Historical references

References to historical events recorded in the Old Testament are common in the New Testament. Such references should be translated in a way that is as meaningful as possible for the new audience, without expanding in a way that would twist or hide the main point of the original message.

Mark 1:2–3   As it is written in Isaiah the prophet, "Behold, I send my messenger before your face, who will prepare your way, ³ the voice of one crying in the wilderness: 'Prepare the way of the Lord, make his paths straight.'"

GNT   It began as the prophet Isaiah had written: "God said, 'I will send my messenger ahead of you to open the way for you.' ³ Someone is shouting in the desert, 'Get the road ready for the Lord; make a straight path for him to travel!'"

The prophet Isaiah spoke as God's mouthpiece, foretelling the coming of the Messiah. Readers who are unfamiliar with the Old Testament might not realise that "I" in this passage does not refer to Isaiah but to God – as a prophet, Isaiah was writing what God had said. The GNT avoids implying the wrong meaning, by making it clear that it is God who spoke these words.

Mark 12:26–27   "And as for the dead being raised, have you not read in the book of Moses, in the passage about the bush, how God spoke to him, saying, 'I am the God of Abraham, and the God of Isaac, and the God of Jacob'? ²⁷ He is not God of the dead, but of the living. You are quite wrong."

"Quite wrong" about what? Quite wrong in believing that people do not rise to life after death. Mark 12:18 sets the context: "And Sadducees came to him, who say that there is no resurrection." Jesus focuses again explicitly on this point in verse 26: "And as for the dead being raised." He makes the point that, long after Abraham, Isaac, and Jacob had died in this world, God said he is their God, thus showing that they must have been raised to life again.

Because of a lack of knowledge about the time when Abraham, Isaac, and Jacob died, and about the covenant that God made with them, the sense may be wrongly thought to be that God is the God of people who are alive in this world now, not of people who have died. But the point here is that people do rise from death. NLT makes this clear: "Long after Abraham, Isaac, and Jacob had died, God said to Moses, 'I am the God of Abraham, the God of Isaac, and the God of Jacob.'"

1 Corinthians 10:1–2   I want you to know, brethren, that our fathers were all under the cloud, and all passed through the sea, ² and all were baptized into Moses in the cloud and in the sea. (RSV)

GNT   I want you to remember, my friends, what happened to our ancestors who followed Moses. They were all under the protection of the

	cloud, and all passed safely through the Red Sea. ²In the cloud and in the sea they were all baptized as followers of Moses.
NLT	I don't want you to forget, dear brothers and sisters, about our ancestors in the wilderness long ago. All of them were guided by a cloud that moved ahead of them, and all of them walked through the sea on dry ground. ²In the cloud and in the sea, all of them were baptized as followers of Moses.

Compare and discuss the GNT and NLT translations.

Hebrews 11:22	By faith Joseph, at the end of his life, made mention of the exodus of the Israelites and gave directions concerning his bones.
NIV	By faith Joseph, when his end was near, spoke about the exodus of the Israelites from Egypt and gave instructions concerning the burial of his bones.
DGN	Because Joseph trusted God, he was able at his death to speak about the future departure of the Israelites from Egypt and to give instructions about what should then be done with his bones. (*DGN* – English translation from the German version, *Die Gute Nachricht*)
CEV	And right before Joseph died, he had faith that God would lead the people of Israel out of Egypt. So he told them to take his bones with them.

DGN and CEV make it clear that, at the time when Joseph spoke, the departure of the people of Israel from Egypt was still a future event.

Hebrews 11:23	By faith Moses, when he was born, was hidden for three months by his parents because they saw that the child was beautiful, and they were not afraid of the king's edict.
NLT	It was by faith that Moses' parents hid him for three months when he was born. They saw that God had given them an unusual child, and they were not afraid to disobey the king's command.

At the time when Moses was born, it was because his parents believed in God that they hid him for three months.... They were not afraid to resist the command of the king that all their male children should be killed. (English translation from the Margi language translation, Nigeria)

1 Peter 2:10	Once you were not a people but now you are God's people.
GNT	At one time you were not God's people, but now you are his people.

The GNT translates meaningfully in the light of Hosea 2:23, which is being quoted in this passage.

9.3 Symbolic actions

In any culture, there are actions that are *symbolic*; that is, they have a special meaning for people of that culture. People who understand the culture will know the meaning of the action; others may be puzzled or may misunderstand.

Example 1

In Mbembe culture, if a speaker said, "He has broken his wife's water pot," an outsider might think that this referred to an accidental breaking. But an Mbembe person would know that this action meant that the man had in fact divorced his wife. This is not a figure of speech. The man did in fact break the water pot. But the action has special significance in the culture.

Example 2

Matthew 21:8 Others cut branches from the trees and spread them on the road.

In Palestine, and indeed in many areas of Africa, palm branches are spread in the road to prepare the way for a chief or important person. But in one area where such a custom was unknown, it was thought that people were spreading branches on the road in order to block the path so that Jesus could not pass. Because of their unfamiliarity with the custom, the hearers thought of the wrong kind of branches. It might have been good to make explicit "palm branches" in order to avoid this wrong meaning. The parallel passage in John 12:13 refers specifically to branches from palm trees.

Example 3

Luke 18:13 The tax collector, standing far off, would not even lift up his eyes to heaven, but beat his breast.

In Jewish culture, "beating the breast" was a symbol of grief or sorrow, in this case sorrow and repentance because of sin. In some cultures, however, the action of "beating the breast" implies pride and defiance. The action may be the same, but the symbolism is different. Care needs to be taken in translating "beat the breast." What exactly was the original gesture? What similar gestures exist in the receptor culture?

Sometimes the purpose of the symbolic action is clear in the source text:

Genesis 17:11 You shall be circumcised in the flesh of your foreskins, and it shall be a sign of the covenant between me and you.

Here a new symbolic custom is being established for the first time and is therefore explained.

Exodus 3:5 Put off your shoes from your feet, for the place on which you are standing is holy ground. (RSV)

The custom of removing your shoes in a holy place was familiar to the original audience, and the speaker is explaining the reason for his command.

Ruth 4:7 Now in those days, to settle a sale or an exchange of property, it was the custom for the seller to take off his sandal and give it to the buyer. In this way the Israelites showed that the matter was settled. (GNT)

In this case, it seems that the custom referred to was no longer practised in Israel by the time that the book of Ruth was written. Therefore, it was unfamiliar to the original audience for whom the book of Ruth was written and the author explains it.

2 Samuel 3:31 Then David said to Joab and to all the people who were with him, "Tear your clothes and put on sackcloth and mourn before Abner."

Here the reference to mourning in the context explains the symbolism of tearing the clothes and of putting on sackcloth.

Mark 7:3   For the Pharisees and all the Jews do not eat unless they wash their hands properly, holding to the tradition of the elders.

This background information is very important for an understanding of the incident that is being described. Mark was writing not only for Jews (who already knew this custom) but also for non-Jews, and therefore he explains the custom.

For discussion

Describe some examples of symbolic actions in your own culture, which might be misunderstood by people from another culture.

9.4 Translating references to symbolic actions

In translating references to symbolic actions, two things must be considered:

- the form of the action itself
- the symbolism or meaning of the action

Consider four different situations that may arise:

- ☐ The action may be known in the receptor language culture and may have the same meaning or symbolism as in the source language culture. In this case, there is no problem.
- ☐ The action may be known in the receptor language culture, but may have no special meaning or symbolism. In this case, there is danger that the main point may be lost.
- ☐ The action may be known in the receptor language culture, but may have a different meaning or symbolism from that which it has in the source language culture. In this case, there is danger that wrong meaning will be communicated.
- ☐ The action itself may be unknown in the receptor language culture.

To avoid communicating wrong meaning, or no meaning at all, it may sometimes be necessary to make the meaning of the symbolic act explicit. For example, in the situation described in example 2 above, Matthew 21:8 might be translated, "Others cut (palm) branches and spread them on the road <u>to welcome him</u>."

Or sometimes it may be possible to use a similar action that is known in the receptor culture that has the correct symbolic meaning. For example, in a certain culture where "beating the breast" symbolised defiance, it was the custom to cross the arms across the breast with a patting motion in order to show sorrow. So this action was used to describe the attitude of the tax-collector in Luke 18:13. Indeed this action may be more similar to the Jewish gesture than to the action that is suggested by the English translation "beat" the breast.

Remember

- In translating symbolic actions, make sure that the correct meaning of the action is also communicated.
- In order to avoid wrong meaning, or no meaning, it may sometimes be necessary to make the significance of a symbolic action explicit.

Exercise 2

In each of the following passages, a symbolic action is mentioned. Use resources such as the Paratext or *Translator's Workplace* programs to look up and compare the *NIV*, *GNT*, and/or *NLT* versions of these verses – some versions make the symbolism explicit. Also look at comments on these verses in *UBS Translator's Handbooks* or in *Translator's Notes* – these resources can also be found in Paratext or *Translator's Workplace*.

For each example, note down

(1) what the symbolic action is;

(2) what this action means or symbolises in this context; and

(3) whether or not the same action would have the same meaning in your own culture. For those passages where the meaning in your own culture would not be the same, discuss how you might translate this concept into your own language.

Matthew 10:14	And if anyone will not receive you or listen to your words, shake off the dust from your feet when you leave that house or town.
Matthew 27:24	So when Pilate saw that he was gaining nothing, but rather that a riot was beginning, he took water and washed his hands before the crowd, saying, "I am innocent of this man's blood; see to it yourselves."
Mark 1:7	And he preached, saying, "After me comes he who is mightier than I, the thong of whose sandals I am not worthy to stoop down and untie." (*RSV*)
Mark 10:16	And he took them in his arms and blessed them, laying his hands on them.
Mark 15:17	And they clothed him in a purple cloak, and plaiting a crown of thorns they put it on him. (*RSV*)

Exercise 3

Instructions, as for exercise 2 above.

Ruth 1:14
1 Samuel 16:13
1 Kings 20:31
Psalm 44:20

Exercise 4

Instructions, as for exercises 2 and 3 above.

Acts 13:3
Acts 14:14
Acts 22:23
Acts 26:1
1 Corinthians 16:20
1 Timothy 5:10
Revelation 11:3

9.5 Points to remember

- ☐ Never assume that, because you, the translator, can understand the translation, other people will necessarily be able to understand it. Remember that you have studied the passage in another language already and have more Bible knowledge than many readers. Test to see whether it is understood by speakers of the language who are not familiar with the Bible.
- ☐ Try to translate meaningfully, so as to give a full understanding of the message. But do not add long explanations or new information to the message. Translate in a way that makes the original intention of the author clear.
- ☐ Opinions differ concerning how much background information may be made explicit in the text. Some versions are very explicit. Some versions do not make anything explicit that is not explicit in the original text – translations of this kind will be difficult for the modern reader to understand without the help of a teacher or commentary. Other versions follow a middle course.
- ☐ Avoid the temptation to leave something out, or to change the meaning so as to make it easier to understand. Instead, try to express the full meaning in a way that can be understood. Consider including a footnote, if necessary.

An example is reported from an early translation project in a language of northern Ghana. Slavery was a common practice in the area at that time. The translator was afraid to include the words "nor thy servant" in the translation of Deuteronomy 5:14, because he was afraid that if the slaves read that servants also should not do work on the Sabbath day, they would use this against their masters and refuse to work. Fortunately, there were others who insisted that this phrase be put in the text before it was printed.

To give a modern example: when translating Romans 1:27, one translator was tempted to omit the reference to homosexuality. Such a thing had never been heard of in the language area, and so it seemed to him a pity to put the concept into people's minds. But he rightly decided that he should include the idea in his translation. To omit it would have been to change the Scripture. The translator has no authority to make any change. It is his duty and responsibility to communicate the exact meaning of the original, unchanged in any way.

9.6 Translation exercise

Study the parable of The Good Samaritan, Luke 10:30–37. What is the main point of the story that Jesus told? What "clues" do the people of your own culture need to understand the point of what Jesus was teaching? After studying the text, retell the story in your own language, without looking at the Bible text. If possible, tell it to one or more speakers of that language and discuss it with them, to see whether they understood what Jesus was teaching.

Record the story as you told it orally, then transcribe it. Work on the transcribed text to develop it as a translation.

9.7 Spiritual hindrances

The parable of The Sower (Matthew 13:1–9, Mark 4:1–9, and Luke 8:4–8) illustrates the fact that sometimes, even if the message is expressed in a meaningful way, it may not be understood because

- sometimes people are not interested;

- sometimes people are too busy with other things to listen; or
- sometimes people already have fixed assumptions and are not open to new ideas.

It is through the work of the Holy Spirit that people come to understand the personal implications of the message and to accept it.

As a translator your responsibility is to make sure that the message is expressed as clearly as possible so that there is nothing in the form of the message that prevents understanding. If people do not understand because the translation is poor, then the translator has failed in his task. Make sure that there is nothing in the translation that hinders the communication of the original author's message.

Remember

- Unnatural language hinders the communication of the message.
- Lack of essential background information hinders the communication of the message. Make sure that the hearer or reader of the translation has the historical, geographical, and cultural information he needs about the original situation in which the message was given.

Planning for translation practice

Part 7 of this training manual discusses issues that need to be considered when a new translation project is being planned. Plans need to be discussed in depth with leaders in the language area concerned. This includes deciding on the first translation goals for this project. It is suggested that prospective translators who are following this manual choose certain passages to translate as an initial translation goal, with consideration of the long-term plans for the project in which they are, or will be, involved as translators. As they study the principles and procedures presented in this training manual, they will apply them to the translation of the passages they have chosen as their initial goal, as well as to the translation practice exercises included in the manual.

Each prospective translator should be linked with a consultant or trainer who will interact with him by reviewing his draft translations, discussing them with him, and giving him feedback.

Some suggested initial goals:

(1) One of the *Wonderful Plan of God* books comprising selections from the Old Testament, with illustrations:

    Book 1: *The Beginning of Everything* (selections from Genesis)

    Book 2: *The Story of God's People* (selections mainly from Exodus)

    Book 3: *A Saviour-King Will Come* (selected prophecies of the coming of the Messiah)

For details on the *Wonderful Plan of God* selections, see the information listed under **BT4 online materials** below.

(2) The Book of Ruth

(3) Christmas story: Luke 2:1–10 and Matthew 1:18–2:12

(4) Easter story: Selected passages from Matthew chapters 26–28 and/or John chapters 18–20

(5) Parables Jesus told; selections from the Gospel of Luke:
>   Story of The Good Samaritan (Luke 10:25–37)
>   Story of The Rich Fool (Luke 12:16–21)
>   Story of The Great Feast (Luke 14:15–24)
>   Story of The Prodigal Son (Luke 15:11–32)
>   Story of The Widow and the Judge (Luke 18:1–8)
>   Story of The Pharisee and the Tax Collector (Luke 18:9–14)
>   Story of The Gold Coins (Luke 19:11–27)
>   Story of The Tenants in the Vineyard (Luke 20:9–18)

(6) Passages from the Gospel of Mark: Mark 4:35–41, 5:1–20, 5:21–43, 6:1–6, 6:6–13, 6:14–29, 6:45–52

The translator could then go on to complete the translation of the whole Gospel of Mark.

(7) In areas where one or more of the denominations represented has a planned system of lectionary readings, take this system into account in selecting (a) the Gospel to be translated first and (b) some specific passages to be translated as initial goals.

Additional resources for "The *Wonderful Plan of God* Selections"

BT4 online materials

For information on *Wonderful Plan of God* selections, see the document 9_Wonderful_plan_of_God-Summary_and_selections-2019.pdf.
(Formatted copies of the *Wonderful Plan of God* selections, with illustrations, are available to view on *Translator's Workplace*. Search for "Wonderful Plan of God" in the library menu and follow the jump links in that file to view each of the booklets in the series.)

See also:
> The video *How to use Bible modules in Paratext*, prepared by Darcie Drymon, demonstrating the Paratext tool that is available for formatting these *Wonderful Plan of God* selections as booklets. This can be viewed at https://vimeo.com/185916082.

Additional information on Bible modules can be viewed at https://lingtran.net/Example+Modules.

Part 2

Translation Procedures

Chapter 10

A Ten-Step Procedure in Translation

This chapter gives an overview of the procedure of translation. The following ten chapters focus on each step in detail. Situations vary and the pattern of work needs to be adjusted to fit the local situation. The description below includes some alternatives.

In summary, to achieve a good quality translation, follow these procedures:

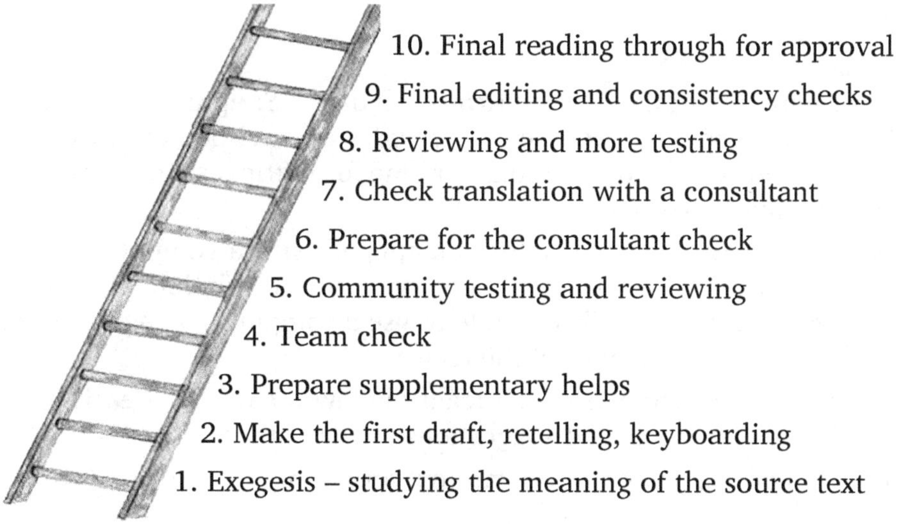

10. Final reading through for approval
9. Final editing and consistency checks
8. Reviewing and more testing
7. Check translation with a consultant
6. Prepare for the consultant check
5. Community testing and reviewing
4. Team check
3. Prepare supplementary helps
2. Make the first draft, retelling, keyboarding
1. Exegesis – studying the meaning of the source text

Figure 1. A ten-step translation procedure.
© 2018 by Seed Company. Used by permission.

Step 1: Exegesis – studying the meaning of the source text

The translator's first task is to study the text carefully, referring to Bible versions, commentaries, and other helps for translators.

Before beginning to translate any Bible book, take time to study the whole book – read the book in at least two different Bible versions. It may also help to listen to an audio recording of the book.

Read the introduction to the book in *Translator's Notes* and in *UBS Translator's Handbooks* (both available in Paratext), in the *NIV Study Bible,* or in a commentary or in other translation helps, seeking to find out to whom, when, and why the book was written. In this way you will gain an overview of the author's purpose in writing the book and of the audience for whom he was writing.

Then focus on natural section and paragraph units in the text, section by section.

See chapter 11 for further details.

Step 2: Making the first draft

The translator, who speaks the receptor language fluently as his first language, makes the first draft of the translation, focusing on one section of the Bible text at a time.

2.1 Oral or written drafting?

Some translators begin by writing their first draft. Others begin by making an oral draft, recording this, and then writing it down. Making an oral draft may help achieve a natural, well-connected text.

An alternative is to make a written draft and then retell the section orally, without looking at the written text. The oral retelling may bring up some natural expressions and some good ways of achieving a well-connected discourse.

See chapter 12 for further details and alternative ways of making the first draft.

2.2 Keyboard the draft

The Paratext computer program is designed specifically for use in Scripture translation, giving access to Bible versions and key resources. It provides an environment in which the translator can keyboard and edit the translation, marking formatting, such as chapter, paragraph and verse breaks, and other features.

In most translation projects today, each translator is equipped with a computer and is trained to use it. Translators usually keyboard as they draft the translation, editing as they work. In situations where a translator is not able to use a computer, a hand-written draft may be keyboarded by another member of the team.

Paratext also makes it possible for members of the team to view the drafts of each book on their own laptops and send comments and suggestions to each other.

See chapter 13 for further information about the Paratext program.

> Suggestion to prospective translators: Use the Paratext program as you do the exercises in this training manual and as you work on draft translations. Develop the habit of looking at the source text in several different versions and using the resources.

2.3 Read the draft aloud

When a section has been drafted and keyboarded, the translator reads it aloud. Or he may ask other members of the team, or other speakers, to read it aloud while he listens.

He may also ask members of the team to retell the section in their own words after they have read it or heard it read. The translator listens to the retelling and makes improvements to the clarity and naturalness of the translation, giving attention to sentence connections and word order.

Step 3: Preparing supplementary helps
(also called "extra-textual helps" or "paratextual materials")

In many contexts, essential background information is needed about the historical and cultural background of the biblical text. This information enables the audience of the translation, living today in their own very different culture, to understand what the biblical author was communicating to his original audience, those who lived thousands of years ago in a very different world. As he drafts, the translator should begin identifying places where background information is needed.

Examples of helps that provide supplementary information along with the biblical text are book introductions and section headings, also footnotes and cross-references. Well-chosen illustrations and glossary entries can also contribute. See further details in chapters 14 and 15.

Step 4: Checking with the translation team

Usually there are several translators on a team. The books to be translated may be distributed so that each translator is assigned certain books to draft. In the case of a long book, parts of the book may be assigned to different translators.

When a translator has drafted the translation of a book or part of a book, the other translators on the team review the draft, make comments, and suggest improvements. The team meets together to discuss these suggestions.

As revisions are made to the translation, the translator enters these into Paratext on his computer. The revision and updating of the text is continued through the translation process.

See further details about the team check in chapter 16.

Step 5: Testing the translation with the receptor community

The goal of Bible translation is to communicate the original meaning of the Scripture text to the new audience, the speakers of the receptor language. It is essential to find out whether or not speakers of the receptor language do understand the translation, and whether what they understand is accurate to the original message. Two ways to do this are the following:

5.1 Testing

Read the translation aloud to representative speakers of the receptor language, speakers who have not been involved in the translation. Ask hearers to retell in their own words what they have heard. Use simple questions to find out whether the hearers have understood the message. Also give the hearers opportunities to ask questions. Invite others to read the portion aloud and retell it in their own words. See chapter 17 for further details.

5.2 Reviewing

Certain members of the receptor language community are appointed as *reviewers* and agree to serve through the project in this role. Their task is to read the draft translations and give feedback to help the translators correct and improve the translation.

Reviewers are appointed from different church denominations and dialects. The translation team receives and evaluates their suggestions and revises the text accordingly. See section 17.6 and chapter 20, step 8, for further details.

Step 6: Preparing for the consultant check – how to make a back translation

A "back translation" is a very literal translation of the draft translation into English or another language of wider communication, a language in which the translation consultant and the translators are able to communicate. It should be prepared by a speaker of the language, someone other than the translator.

The back translation gives the translation consultant an initial insight into how the passage has been translated. It helps reveal whether the translation is communicating the meaning of the original text accurately and effectively. See further details in chapter 18.

Step 7: Checking the translation with a consultant

The role of a translation consultant is to guide translation teams in the procedures needed to achieve a good quality translation, and to encourage them along the way. Ideally, the same consultant is linked to the project for several years.

The consultant is responsible for training the team. He shows the translators how to find the translation helps that are available for each book, and how to use these helps well. He also shows them how to use the translation resources on Paratext and elsewhere to find solutions to translation problems.

The consultant is also responsible for helping to check the accuracy of the translation, working with the translators to check for faithfulness to the original Hebrew, Aramaic, or Greek text. He also does sample comprehension testing with other speakers.

See further details about the consultant check in chapter 19.

Step 8: Reviewing and more testing – focus on reviewing

Those appointed as reviewers continue to receive the draft translations and to give feedback to the translators. As more books are translated and consultant checked, the reviewers are kept busy receiving the draft copies and giving their feedback.

It is helpful if reviewers can meet with the translation team, or part of the team, from time to time, to read through passages together and discuss translation issues.

Continue to test the translation with representative speakers of the receptor language. Find out whether it is communicating the true meaning of the biblical text clearly. Find out whether what the hearers understand is indeed the meaning that the original author was communicating. Is the language natural and is the style acceptable? Is the right kind of language, the right register of language, being used?

This is also an opportunity to explore further and find solutions to issues that may have been raised during the time of checking with the consultant.

See section 17.6 and chapter 20, step 8, for further details about reviewing.

Step 9: Final editing and consistency checking – preparing for publication

The translation team will again read carefully through the whole text, checking for accuracy, clarity, and naturalness.

Computer-based tools are used to help check the consistency of the translation of parallel passages in different Bible books, the consistency of Old Testament quotations in the New Testament, of the translation of key biblical terms, also of spelling (including consistency in spelling proper names), capitalisation, punctuation, and format. See further details in chapter 20, step 9.

Step 10: Final reading through for approval by the receptor language church and community representatives

This is the opportunity for representatives of the churches and community to meet and read selected portions of the translated text. It is important that the translation has their approval before it is sent for publication. It is ideal if the consultant can also be there for at least part of the time.

It is helpful to read selected passages aloud using a projector to show the text on the screen. This keeps everyone focused and enables them to see the written translation as well as to listen to it being read. It also helps catch any spelling mistakes. Participants can see any changes being made and so ensure that they are made correctly.

The goal is to make sure there is consensus in approving the text before the translation goes for publication. See further details in chapter 20, step 10.

> These ten steps present a basic version of the translation process. Situations differ and the order of the steps may vary. For example, with experienced translation teams, the consultant check often comes after testing and reviewing have been done. With translation teams in the early stages of a project, it is good to do the consultant check before wider testing.
>
> Many of the steps overlap. Some steps, such as preparation of helps that supply supplementary information and work on key terms, continue through the program.
>
> Some steps may need to be done more than once. For example, if the translation is extensively revised, the revised draft will need to be tested and checked by a consultant again.
>
> Chapters 11 through 20 explain and illustrate each of these steps in more detail.

Additional resources on "A Ten-Step Procedure in Translation"

BT4 online materials

10_Translation_procedure_10_steps.pptx
10_Bible_translation_process_for_written_and_oral_products.pptx
10_Ten_translation_steps.pdf

Chapter 11

Step 1: Exegesis – Discovering the Meaning of the Source Text

Exegesis involves the careful study of a Scripture text. It is the process by which someone discovers what the original author intended to communicate.

This chapter describes the procedure that translators need to follow as they study the text, preparing to draft a translation. Begin by looking at the big picture, the whole book, before focusing on smaller units of text. Also look at how this book fits into the structure of the whole Bible.

11.1 First study to get an overview of the whole book

11.1.1 Examine the historical situation in which the book was written

Who is the author? When was it written?

Who were the original recipients? To whom was the author originally writing? What was their situation at that time?

What was the relationship between the author and his audience?

What historical situation caused the author to write the book? What was his purpose in writing the book? What is the message that he is aiming to communicate?

> **Finding the information**
>
> The *New International Version Study Bible,* published by Zondervan, provides a helpful introduction at the beginning of each Bible book. This includes background information about the author, the date of writing, and the situation at the time that the book was written. It also provides an outline displaying the main divisions and parts of the book. This helps the reader gain an overview of the whole book that will help in understanding, and translating, the smaller units and details of the book.
>
> Other sources of information
>
> - Introductory information in the *UBS Translator's Handbooks* or *Translator's Notes* and other helps available on Paratext or *Translator's Workplace.*
> - The book introductions in the *Good News Translation* or the *Contemporary English Version.*
> - If geographical locations are mentioned, look at a map of the area concerned; for example, maps found at the back of the *NIV Study Bible.*
> - Oasis International. 2016. *Africa Study Bible, NLT.* Carol Stream, IL: Tyndale House Publishers. "The *Africa Study Bible* combines the *New Living Translation* with study tools that reflect uniquely African insights and experiences."
> - Halley, Henry H. 2014. *Halley's Bible Handbook.* Completely revised and expanded edition. Grand Rapids, MI: Zondervan.

11.1.2 Identify the major units of the book; familiarise yourself with the structure of the book

Study the outline of the book. How does the narrative, or the argument, progress?

Are there certain concepts, perhaps certain key words or other forms that recur at various points through the book? How are the major parts of the book connected? (This is especially important for long books.)

What is highlighted or emphasised?

11.1.3 Read and/or listen to the text of the whole book

Read the text in the language and version with which you feel most comfortable.

Observe what the author says about his purpose, the recurring topics that he writes about, and the feelings that are expressed.

Some find it helpful to listen to an audio version of the book. Recordings in different Bible versions are available online.

Alternatively, watch a video for those books for which videos are available, such as Genesis or the Gospel of Luke. It is, of course, important to remember that these films are only attempts at visualisation. But they may be helpful in portraying the cultural background of the text and in giving one interpretation of the text. See the information about videos at the end of this chapter.

Application exercise

This exercise should be done by a translator at the point when he is preparing to begin the translation of a Bible book.

Study to get an overview of the book you are about to translate, following the guidelines above. Then draft, in your own language, a summary of what you have learnt about the purpose and content of the book. Discuss this with your consultant or other members of your team. This may form a basis for a book introduction (see section 14.1).

11.2 Focus on a section at a time, studying the text in detail

Major English versions of the Bible such as the *New International Version* (*NIV*), the *New Living Translation* (*NLT*), the *Good News Translation* (*GNT*), and the *Contemporary English Version* (*CEV*), divide the Bible text into units called "sections," each section having a section heading. These can easily be viewed in Paratext or *Translator's Workplace*.

The English versions agree much of the time on where section breaks are made, although occasionally they differ. It is suggested that you usually follow the section divisions in the version you have chosen as the primary source text.

It is still good to observe differences in section breaks and section headings in other Bible language versions, both English versions and versions in languages of wider communication in your area. There may be reasons for following alternatives at certain points. There is a tool in Paratext by which you can view a display of the section divisions and alternative section headings in different versions. See "Tools/Checklists/Section Headings" in the Paratext menu.

11.2.1 Read the section in different versions

Study the section in two different Bible versions:

a. The version you have chosen as your primary source text. This could be the original Hebrew or Greek text, or a reliable translation that reflects the form of the original language to some degree. The *New International Version* (*NIV*) is suggested. (See discussion in section 3.4.)

b. Also study a version that is more meaning-based, such as the *Good News Translation* (*GNT*), or the *New Living Translation* (*NLT*).

Compare with other versions too. Programs such as Paratext and *Translator's Workplace* make it possible to view several versions at the same time. (See figure 2 in chapter 13.) If you have access to versions in different languages with which you are familiar, use these too.

11.2.2 Identify the main theme of the section

Answer the question, "What is the section about?" This will also help you to make a tentative section heading. The section heading should reflect the theme of the section.

11.2.3 Study the section in detail

a. How does this section relate to what comes before and what comes afterwards? For example, does it describe the next event in a sequence of events?

b. Consider what marks the section as a unit. Are there forms that indicate the opening or ending of a section?

c. Compare the two (or three) versions you are using as your primary source texts, noting differences. Study the differences between these versions. Are most of the differences alternative ways of saying the same thing, or are there differences in the meaning? If there are differences in the meaning, that is, different interpretations of the original text, you will need to study these differences and decide which to follow.

d. Are there any textual differences in the passage?

Have any of the versions you are using as your primary source texts followed different readings in the original language manuscripts? When this happens, there will be a footnote in at least one of your source versions. This will also be noted and discussed in the *UBS Translator's Handbooks* or other resources to which you refer.

It is recommended that you follow the same text as your primary source text, for example, the *NIV*. This issue may need to be discussed with church leaders in the area and a statement should be included in the translation brief for the project. See further chapter 43, point 2.

e. List questions to be investigated and potential problems. For example,
   - Are there cross-cultural differences?
   - Are there concepts mentioned that will not be known to the receptor audience?
   - Are there any symbolic actions?
   - Are there complex constructions to unravel?
   - Are there abstract nouns expressing events?
   - Are there any ambiguities or unclear meanings?
   - Are there idioms or figures of speech?
   - Are there any "of" constructions, ellipses (shortcuts), passive verbs, or other issues?

f. Identify key biblical words that need in-depth study. For further discussion of key biblical terms, see chapter 24.

11.2.4 Find the facts

To find help, use your resources. Look up other English Bible versions and Bible versions in any other languages that you are using. Use reference helps, such as study Bibles, dictionaries, commentaries, articles, *Translator's Notes*, *UBS Translator's Handbooks*, *Exegetical Summaries*. Many of these can be accessed in Paratext or *Translator's Workplace*.

Go through the points you have underlined or written down, looking for a way to resolve them. Use the following methods:

a. If the meaning of a verse is not clear, study the text in other Bible versions.

Also study parallel passages in other Bible books, or other passages that may be relevant. In the *Good News Translation*, parallel passages, where relevant, are listed under the section heading for each section.

b. If there are alternative interpretations, consider these carefully. Refer to commentaries for help. Make good use of the *UBS Translator's Handbooks* or *Translator's Notes*, or other translator's aids available for the book.

c. If the meaning of a word is not clear, look up the word in your dictionary.

d. If the problem is something to do with Jewish culture or religion, use your Bible dictionary.

e. Try rewriting the verse in simple English (or another language of wider communication). Use the techniques you are learning for discovering the meaning. For example, it may help to re-express any event ideas as verbs or to break long, complex sentences into shorter sentences. See the chapters in part 4 of this manual.

f. If you have difficulty in finding a solution, discuss the problem with someone else, such as your consultant or a friend who has good Bible knowledge.

g. Think – or talk – through the whole passage. Review how the parts connect together; study the connections.

h. If the passage includes quoted conversation or other interaction between people, consider the attitudes and emotions that are being expressed.

After you have thoroughly studied the meaning of the passage, you are ready to re-express this meaning in the receptor language; you are ready to make the first draft.

11.3 Ancient wisdom on exegesis

The following words occur in the "Prologue" addressed "to the Christian reader" in the first printed Bible in the English language, the Coverdale Bible, published in 1535. This prologue follows the dedication to Henry VIII at the front of the Bible. A transcription of the "dedication" and "prologue" can be viewed online at http://www.bible-researcher.com/coverdale1.html.

A golden rule of interpretation	A translation of these words into modern English
It shall greatly helpe ye to understande Scripture,	It will help you very much to understand the Scriptures
If thou mark	if you pay attention
Not only what is spoken or wrytten,	not only to **what** is spoken or written,
But of whom,	but also **of whom**,
And to whom,	and **to whom**,
With what words,	with what **choice of words**,
At what time	at what **time** in history,
Where,	**where**,
To what intent,	for what **purpose**,
With what circumstances,	and in what **circumstances**;
Considering what goeth before	consider also **what is said before** (in the previous verses and elsewhere in the Bible)
And what followeth after.	and **what is said after** (in the following verses).

Additional resources on "Discovering the Meaning of the Source Text"

BT4 online materials

11_Exegesis-Introduction.pptx
11_Exegesis-Resources_for_Bible_translation.pptx
11_Exegesis-Translating_poetry.pptx
11_Exegesis-Procedures_in_brief-Handout.pdf

Websites

Carson, Don A. 2016. Rightly dividing the Word of God. Video presentation at SS Gospel Centre, Petaling Jaya, Selangor, Malaysia, July 2016. View at https://www.youtube.com/watch?v=xHjD0TuuOmk.

Faith Comes By Hearing – A website to explore: https://www.faithcomesbyhearing.com/.

YouVersion has audio Bible versions in 15 English versions and more than 900 other languages. (These are available online and as an app at https://www.bible.com. See https://www.bible.com/audio-bible-app-versions, for the full list of languages. See also BibleGateway.com/.)

For further reading

Fee, Gordon D., and Douglas Stuart. 2014. *How to read the Bible for all its worth*. Fourth edition. Grand Rapids: Zondervan.
(Also available to view in *Translator's Workplace*.)

Chapter 12

Step 2: Making the First Draft

> **Remember**
> - When preparing to translate, the first step is always to study the meaning of the source text.
> - When the meaning of the text is clear in your mind, the second step is to re-express that meaning in a way that is natural and clear in the receptor language.

The translation into the receptor language should be done by someone who speaks that language fluently as his first language for the following reasons:

- A first-language speaker of the receptor language has natural control of the full range of lexical and grammatical resources of his language. He knows the nuances and idioms of the language and uses the discourse features of the language instinctively.
- A first-language speaker knows the culture and beliefs of his own people. He will be able to assess the assumptions and presuppositions that the audience will bring to the text – an important factor in successful communication.
- Without such translators, there will be no sustainable ongoing translation project. The project will always be dependent on the presence and leadership of outsiders. There will be little possibility of revision and improvement of the translation, or of ongoing translation work towards, for example, a complete Bible.

> Before beginning the translation of the text of the book you plan to translate, consider drafting a brief introduction to the book. This is especially helpful for those epistles that are written to a named audience with a specific purpose, responding to a local situation. See suggestions on book introductions in chapter 14.

12.1 Procedure for drafting, section by section

(1) Having studied the meaning of the section in detail, remind yourself of the following:
- What was the author's purpose in writing this text?
- Who was the intended audience of the original message?
- Who is the audience for whom the translation is being made?
- What type (genre) of text is it? For example, narrative, poetry, letter, informal conversation, formal speech? See further chapter 38.

(2) With the intended audience of the translation in view, think through the translation of the section – think of it as a whole; think about how the parts connect together.

(3) Then keyboard or write the translation. Or use the alternative method suggested below of making an oral recording first and then transcribing it.

(4) Read through the translation aloud.

(5) Review, reread, retell, revise, check the details and the naturalness, keeping the intended new audience in focus.

The next step will be to test the translation with representatives of the new audience – see further details in chapter 17.

12.2 An alternative method: Make the first draft orally, speaking it into a recorder

Some translators have found it helpful to make the first draft of the translation orally. First study the source text to get the correct meaning clear in your mind, as described for step 1 above. Then set books aside and retell the passage in your own words, without looking at the source text, recording this retelling as you speak. You can then replay the recording and keyboard or write down the translation from the recorded draft. Then refer again to the source texts and work on this draft to improve its accuracy, clarity, and naturalness.

An alternative approach is to make the first draft in writing, then put that written draft aside and speak a freely told version of the passage, recording it as you speak. Then compare the freely told version with the written version. The freely told version may be more natural in the way the material is arranged and in the way sentences are connected. Sometimes the translator uses natural expressions and idioms that he did not think of when he made the written version. He can use this wording to improve the naturalness of his translation.

Yet another way to use freely told oral versions with good results was used in developing the translation for the Twi people of Ghana. The missionary, Johann Gottlieb Christaller, working in the mid-19th century (about 1854), trained two Twi men to translate. He would explain a Bible passage to them and they would then discuss and write down their translations. Christaller also told the story to another speaker, who retold it to a group of school children. These, in turn, wrote the story down in Twi from memory. Christaller then made a draft translation using all these different versions.

"The Twi Bible was a masterpiece, and remained for a long time the best Bible translation in any African language; it became popular at once and has remained so till today" (Debrunner 1967:143–144).

> Experiment with different methods! Try different ways of drafting the translation until you find the way that gives you the best results in your situation.
>
> Three PowerPoints describing methods of drafting are listed at the end of this chapter.

12.3 Adaptation

Adaptation is taking an existing translation and revising it to meet the needs and preferences of a different audience, often for a group of people who speak a related dialect or language.

Adaptation should only be considered in situations where (a) the grammar and other aspects of the form of the receptor language are very similar to that of the source language, and (b) the source language translation is a high-quality translation (accurate, clear, and natural), well received in the language area for which it was prepared.

Historically, the software program named CARLA (Computer Assisted Related Language Adaptation) has been used with various degrees of success. Information concerning a program named *Adapt It* is available to view on the website https://adapt-it.org/. This program is under development and is currently being evaluated.

A method that is currently being experimented with is to use the interlinearizer tool in the Paratext program. This method requires that the translator, a first-language speaker of the receptor language, also has a good knowledge of the language from which the adaptation is being made. The translator types in the equivalent words from his language under each word of the source language text. Then the program begins to guess the equivalent words for other verses. As the translator corrects these guesses, the system adjusts to take these corrections into account, and the proposed forms become increasingly correct. The first draft that results from this process must then be thoroughly revised, tested, and checked in the usual ways. For further information on the interlinearizer tool, see chapter 18, point 6.

In all projects where adaptation contributes to the preparation of the first draft, the following points should be observed:

- Suitably qualified speakers of the receptor language must be appointed and fully trained in Bible translation principles and practice.
- The translation team must have full control of the editing and revision procedures, as in other translation projects.
- Procedures for team checking, testing, and consultant checking should be followed, as with other translation projects.
- The receptor language audience must be given every opportunity to make the translation their own, adapting the style as appropriate for the receptor language situation.

12.4 A review of necessary conditions for achieving a good quality translation

Even when the translator is a first-language speaker of the receptor language, to achieve a good translation, attention must be given to the following points:

a. The translator must have a good understanding of the source message. Exegetical preparation should be done before the first draft is made. It is not satisfactory to draft the translation before studying the text carefully.

b. The translator must have access to materials that will help him in exegesis and translation, both in printed and electronic form. He will be trained by his advisors or consultants to make full use of these resources.

c. The translator must be well trained in translation principles, including ongoing on-the-job training in the application of these principles.

d. The translator must develop an awareness of the grammar and other features of his own language, including study of the discourse structure. If the translator has not learnt to value the beauty and intricacy of his own language, he will tend to follow the structure of the source text. See further information in chapters 39, 40, and 41.
e. The translator must learn to work as part of a team. Input from others in improving the first draft is always needed, and translators must be open to this.
f. The translator must learn to seek feedback on his translation. Translation that has been drafted should be reviewed by other translators on the team, tested with other speakers, and checked with a consultant. The translator will learn a lot from the testing and checking process, and so he will begin to produce better first drafts that will not need so much revision.
g. The translator must remember that the first draft is only a first draft. Changes will be needed before a polished translation is achieved. Test and revise. Test and revise again.

12.5 Translation practice

Translators in training should now apply steps 1 and 2 to the text that has been chosen for first translation practice. See the note on "Translation practice" at the end of chapter 9. If there is more than one speaker from a given language taking the training course, it is suggested that, for this first exercise, they all translate the same passage and then compare translations. This gives opportunities for team members to develop the skills of listening and learning from each other, and working together to get the best results.

Additional resources on "Making the First Draft"

BT4 online materials

12_Drafting_and_oral_retelling.pptx
12_More_about_drafting_a_translation.pptx
12_Using_adaptation_to_make_a_first_draft.pptx
12_Chart_to_track_translation_progress.pdf

Websites

Adapt It. https://adapt-it.org/
   (Computer program.)
Audacity. https://www.audacityteam.org
   (An easy-to-use, multi-track audio editor and recorder.)
Oral Bible Translation with Render. http://www.renderpartners.com/
   (Software for Oral Bible translation.)
Scripture App Builder: https://software.sil.org/scriptureappbuilder/

For further reading

Wendland, Ernst R. 2013. *Orality and the Scriptures: Composition, translation, and transmission* Publications in Translation and Textlinguistics 6. Dallas: SIL International.

Chapter 13

Keyboarding the Translation – An Introduction to the Paratext Program

This chapter provides a short introduction to the Paratext program, a translation editing program jointly developed by the United Bible Societies and SIL International. At the time of writing, Paratext is the most widely used program for keyboarding, editing, and checking Scripture translations.

The Paratext program is designed for three main purposes:

- To give the translator ready access to the source text in the original Hebrew and Greek texts and in a selection of English and other language Bible versions that may be relevant for his situation. It also gives access to many other resource helps for translators. New features are under development.
- To provide an environment into which the translator can keyboard the translation, marking formatting, such as chapter and verse breaks, paragraph breaks, and other features.
- To provide tools for checking consistency of spelling and other features.

Paratext provides a way to keyboard the translation, and then to edit and improve the translation further. It makes it possible for members of a translation team, and others involved, to view the translated text in its latest form. The team members may be widely separated but they can all view the same text on their computers.

Take every opportunity to observe Paratext in use. If you are preparing to serve as a translator, in due course you will receive full training.

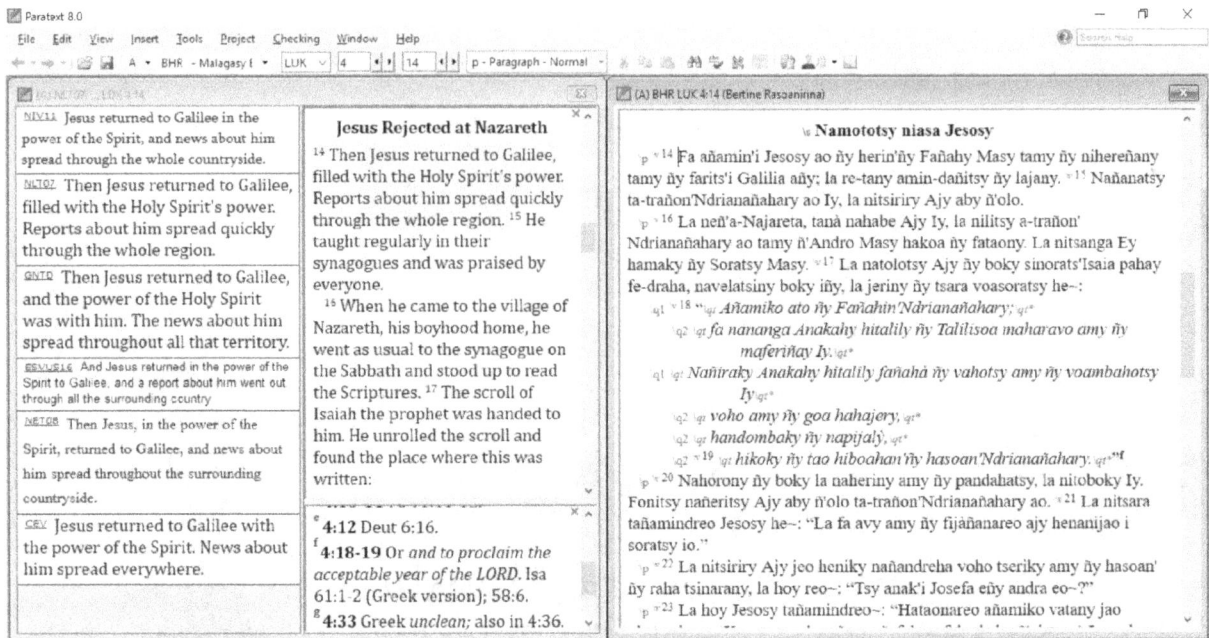

Figure 2. Display of a Paratext translation screen in the Malagasy-Bara language of Madagascar. © 2018 by Berthine Rasoanirina. Used by permission.

The following facilities are available in Paratext:

- Access to multiple Bible versions, which can be viewed and compared side by side;
- Access to the original Hebrew and Greek texts and to Bible language dictionaries;
- Access to resources such as *UBS Translator's Handbooks* and SIL *Translator's Notes*;
- Access to tools for checking consistency of the translation in spelling, punctuation, formatting, use of key biblical terms, transliteration of proper names, and other issues on which consistency is needed;
- Access to a tool that identifies passages that reoccur in different parts of the Bible;
- Facility to enter and edit translated (or back translated) text;
- Facility to share translation drafts with other team members, and to make backups for safe-keeping;
- Facility to attach notes to the draft translation on points that need to be further discussed and decided, with a way to track the responses from other team members; and
- Facility to produce an interlinear word-for-word rendering, which may be helpful to a consultant.

It is good for the translation to be keyboarded as soon as possible, so that it is available in a form that can easily be reviewed, revised, backed up, and shared.

Additional resources on "Keyboarding the Translation – An Introduction to the Paratext Program"

BT4 online materials

13_Introducing_the_Paratext_program.pptx
13_Learning_to_keyboard_your_translation.pptx

Website

Learning about Paratext: https://paratext.org/support/learning/. This site includes videos introducing the latest update of the Paratext program and providing training in its use.

Chapter 14

Step 3: Supplementary Helps – Book Introductions and Section Headings

We have seen that the reader of a translation may need to know certain background information if he is to understand the message that the original author intended to communicate. He may need to know relevant facts about the way that people lived at the time this book of the Bible was written, and about the historical situation at that time.

This chapter and the following chapter give suggestions on ways in which such information can be provided for the reader.

14.1 Book introductions

Some Bible versions include a brief introduction to each book. Examples in the *Good News Translation* can be viewed on Paratext. The introduction will usually identify the original author and the audience that he was addressing, and will include a brief statement about the time and historical situation when the book was written.

Introductions may include information that is relevant and helpful for the correct understanding of the message of the book. For example, to understand the message of Galatians, it is necessary to understand the function of circumcision in the Jewish culture. A brief explanation of what circumcision means in Jewish culture could therefore usefully be included in an introduction to the book.

In writing each of his epistles, Paul had a specific audience in mind, but it seems he anticipated that what he wrote would also be used beyond this initial audience:

> To the church of God that is in Corinth, to those sanctified in Christ Jesus, called to be saints *together with all those who in every place call upon the name of our Lord Jesus Christ*, both their Lord and ours (1 Corinthians 1:2; italics added)

For longer books, it is helpful to include a brief outline of the main divisions and themes of the book.

14.2 Section headings

In modern versions of the Bible, the text is arranged in sections and paragraphs. These divisions are helpful both for private study and for choosing passages for reading aloud. Each section describes one incident or discusses one topic. A good pattern to follow is that of the *NIV* or *GNT*. In these versions, the section headings

- break the text up into meaningful, complete units, indicating the main theme of the section;
- help the reader to find a specific reference more easily; and
- help to avoid long pages of unbroken print that might look difficult to a new reader.

Each section heading should express the theme of the section that follows. The heading should give the reader some context, so that he knows what topic to expect in the section, sometimes also introducing the participants who will be involved. But it should not tell everything that is in the section – it does not provide a summary of the section.

Section headings will also reflect the main trends and emphases of the book. For example, in the Gospel of Matthew, an important theme is the fact that Jesus came not only to the Jews but to people of other nations as well. Section headings such as these reflect this:

Matthew 2:1–12   Strangers from far away come to see Jesus

Matthew 8:5–13   Jesus heals the servant of a Roman soldier

Matthew 15:21–28 Jesus heals the child of a woman who is a foreigner

Paratext provides a tool to view the alternative section headings used in different Bible versions. See the chart below. This can be found in the Paratext menu: "Tools/Checklists/Section Headings." Looking at alternative headings will help the translator find the form that is best for his translation.

Section Headings (Acts 1:1–4:37)				
	NIV	***ESV***	***NLT***	***GNT***
1:1	Jesus Taken Up Into Heaven	The Promise of the Holy Spirit	The Promise of the Holy Spirit	
1:6		The Ascension	The Ascension of Jesus	Jesus Is Taken Up to Heaven
1:12	Matthias Chosen to Replace Judas	Matthias Chosen to Replace Judas	Matthias Replaces Judas	Judas' Successor
2:1	The Holy Spirit Comes at Pentecost	The Coming of the Holy Spirit	The Holy Spirit Comes	The Coming of the Holy Spirit
2:14	Peter Addresses the Crowd	Peter's Sermon at Pentecost	Peter Preaches to the Crowd	Peter's Message
2:42	The Fellowship of the Believers	The Fellowship of the Believers	The Believers Form a Community	
2:43				Life among the Believers
3:1	Peter Heals a Lame Beggar	The Lame Beggar Healed	Peter Heals a Crippled Beggar	A Lame Beggar Is Healed

3:11	Peter Speaks to the Onlookers	Peter Speaks in Solomon's Portico		Peter's Message in the Temple
3:12			Peter Preaches in the Temple	
4:1	Peter and John Before the Sanhedrin	Peter and John Before the Council	Peter and John before the Council	Peter and John before the Council
4:23	The Believers Pray	The Believers Pray for Boldness	The Believers Pray for Courage	The Believers Pray for Boldness
4:32	The Believers Share Their Possessions	They Had Everything in Common	The Believers Share Their Possessions	The Believers Share Their Possessions

Consider the following practical points about preparing section headings.

14.2.1 Providing necessary background information in the heading

Sometimes essential background information that is not supplied in the text can be included in the heading. For example, Mark 15:1–5 describes how Jesus was brought to stand before Pilate. But there is no mention in Mark's Gospel of who Pilate was, although this is explicit in the text of the parallel passages in Matthew and John. A suitable heading before Mark 15:1 might be the following:

How they bring Jesus to stand before Pilate, the Roman who is governor

In the story of the Good Samaritan (Luke 10:30–37), part of the significance of the story lies in the fact that Samaritans were not true Jews and were despised by the Jews. Some indication of this could be provided in the following heading:

Story about a stranger from Samaria

Sometimes it may be appropriate to supply a clue in the section heading that will help the reader towards a correct understanding of the text. For example, before the section John 1:1–18, one translation had the following heading, preparing the reader to understand that "the Word" in the following text refers to Christ:

Matter about Jesus Christ, who is the Word of God

14.2.2 When to prepare the section headings

The best time to prepare the section heading is at the time that you translate the section. At that time, the content of the section is fresh in your mind.

After completing the translation of the whole book, review the section headings throughout the book to see how they relate to one another. The section headings should reflect the themes of the whole book, showing the sequence of events or the development of teaching points.

14.2.3 The form of section headings

Section headings should be fairly short. But they should not be confusing or obscure. It is better to have a longer heading that will be clearly understood, than a short confusing one.

Here are some alternative forms used in section headings in English versions:

Complete sentences

Statement:	Jesus sends out the twelve disciples (Mark 6:7)
	Jesus feeds five thousand men (Mark 6:30)
Question:	Who is the greatest? (Mark 9:33)
Command:	Turn from your sins or die (Luke 13:1)

Incomplete sentences

Confessing and rejecting Christ (Luke 12:8)

Understanding the time (Luke 12:54)

Noun phrases

The transfiguration (Luke 9:28)

Jesus and Beelzebul (Luke 11:14)

The lost sheep (Luke 15:1)

Prepositional phrases – for example, identifying the location where a certain event took place

In Cyprus (Acts 13:4)

In Antioch in Pisidia (Acts 13:13)

In Iconium (Acts 14:1)

Some languages prefer to use a complete sentence rather than a prepositional phrase.

Barnabas and Paul visit Cyprus (Acts 13:4)

Some languages prefer forms such as the following:

How John baptised Jesus (Matthew 3:13)

Word that Jesus taught people about praying (Matthew 6:5)

Word about how Jesus healed many people (Mark 1:29)

How Jesus fed five thousand men (Mark 6:30)

Story about the sheep that was lost (Luke 15:1)

The natural order may be different from that of English.

How Jesus healed many people, its word (Mark 1:29)

The sheep that was lost, its story (Luke 15:1)

Care needs to be taken to use the appropriate form of the verb.

In English the present tense is sometimes used in headings referring to a past event. This is called the "historical present." Some languages prefer to use future tense or past-completed forms of the verb in headings.

> Experiment to find what fits best! Test to see what is understood and approved by those for whom the translation is being prepared!

14.2.4 Pronoun reference in section headings

Use names rather than pronouns in section headings. This is because readers may begin reading at the beginning of a new section.

14.2.5 Capitalisation and punctuation in section headings

Option 1: Capitalise the first letter of the heading, and then only words that are always capitalised, such as proper names (this is called "sentence capitalisation").

Option 2: Capitalise the first letter of the heading, and all main content words (nouns and verbs), but not grammatical connecting words (this is called "headline capitalisation").

Option 1 above is the easiest to apply consistently and the easiest for new readers to read. It is not recommended to write all letters of the heading in capital letters as this is harder for new readers to read.

Do not put a full stop (period) at the end of section headings. If the section heading is in the form of a question, put a question mark. If the section heading is an exclamation, put an exclamation mark.

Remember

- Section headings mark natural breaks in the larger text. They help the reader to know the theme of a passage.
- All the above kinds of supplementary helps provide the reader with information that will help him understand the text in the way that the original author intended it to be understood.

Additional resources on "Book Introductions and Section Headings"

BT4 online materials

14_Supplementary_helps_1-About_extra-textual_helps.pptx
14_Supplementary_helps_2-Book_introductions.pptx
14_Supplementary_helps_3-Section_headings.pptx
14_Bible_book_introductions.pdf
14_Section_headings_in_Ruth-Comparing_versions.pdf

For further reading

Barnwell, Katharine. 1994. Supplementary helps in Scripture publications. *Notes on Translation* 8(2):8–13.

Clark, David J., and Christer Asberg. 2006. Section headings: Purposes and problems. *The Bible Translator* 57(4):194–202.

Fry, Euan M. 1983. The use and value of section headings. *The Bible Translator* 34(2):235–239. http://www.ubs-translations.org/tbt/1983/02/TBT198302.html?seq=37.

Hoover, Joseph. 2008. Parable of the lamp: A dysfunctional section heading. *The Bible Translator* 59(4):190–194.

Loewen, Jacob A. 1985. A new look at section headings. *The Bible Translator* 36(2):237–241. http://www.ubs-translations.org/tbt/1985/02/TBT198502.html?num=237&x=0&y=0&num1=.

van Klinken-Rijneveld, Liesbeth. 2007. On the purpose of section headings: A functional approach. *The Bible Translator* 58(4):191–200.

Wendland, Ernst R. 1993. On preparing a reader-friendly format: With emphasis on section headings. *Notes on Translation* 7(3):13–27.

Zogbo, Lynell. 1990. Writing introductions to the books of the Bible. *The Bible Translator* 41(2):228-230. http://www.ubs-translations.org/tbt/1990/02/TBT199002.html?num=228&x=0&y=0&num1=.

Chapter 15

Step 3, *continued*: Supplementary Helps – Footnotes, Cross-References, Parallel Passages, Glossary, Illustrations, Maps, and More

15.1 Footnotes

Footnotes can be used for the following purposes:

- To provide background information or explanation that cannot be included acceptably in the text itself
- To provide an alternative translation, occasionally; for example, John 7:37–38 in *NIV* and *GNT*
- To note an alternative textual reading in the original language manuscripts, when there is a particular reason for noting the alternative. In general it is recommended to follow the same readings as the Bible version that has been chosen as the primary source text, for example, *NIV*.
- To indicate where the order of the words in the text has been changed in order to achieve a meaningful translation. The more literal form of the source text can be given in the footnote with an explanation, if needed.

Too many footnotes distract the attention of the reader from the text and can be confusing rather than helpful. Limit the use of footnotes to points that it seems helpful and necessary to include. Discuss this with your consultant.

The Paratext program provides a way to format footnotes so that they are clearly distinct from the text.

15.2 Cross-references

A cross-reference identifies another passage of Scripture that is relevant to the passage in focus. The occasions for cross-references include

- identifying a passage that describes a historical event that is referred to, for example, Matthew 24:38 refers to the story of Noah, found in Genesis 6:5–8:22; and

- identifying the source of a quotation, often an Old Testament passage quoted in the New Testament. For example, Acts 13:33–35 refers to Psalm 2:7, Isaiah 55:3, and Psalm 16:10; Romans 1:17 refers to Habakkuk 2:4. Such quotations are often introduced by the phrase literally translated, "it is written." Quotations may include prophecies that have been fulfilled, as, for example, in Romans 15:12, referring to Isaiah 11:10.

Cross-references included in English versions vary. Those in *NIV*, *GNT*, and *NLT* are good models to consider.

Cross-references are usually placed at the bottom of the page, as footnotes.

15.3 Parallel passages – a special kind of cross-reference

In the Gospels, especially the synoptic Gospels, there are passages where the same event is described in more than one Gospel, with similar wording. For example, the parallel passages describing how Satan tempted Jesus are Matthew 4:1–11, Mark 1:12–13, and Luke 4:1–13.

Similarly, there are many parallel passages in the Old Testament. For example, Isaiah 2:2–4 and Micah 4:1–3.

The *NIV* and *GNT* provide the references for parallel passages immediately below the section heading for the passage concerned. Consider following this model.

It is helpful to compare parallel passages as you translate.

Paratext has checklists that enable you to select and compare the following points:

- all parallel passages
- parallel passages within the New Testament, including parallel passages in the synoptic Gospels
- Old Testament passages quoted in the New Testament
- parallel passages within the Old Testament

15.4 Glossary

Some editions of the Bible, such as the *GNT*, have a glossary at the back of the book. This is a list with explanations of concepts and objects that may be unknown in the receptor language area.

A glossary can be useful for explaining such terms as "Pharisee," "Sadducee," "Son of Man," and many others. In an edition of the New Testament only, it can also be used to provide brief background information about the main Old Testament characters who are mentioned in the New Testament.

Words for which an explanation is included in the glossary can be marked with an asterisk (*) in the text. But it should be remembered that many readers will not refer to the glossary at the time that they are reading the text. The text itself should still be translated in as meaningful a way as possible.

Sample glossaries are available on *Translator's Workplace*, providing information that can be adapted for specific situations, as needed.

15.5 Illustrations

Well-chosen, well-placed, historically accurate pictures can be a real help to the reader. Objects or activities mentioned in the biblical text that are unknown in the receptor language culture can often be represented by pictures. Pictures are not just decoration; they help the reader to understand the meaning of the text.

Pictures used in Scripture publications must be
- clear and easy to understand; test each picture you plan to use by showing it to representative speakers of the receptor language to discover whether it is readily understood;
- accurate and true to the biblical culture.

Sometimes it is helpful to include a brief explanatory note under a picture. This is called a "caption."

An edition of the Bible that uses illustrations to aid the understanding of the reader in this way is the *RSV* edition, published by Collins for the British and Foreign Bible Society with illustrations, by Horace Knowles. The introduction to this edition explains: "Instead of the usual type of story-picture, there are simple little drawings that look more like up-to-date visual aids than illustrations.... They have been fitted into the text just at the place where help is needed."

Examples:

- Animals and plants referred to in the Bible text that may be unfamiliar to the reader: camel, bear, nard, hyssop, fig tree, vine with grapes;
- Activities that may be unfamiliar in the receptor language culture: a shepherd with sheep, people ploughing using oxen, a watchtower in a vineyard, a sower sowing seed by scattering it by hand; and
- Things to do with the Jewish religious system: the tabernacle, priests and Levites in their official dress, altars.

The original set of illustrations by Horace Knowles has been augmented by Louise Bass, to include additional pictures that may be useful to illustrate cultural differences, using the same style of drawing. This set of illustrations is copyrighted by the British and Foreign Bible Society. Translation projects wishing to use these illustrations should consult with the Bible translation organisation with which their project is affiliated. A CD of the full set of Horace Knowles and Louise Bass illustrations is available. Those involved in preparing Scripture for publication will be able to advise on current procedures.

Sets of biblical illustrations to explore

Illustrations by Horace Knowles and Louise Bass © 1954, 1967, 1972 by The British and Foreign Bible Society. Amendments and additions by Louise Bass © 1994 by The British and Foreign Bible Society.

David C. Cook, © David C. Cook Publishing Co.
(Obtain permissions from the publisher's website at https://davidccook.org/david-c-cook/permissions/.)

Darwin Dunham illustrations, © United Bible Societies, Africa Regional Centre, Nairobi, Kenya.

Graham Wade illustrations, United Bible Societies, Africa Regional Centre, Nairobi, Kenya. (The website http://fmosoft.com/, gives accesss to copyright-free maps and other resources.)

Additional resources on "Footnotes, Cross-References, Parallel Passages, Glossary, Illustrations, Maps, and More"

For more information, consult the publications department of the Bible translation organisation to which your project is attached, or contact publications_intl@sil.org.

BT4 online materials

15_Supplementary_helps_4-Illustrations_and_maps.pptx
15_Supplementary_helps_5-Footnotes_glossary_parallel-passages.pptx

For further reading

Barnwell, Katharine. 1990. Choosing illustrations for Scripture publications. *Notes on Translation* 4(2):2–17.

Blight, Richard C. 2005. Footnotes for meaningful translations of the New Testament. *Journal of Translation* 1(1).
(Can be viewed at https://www.sil.org/resources/publications/jot/1.1.See also https://www.sil.org/resources/publications/entry/40266.)

Blight, Richard C., and Katharine Barnwell. 1999. *Supplementary information for Scripture publications*. Dallas: SIL International.
(Available on *Translator's Workplace*.)

Blight, Richard C., and Katharine Barnwell. 2005. *How to prepare a glossary and a topical index*. Dallas: SIL International.
(Available on *Translator's Workplace*.)

Chapter 16

Step 4: The Team Check

16.1 Different kinds of checks

The translator who makes the draft translation will himself do the first checks – carefully reading over the draft translation and running the basic spelling and formatting checks in Paratext.

The next major check is the "team check." This is step 4 in "A Ten-Step Procedure in Translation."

Wherever possible, there should be more than one trained translator working on a translation project. The translators may be translating different books or perhaps different parts of a long book. It is therefore important to have an opportunity for all the translators to sit together and check each translated book together, soon after it has been drafted. This is important for checking the accuracy of the content and the consistency in using the agreed systems for spelling and formatting.

Another check is the check with a translation consultant. See chapter 19 for further information about checking the translation with a consultant.

16.2 Team check

Some of the most helpful comments and suggestions come from other members of the translation team. If there are two or more translators on the team, they exchange their work to receive comments and suggestions from each other. Many teams find it helpful to exchange comments in writing first, using the "Notes" feature in Paratext, and then to sit together to read the translation aloud and to discuss points that are not yet settled. Experiment to find out which method is most effective for your team.

When sitting together for the team check, changes can be made directly on the master text in Paratext. It is ideal if the text of the translation being checked can be projected on a screen or wall. In this way, all involved can see the revisions being made and continue to comment. The "Paratext-Live" tool in the Paratext program also makes this possible.

The team check is also an opportunity to discuss and check the translation of key biblical terms. Members of the translation team need to coordinate on the translation of these terms so that they are translated consistently, according to context, in all books of the Bible. The team needs to keep a record of the decisions made and to review these together periodically.

For discussion

(1) Is it better to do the team check sitting together, or for each team member to do it on his own and send notes for the rest of the team to consider?

(2) When should team checks be done? How often should the team members meet for team checks?

(3) If the team consists of some older members and some younger members, what can be done to encourage all to contribute and to listen and respect the views of others?

16.3 Points to consider in the team check

Is the translation accurate?

> Compare the translation verse-by-verse with the source texts.
> Is there any part of the meaning that has been missed out?
> Does the translation add anything to the original meaning?
> Has the meaning been changed in any way?

Is the translation clear?

> Is there anything in the translation that may be confusing to the intended audience?
> Is there anything in the translation that could be misunderstood?
> Is it clear who did what?
> Are there any idioms or figures of speech that have been translated word-for-word instead of by their true meaning?
> Is the connection of thought clear in the passage?

Is the translation natural?

> One member of the team reads the translation aloud while the other members of the team listen without looking at the translation or the source text. They listen for any places that sound unnatural or foreign. They listen to the way that the whole passage connects together. Does it read smoothly? The team can also experiment with retelling the text orally.

Is the spelling, punctuation, and formatting consistent?

> a. Check the spelling, especially any points that need particular attention. For example, in languages that have special marks (diacritics) to distinguish certain letters (such as dots under some vowels), these marks may be missing. Check for consistency. Also check to ensure that all necessary tone marks are included.

b. Check the spelling of proper names. Have these been spelt consistently according to the agreed system? Paratext includes a tool to help check consistency in the spelling of proper names.
c. Check the use of capital letters. Have capital letters been used consistently? It is helpful to decide early what phrases should be written with capital letters (such as Son of Man, Book of God, House of God). Keep a list of these phrases. This will help you to be consistent and will save work later.
d. Check the punctuation.

   Are full stops and commas written where they should be?
   Is there a question mark at the end of all questions?
   Are direct speech quotations enclosed in quotation marks "..." (or in whatever way you have decided to mark them)? Check especially that there are quotation marks at both the beginning and end of all quotations.
   If brackets or parentheses ( ) have been used at all, check that there is a closing bracket whenever there is an opening one.
e. Check the chapter and verse numbers. If any have been missed, be careful to insert them in the right place.

   There are tools in Paratext to help with most of these consistency checks. Take opportunities to learn to use these tools effectively.

Figure 3. Team check in progress.
© 2018 by John Afro Enang. Used by permission.

Additional resources on "The Team Check"

BT4 online materials

16_Team_check.pptx

Chapter 17

Step 5: Testing the Translation with the Receptor Community

> **Why is it necessary to test a translation?**
>
> 1. To discover whether the translation is truly accurate, clear, and natural. Does it communicate the true meaning effectively to the intended audience, that is, to representative speakers of the receptor language?
> 2. To find ways of improving the translation.
> 3. To give the speakers of the language opportunity to share their ideas and express their views on the translation. They become aware that the translation belongs to them and that their comments are valued.

What is the difference between "checking" and "testing" the translation?

- "Checking" describes the work that the members of the translation team do among themselves. It involves the careful examination of every aspect of the translation to make sure that it is as correct as possible in every way. Checking is a tedious task, but a very necessary one.

- "Testing" is the process of taking the translation out to other speakers of the language, to find out whether it is understandable to them, and whether the message it communicates is accurate. In some parts of the world this is described as "checking with an uninitiated native speaker (UNS)." Different ways of testing the translation will be described in this chapter.

- "Reviewing" is done by certain members of the receptor language community who are appointed as reviewers. Their task is to read the draft translations and give feedback to help the translators correct and improve the translation. Their contribution is particularly important in trying to ensure that the translation is acceptable to different denominations, speakers of different dialects, and other groups in the community.

Some ways of testing the translation include the following:

17.1 Reading the translation aloud

a. In discussing the procedure for drafting a translation (section 12.2), it is recommended that, after drafting the translation, you *read it aloud to yourself*, listening to how it sounds. You may notice things that you had not noticed when you looked at the written translation. For example, you may notice that there is a need to improve the connections between sentences and between paragraphs.

b. *Read it aloud to yourself again a few days later.* You may notice then some points that you did not notice the first time.

c. *Read the translation aloud to someone else.* Ask that person to point out anything that sounds unclear or unnatural.

d. *Record your reading on a recording device.* The translator (or someone else) reads the translation onto a recording device, so that people can hear the translation as well as read it. Readers have commented that, as they practise reading the translation, preparing to record it, they notice mistakes in the translation that they had not noticed before. The recording is also a good way of making the translation available to others who are unable to read. The programs *HearThis* or the *Scripture App Builder* are available to facilitate recording. See the websites: https://software.sil.org/hearthis/ and https://software.sil.org/scriptureappbuilder/.

17.2 Listening to readers

The purpose of this test is to find out which parts of the translation people find difficult to read. If someone finds a passage difficult to read, it is usually because

- the meaning was not clear; or
- the language used was unnatural, unexpected, or ambiguous.

For this test, you need the help of people who can read fairly well. Make it very clear to the reader that you are not testing his reading ability to see if he is a good reader, rather you are testing the translation, to see how the translation can be improved.

Watch for differences between the written text and what is read, such as the following:

- If the reader stumbles, or misreads, check to see what caused the mistake. Consider how to improve the translation so that it reads more smoothly at that point.

- From time to time, the reader may change a few words without being aware he has made a change. Sometimes this happens because the reader is tired or careless. But often it is because there was something unnatural in the translation, and the reader automatically changed it to something that seemed to him to fit better in that place. It may be possible to improve the translation at that point.

- There may be some places in the text where the reader reads something quite different from what the translator intended. He may read a word with the wrong "tone," which changes the meaning, or it may be some other change. If the reader mispronounces a word so that the meaning is changed from what the translator intended, this shows that the translation is not clear. The reader did not understand the correct meaning. The translation needs to be improved.

Take every opportunity to listen carefully to people reading the translated Scriptures, for example, in readings in church. By doing so you can learn whether the translation is clear to those who are reading it or not.

Remember

Always make it clear to the reader that you are not testing the way he reads. Explain carefully that you are looking for ways to make the translation better.

17.3 Tell-it-again test

The purpose of this test is to discover places in the translation where the meaning is not clear, or where the readers might have understood a wrong meaning. It can also give good ideas for improving the translation.

a. Choose a fairly short passage (about three or four verses at a time).
b. Read this to someone *who does not already know the story*. Or, if the person is able to read, let him read the story himself.
c. Ask the hearer to retell what has just been read, using his own words. Record what he says, if possible.
d. Listen and notice the following:

- Whether any part of the meaning is missing. Maybe that part was not clear.
- Whether the person understood something different from what the translator intended to be understood. This also shows that the translation is not clear.
- Whether the person uses some good expressions to retell the meaning. Write these down. They can be used to make the translation clearer and more natural.

e. Repeat the test with several different people. Do not ask anyone to retell a passage that he has already heard someone else retell.

The test can also be used with a group of people. Discussion between the people in the group will bring interesting points to light.

The advantage of recording the retelling is that the recording can be replayed later. The person doing the test then has another opportunity to note down any expressions that he did not have time to write down during the testing session.

17.4 Questions and answers

The purpose of this test is to find out whether the meaning of the translation is accurate and clear.

a. Choose a passage and prepare a list of questions. The questions should be short. They should be questions that require short, factual answers.

Sample Questions on Mark 2:1–12

- *Where* was Jesus standing while he was preaching?
- *Who* was listening to him?
- *Who* came there and wanted to reach him?

- *Why* could they not reach him?
- *What* did they do?
- *What* did Jesus say to the paralysed man?

  b. Read the passage to someone (or to a group of people) and ask them to answer the questions. Write down the answers that are given.
  c. Repeat with several other people.

Make sure that the questions are clear. If your helper does not understand what you are asking him, then the answer will not be helpful to you. It may even lead you to wrong conclusions. The questions can also be used in a group Bible study situation.

There are sets of questions prepared in English for some Bible books. These will help you in preparing questions in your own language.

If a certain question is answered wrongly by several different people, this shows that the text is not clear at that point.

Avoid these things when using questions:

- Do not ask "Did you understand this passage?"
- Do not use questions to which someone can answer just "yes" or "no."

Remember

As with other tests, explain carefully to everyone who is answering the questions that you are not testing them (to see if they are clever or have the right answer), but rather you are testing the translation, to find out if it communicates clearly.

Exercise

Below is the back translation of a sample first draft translation of Mark 1:16–20. Imagine that you are testing this translation. You have asked another speaker the following set of questions and have received these answers. From these answers, what points in the translation seem to be unclear and probably need improvement? You will need to refer to the *NIV* and *GNT*, or other translations, as source texts.

Sample first draft translation for testing:

> ¹⁶ One day Jesus was walking beside the water of Galilee. As he was walking along he saw Simon and the brother of Andrew throwing nets into the water. They were doing this because they were haleyes. ¹⁷ Jesus called out to them, "Come and follow me and I will help you to catch men." ¹⁸ At once they got up and left their nets and followed him. ¹⁹ Then they went a little further and found James and John who were mending their nets. ²⁰ Jesus called them also and they got up at once and followed him, leaving their father with the servants in the boat.

Question: Where was Jesus walking?

Answer: He was walking beside a lake.

Question: Who did he see there?
Answer: Simon and the brother of Andrew.

Question: Who was Simon's brother?
Answer: I do not know.

Question: What were they doing?
Answer: Throwing nets into the sea.

Question: Why were they doing this?
Answer: Because they were heleyes.

Question: What are heleyes?
Answer: I do not know.

Question: Why would a person throw nets into the sea?
Answer: Maybe the nets were worn out.

Question: Why did Jesus say they should follow him?
Answer: He wanted them to help him arrest some men.

Question: What did Simon and Andrew do then?
Answer: They went with Jesus.

Question: Who else did Jesus see?
Answer: He saw James and John.

Question: Who was the father of James and John?
Answer: I don't know.

These responses indicate that some information has been omitted and that there are some misunderstandings, showing that the translation needs to be corrected and improved.

17.5 Comparing alternative ways of translating

As translator, you will sometimes be considering alternative ways of translating a certain text. You want to find out which of the alternatives best communicates the correct meaning to the audience for whom the translation is intended. You also want to discover any differences in meaning between the alternatives, and whether one of the alternatives is more accurate to the meaning of the original text.

Ask those helping which of the alternatives they understand best. Ask them to tell you the meaning they understand in their own words. This will help to show whether the correct meaning is indeed being communicated.

This method can be used with individual helpers or with a group of people, possibly in a group Bible study. It may give rise to useful discussion. Participants in the discussion may suggest other alternatives that are better than those suggested. Such suggestions should be carefully noted.

17.6 Reviewing

Reviewers are appointed as representative speakers of the receptor language who will give feedback to the translation team. All church denominations in the language area should be invited to appoint reviewers. Reviewers may also be appointed to represent a specific dialect area, or some other social group.

Who can be a reviewer?

Reviewers should be fluent speakers of the receptor language. They need to be genuinely interested and committed to the work so that they can continue to give feedback as further books are translated.

What is the task of the reviewer?

Reviewers study the translation, reading it carefully, section by section, to see if there are any errors or omissions. They give suggestions for improving the translation, to make it clearer and more natural. They may be asked to give feedback on specific issues, such as choice of key biblical terms, or on the style of language used in the translation.

What training does a reviewer need?

If the writing-system for the receptor language has been recently developed, reviewers will need training in understanding and applying this writing system. They will need opportunity for practice so that they can read the translation fluently and easily.

Reviewers should also receive basic training in translation principles and procedures, so that they understand how their contribution fits into the whole process. They should be aware that they are making a very important contribution to the project.

How do reviewers work?

Reviewers may work individually, and may also meet to work together from time to time as groups. Meeting as a group helps to stimulate thinking and to discover where there may be different viewpoints to consider.

17.7 Draft editions – audio and/or written

A draft version for wider testing is prepared after the consultant check (see chapter 19) has been completed. The translator has gathered the comments and suggestions that have come through the checking and testing processes, and has revised the draft, entering the changes in Paratext.

Draft editions can be produced either in audio form or as a printout, ideally in both forms. Printed copies should be clearly marked as "draft editions" and should be accompanied by a note inviting further comments and suggestions, which will be sent to the translators. The same information should be included in audio recordings. Audio recordings can also be accompanied by digital text, so that the hearer can read the text as he listens. See https://software.sil.org/scriptureappbuilder/.

Audio recordings, in a form that can be shared on a mobile phone, have become popular. People listen and begin to discuss the translation – the translation team listen eagerly to the discussion and use the feedback to polish the translation ready for the final publication.

Draft versions are distributed to pastors and church leaders, and to anybody who is willing to read and use the translation. The way in which this draft version is used, and the reaction of the readers and hearers, will help the translation team to know whether the translation is now ready for full publication. Recordings of draft versions can be set so that they delete after a certain date.

Before the New Testament or whole Bible is published, at least one or two books should be printed as draft editions. Much can be learnt from comments and suggestions that arise from the use of these draft versions, so that the final version can be improved.

17.8 Using translation in Bible study groups

Use of the draft translation in Bible study groups, also in family devotional times or fellowship meetings, is a good way to gather feedback on the translation. These should be informal study situations so that participants are able to ask questions and discuss freely. Translators or reviewers who take part in such groups will be able to note any places where the text was not well understood, also good alternative ways of expressing the text.

17.9 General notes on testing translations

- Start testing early in the translation project. What you discover through testing the first translated passages will help you to make a better first draft of later passages and will save you time later. Starting testing early also helps to make members of the receptor community aware of the translation project from the beginning, and encourages their involvement.
- Test widely:
    with Christians and non-Christians
    with young and old
    with men and women
    with those who are able to read and those who are not
- Keep a chart of the testing process, recording which passages you have tested, and in which ways. Also record the date(s) when a particular passage was tested. Every passage should be tested by several methods. Difficult passages may need to be tested, revised, and retested several times.
- Use the "Notes" tool in Paratext to keep a verse-by-verse record of issues that need further discussion and decision. Plan time for team checking to review the feedback received and to polish the final text ready for publication.

> **Remember**
>
> Proper testing is an essential part of the translation work.
>
> Summary of eight ways of testing your translation:
> 1. Reading aloud
>   2. Listening to readers
>   3. Tell-it-again
>   4. Questions and answers
>   5. Comparing alternative ways of translating
> 6. Feedback from reviewers
>   7. Draft versions
>   8. Use of the translation in Bible study groups

Additional resources on "Testing the Translation with the Receptor Community"

BT4 online materials

17_Testing_1-Why_test.pptx
17_Testing_2-Tell-it-again.pptx
17_Testing_3-Asking_questions.pptx
17_Testing_4-More_ways_to_test.pptx
17_Testing_5-Tips_on_testing.pptx
17_Testing_6-Genre_questions.pptx
17_Checking_concert_experiment.pdf
17_Reviewers-Their_role_and_contribution.pdf
17_Testing_questions-Luke_10_25-37.pdf

Websites

HearThis or the *Scripture App Builder*
   (Programs that are available at https://software.sil.org/hearthis/, and https://software.sil.org/scriptureappbuilder/.)

For further reading

Iyoku, Samuel. 1977. Check the Word. *The Bible Translator* 28(4):404–407. http://www.ubs-translations.org/tbt/1977/04/TBT197704.html?num=404&x=0&y=0&num1=.

Loewen, Jacob A. 1972. Criticism can be helpful. *The Bible Translator* 23(2):234–240. http://www.ubs-translations.org/tbt/1972/02/TBT197202.html?num=234&x=0&y=0&num1=.

SIL Africa Area Translation Department. 1985. How to use testing questions for testing translation. Africa Area Translation Aids 5. Nairobi: SIL International. (Available on *Translator's Workplace*.)

Chapter 18

Step 6: Preparing for the Consultant Check – How to Make a Back Translation

18.1 What is a "back translation"?

A *back translation* is a very literal rendering of a translated text into English or another language of wider communication in the area concerned, a language in which the translation consultant and the translators are able to communicate with each other. It uses the vocabulary of English (or the language of wider communication) while reflecting as closely as possible the content and grammatical structure of the translated text in a form that someone who does not speak that language can understand.

A back translation is not a proper translation. It will not sound natural in English because it reflects the grammatical patterns used in the language of the translation, not those of English.

Here is an example of an early draft translation of Luke 1:26–33 in the Hohumono language of Nigeria, with back translation, as it might appear in Paratext, side by side with the translated text:

Rezeb a remare a Jizos o	Foretelling of birth of Jesus
26 Bhaa ihuhun hobhorayen a reme hohumo a Erisabe, Obhazi othom enjer Gebira bhaa Nazaret, usa gwen bhaa Gariri o. 27 Eethom onyi wunagwa gw' ora orom-hozeng, rehon aase ora Meri. Orom gw' eepo rebhan ora Josef, gw' ozeng bhaa emarethai a Ovai Dever o. 28 Gebira opa eehobhe bho eero, 'Rajuno haraku ara agwo! Obhazi oku ara agwo ofene bho oothaa roso-aone sá rokpoi o!'	26 In month sixth of pregnancy of Elizabeth, God he-sent angel Gabriel to Nazareth, town one in Galilee, 27 he-give young lady who she had man not known, name of her is Mary. Man who he she proposed marriage he was Joseph who he came from family line of king David. 28 Angel the went to her there he she said, "Greetings, you whom God he has greatly he looked good face! The Lord he-is with you."
29 Meri rofem sa-reevuvura bhaa hezeere bho, bhaa ramon a hithere aaje, okubho otun bhoven fá reya sem reja. 30 Asi enjer gwe sa-eero, 'Meri, ho-za oohara, ozama afong roso-aone ara Obhazi o. 31 Agwo akura ahumo reme, amar wun-orom gwá ara aafi Jizos o. 32 Ame óra onoo a hekpeere ada bheeya Wun-orom ame Gwé Obhang ota. Jihova Obhazi eenyi hisee a ibhobhe ase aagwe Dever o. 33 Ame ofene obhob don a Jekob bhaa ikpakpa-ikpa, ibhobhe a hevai aase rekpune hi-ma iyina.'	29 Mary's heart it she confused very greatly from words of his, she was she thought something that greeting this it show. 30 But angel the he her told, "Do not you fear Mary, because you have found face good with God. 31 You you will you carry belly, you will bear child-man who you shall name him Jesus. 32 He will be person of greatness and they will him call Son of Who He is High Most. Jihova God will him give throne of father his David. 33 He he will again he rule Israel for ever; government of kingship his end not it would it have."

18.2 The purpose of a back translation

The purpose of making a back translation is to help a translation consultant, or someone else who does not know the language, to discuss the translation with the translator. Although it will not give the consultant a full understanding (as he would have if he knew the language), it will give some insight and serve as a beginning point for further discussion and explanation.

It is important that the back translation is well made, following the principles described below. Otherwise, it will mislead the consultant.

Provided that the back translation is made by someone who is not one of the translators, back translations are also another way of discovering how another speaker is understanding the translation. Places where the translation is inaccurate or unclear are often discovered through back translations.

18.3 Who should make the back translation?

The back translation should be made by a first-language speaker of the receptor language. It should be made, if possible, by someone who does not know the Bible well, and who is not already familiar with the passage concerned. Then it is more likely to reflect what this translation is communicating, without being influenced by the back translator's previous knowledge of the passage.

There are two reasons why the back translation should be made by someone other than the translator:

- The translator has previous knowledge of the passage; he has already studied it well.
- The translator knows what the translation is meant to say. He sincerely thinks that it gives the correct meaning (otherwise, he would not have translated that way). But we need to know whether the correct meaning is in fact understood by another speaker.

The person who makes the back translation needs to be trained. See point 7 below.

18.4 Oral or written?

A back translation can be done orally during a consultant checking session. This gives opportunity for the consultant to ask for further explanation, where needed. There is also opportunity for discussion. An oral back translation made during a consultant checking session also helps the consultant to know whether the language-speaker making the back translation is understanding the translation easily.

Alternatively, the team may arrange for a written back translation to be prepared so that this can be sent to the consultant in advance of the consultant session. The advantages of having a written back translation for consultant checking are discussed in chapter 19, point 4.

18.5 Viewing a back translation in Paratext

In Paratext it is possible to open a "back translation" project that corresponds with the receptor language translation. The back translation can be keyboarded into this project and displayed as a Paratext window. The windows are arranged so that the back translation is viewed side-by-side with the translation and can easily be compared.

Advantages of having the back translation in electronic form include the following:

- The back translation can be updated as revisions are made in the translation, so that it provides an updated record of the translation.
- It can be sent to the translation consultant in advance of consulting sessions, using the Paratext "send/receive" function. The consultant can then prepare for the session ahead of time. He can also send notes to the team before the session so that many points can be reviewed and resolved before the session. Then face-to-face time during the consulting session can focus on points that need discussion.
- Back translations in electronic form are more readily available. (Hand-written back translations may not be found when they are wanted!)
- They can also be easily shared with those who may be translating into related languages, sharing good translation suggestions and inviting feedback.

18.6 The interlinearizer tool in Paratext

The Paratext program has a way to generate an interlinear word-by-word gloss of a translation. The computer guesses the meaning, based on word frequency. To begin with the guess is often wrong, but as the user corrects the gloss verse by verse, the computer remembers the corrections, and the gloss becomes increasingly accurate. The person who corrects the gloss should be a first-language speaker of the receptor-language.

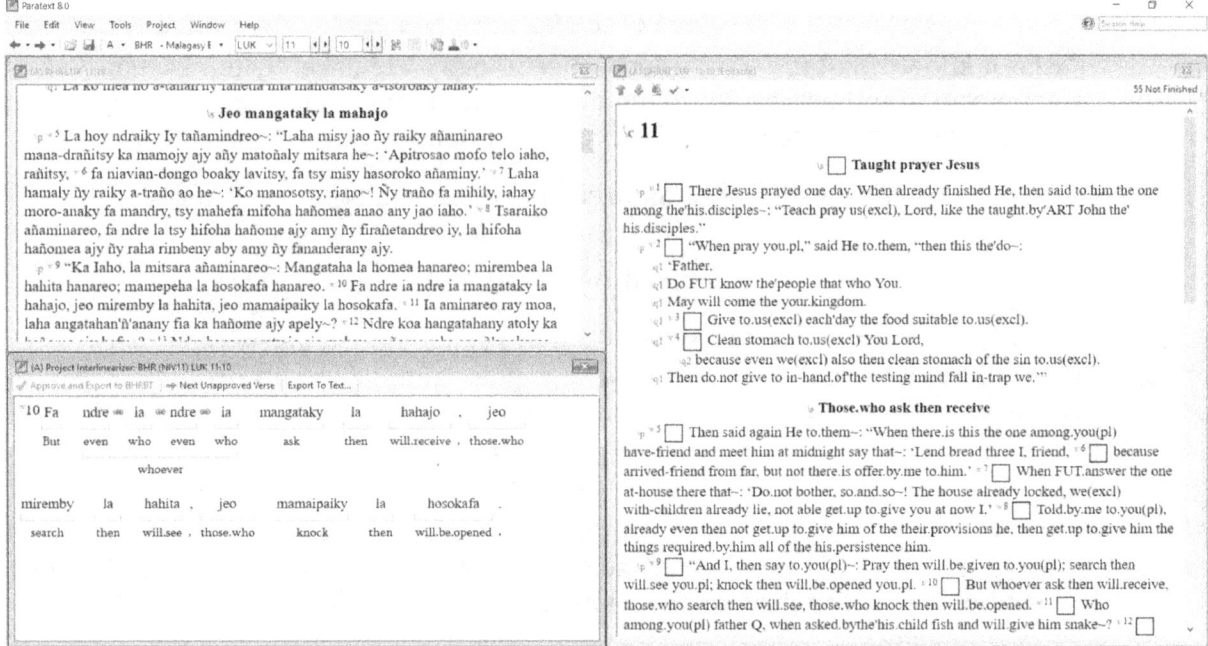

Figure 4. This screenshot illustrates the display for showing a back translation and the "interlinearizer" window, in the Malagasy-Bara language of Madagascar.
© 2018 by Berthine Rasoanirina. Used by permission.

By contrast, a regular back translation is done entirely by a human being, a first-language speaker of the language of the translation. It reflects what this speaker understands as he reads the translation. It reveals whether or not he is understanding the message that the original author was communicating to his original audience.

Both the back translation done by a human being and the computer-generated interlinear gloss are useful, but for different purposes.

An example of an interlinear, very literal back translation (word-for-word key), generated using Paratext:

Anọng	*p'akkẹrẹ*	*nnwẹr*	*nwoma,*	*ode*	*kaam*	*Paul,*
People	who-write	paper	this,	it-is	I	Paul,

kw'nyim	*mgbakkohbhọ*	*okurọ*	*k'eso ch'Jisus*	*Kraist,*
who-I-lie	chains	because	for head of-Jesus	Christ,
[I am in prison]			[because of Jesus]	

omaana	*Timoti,*	*agbaanakka*	*kwamina.*
and/with	Timothy,	brother	our.

Mọkkẹr	*onang*	*Philemon,*	*oyodikkobh*	*kwamina*
We-write	give	Philemon	friend	our

kw'mosokọ	*ettem,*	*kw'mọtọnọ*	*osi*	*ọtọhm.*	*Mobira*
whom-we-place	heart	who we-together	do	work.	We-also

ozima	*Aphiya,*	*agbaanakka*	*kwamina*	*k'epanọng*	*ọttara*	*Akipus,*
greet	Apphia,	sibling	our	female	and	Archippus
		[lit. our female sibling]				

kw'ode	*mach'oyok-osojanong*	*kwamina*	*kw'moṭoṇo*
who-is	like-fellow-soldier	of-ours	whom-we-together
osi	*erima*	*ch'oṭohm*	*mva.*	*Mobira*	*ozima*	*ẹkkọbazikaan*
do	fighting	of-work.	this	We-also	greet	church-group
maphyir	*ch'ettong*	*ny'ọsọhm*	*kwọ.*	*Tte*	*Ibinọkpaabyi,*	*kw'ode*
all	who-gather	in-house	your.	May	God,	who-is
Ttatta kwamina,	*ọmaana*	*Ọvaar*	*Jisus*	*Kraist,*	*mado*
Father our	with	Chief	Jesus	Christ	bless
bọnga,	*mabira*	*anang*	*bọnga*	*ọdaam.*
you-plural	also	give	you	peace/contentment

A consultant may find a word-for-word key of this kind difficult to understand. This may be especially so when the following points apply:

a) The language from which the key is being made has a grammatical structure that is very different from English, especially in respect of word-order.

b) The consultant is not familiar with languages of that language family.

When these conditions are true, then the consultant may ask the translation team to provide a freer back translation, oral or written, in addition to the interlinearizer version.

18.7 Training back translators

A good way to train a back translator is to ask him first to make a back translation of some natural, non-biblical receptor language texts. In this situation, there will be no temptation to be influenced by an existing English (or other major language) translation or by theological bias. Encourage the back translator to read one sentence at a time, and then write the meaning, phrase by phrase. By trial and error, giving him feedback at each attempt, help him to find just the right level of literalness – literal enough to reflect the receptor language structure, and free enough to communicate the meaning.

Starting with a non-biblical text is helpful because the back translator works only from this text. He is not tempted to look at a Bible to see what it says, or to be influenced by his memory of the passage. Many people feel freer when working with a non-biblical text.

Experiment! Try out different people. Some people prove to be very good at making back translations, and even enjoy doing it, while others never seem to develop the skill.

The translator or another member of the team should go over the back translation carefully before it is sent to the consultant, to ensure that it represents the translation accurately. He may use a different colour to add notes where necessary. Even in this process, the translator may discover some errors in the translation and correct them himself. These can be discussed and corrected by the team before the translation goes to the consultant.

Ask your consultant to give you feedback concerning back translations you have made.

18.8 Some details to remember

☐ The back translator should not look at any text except the translation while making the back translation. All Bibles should be closed. Do not under any circumstance look up to see what other versions say. The back translation should reflect only what this translation says.

- ☐ A back translation should be as literal as possible while still making sense. Make necessary adjustments to make it readable and understandable. But it should not read as a smooth translation. Rather it should reflect the structure of the language of the translation.
- ☐ The back translation should be phrase-for-phrase (rather than word-for-word).
- ☐ Keep paragraph, sentence, and clause breaks, with punctuation as in the translation.
- ☐ Keep the order of sentences and clauses as in the translation.
- ☐ Where there is an idiom or figure of speech, put the meaning in the text, with the literal form in square brackets. Alternatively, if the back translation is being done interlinearly, put the literal form under the language and the actual meaning in brackets. For example,

Mbembe: *kaam anong kinchi*
         I   people do-not-eat   [I do not cheat people]

Mbembe: *otor be otohng*
         he-pulled them ears   [he-warned them strongly]

If an idiom occurs frequently, it is not necessary to repeat the note every time it occurs.
- ☐ Include grammatical information in square brackets, where needed. For example, indicate whether a pronoun back translated as "you" is singular or plural.
- ☐ Where two or more words are needed to back translate one word in the translation, link the words with hyphens.
- ☐ Where two or more alternative words are needed to indicate the area of meaning of a word in the translation, separate these words with a slash. Examples: love/kindness, he/she.
- ☐ If words from the receptor language are included in the back translation because they seem untranslatable, put an explanatory note enclosed in square brackets after the word.
- ☐ Add notes wherever needed to explain anything different or unusual in the translation. Add notes to explain background cultural information. The notes may be at the end of the verse. Or you can use the footnote function if the back translation is being keyed on a computer.

Remember

A back translation helps someone who does not know the language of the translation to understand how the meaning is expressed in the translation. Include explanatory notes where needed.

Additional resources on "How to Make a Back Translation"

BT4 online materials

18_Back-translation-Best_practices.pptx
18_How_to_make_a_back-translation.pptx
18_Sample_back-translation-Ruth_1_1-13.pdf

Chapter 19

Step 7: Checking the Translation with a Consultant

> The role of a translation consultant is to help Bible translation teams succeed in their task of producing a good quality translation that will meet the needs of the receptor community. The consultant seeks to train, guide, and encourage translation teams in many different ways.

19.1 What is the purpose of checking with a translation consultant?

The consultant checking process provides guidance and support to the translation team, helping them to follow good procedures and to ensure that the translation meets required standards before publication.

The consultant seeks to help the translators develop their skills in translating, and in checking and improving their own translations. As they develop these skills, the team will catch more and more errors themselves and will make their own improvements. The translations submitted for checking will be better and better as the project proceeds.

The consultant works with the team to help check the translation for accuracy to the original Hebrew, Aramaic, or Greek text, and for clarity in communicating the biblical author's intended meaning to the new audience. He also interacts with the team on language issues, encouraging the use of the rich resources of the receptor language.

Before translated Scripture can be accepted for publication by a Bible publishing agency, the agency will require confirmation from a qualified translation consultant that the translation is indeed ready for publication, having met the standards required. This is true of translation programs under the auspices of all Bible translation organisations that are members of the Forum of Bible Agencies International.

19.2 What needs to be checked?

All translated Scripture needs to be checked, also all supplementary information that is included in Scripture publications, such as book introductions, section headings, footnotes, and glossaries.

19.3 When should translation checking be done?

Draft translations that have been team-checked and have been through initial testing and reviewing, are ready for checking with a consultant. Consultant checking should then be done as soon as possible – this is important for the development of the translation team and for their encouragement.

During the early stages of a translation project, consultant checks should take place frequently, as this is part of the training for the team. The checks should be done meeting together face-to-face whenever possible.

Later, when the team has experience and has established good habits of translation, some of the checking can be done over the internet, with occasional face-to-face meetings.

Try to keep up to date with arrangements for checking, so that unchecked books do not accumulate. Arrange for checking of each book as soon as possible after it is ready.

It is helpful if the same consultant can continue to serve a team throughout the project. In this way, the consultant can build strong relationships with the translators, getting to know their strengths and weaknesses and helping them develop. He also builds up his knowledge of the receptor language and culture. However, it is often not possible to keep the same consultant, and it should be remembered that different consultants have different strengths and can train the team in different skills.

19.4 How do the translation team and the consultant work together to check the translation?

Usually a consultant spends time with the translation team in the area where the receptor language is spoken. He sits with the team to work through the translation verse by verse. Sometimes there may be checking workshops, when several teams come together to check the same book, benefitting from the fellowship and interaction.

Except in rare cases, the consultant is not a speaker of the receptor language, so he uses a back translation to gain insight into the meaning of the translated text. This provides the starting basis for discussion with the team.

As explained in chapter 18, there are two kinds of back translation: oral (spoken) and written. It is usually recommended that the team prepare a written back translation in advance of the checking session, for the following reasons:

- This enables the consultant to prepare before the time together with the team. He has opportunity to research exegetical points where necessary.
- The consultant can send comments to the team in advance, using the "Notes" tool in Paratext. The team will be able to cover some issues before the checking session so that the time together can be spent on the more challenging points that need discussion.
- It gives the consultant an opportunity to look at discourse patterns and other grammatical features in a larger body of text.
- It makes it possible for the consultant to compare different parts of the translated text, such as parallel passages in the Gospels.
- Through looking at the back translation before the consultant session, the translators themselves can observe points in the translation that need revision.

- Additional oral back translation can still be requested during the checking session, when needed to gather feedback from other speakers.
- The back translation (after being checked and edited) can be shared as a help to other translators, especially those working in related languages.

Many translation consultants testify to the value of receiving a written back translation before the session.

There may, however, be circumstances where using an oral back translation is acceptable. This may include situations where the project is at an advanced stage and where the consultant has already been working with the project for some time and is familiar with the local situation and with features of the receptor language.

19.5 Preparing for a consultant check

In preparation for checking sessions, in addition to a back translation, the consultant may ask the team to provide the following items:

- A list of proposed translations of key biblical terms – explaining the terms tentatively chosen and reasons for the choice. It may be helpful to refer to the list provided in Paratext.
- Some freely told (not translated) texts in the receptor language, with an interlinear gloss. Also copies of any notes that have been written up about the discourse structure and other features of the receptor language.
- Notes on any points that the team would like to discuss or areas on which they would appreciate further training. This could include how to use certain resources.

19.6 Other activities during consultant checking visits

A consultant visit provides opportunity to review the plan and progress of the translation project and to discuss plans for the next weeks and months. The consultant will invite the team to share their difficulties and concerns and will look for ways to resolve these needs.

It is a time to review the plan for which books of the Bible the team will translate next, taking the opinions of church leaders into account. Each team member needs to be clear on his specific assignment and responsibilities. Consultants can help the team access commentaries and other helps that are available for the Bible books that are about to be translated. They may also be able to bring resources to share with the team, focusing on translation procedures or issues with which the team are involved. For example, PowerPoints or Bible background videos.

Consultants welcome opportunities to meet with the project Translation Committee and to support the project in public relations in the language area. This is an opportunity to address any problems and to encourage wider partnership. Ideas for promoting the use of translations can also be shared. If any church denomination, or dialect region, is not using the translated Scriptures, the consultant can participate with members of the committee or translation team in paying a courtesy call on the leaders of that church or area to explain the program and answer questions.

Translation teams are encouraged to tell their consultants ways in which they can help. Consultants are ready and eager to help the team achieve their goals.

Translation checking in progress . . .

Figure 5. Translation checking.
© 2018 by Charles Nkanu David. Used by permission.

Additional resources on "Checking the Translation with a Consultant"

BT4 online materials

19_Checking_translation_with_a_consultant.pptx
19_How_translation_consultants_can_help.pptx
19_Planning_for_a_consultant_check.pptx
19_The_role_and_function_of_a_translation_consultant.pdf
   (Also available to view in *A Handbook for Translation Consultants*, in *Translator's Workplace*.)

Website

The Forum of Bible Agencies International "Statement on qualifications for translation consultants."
   (Can be viewed at https://forum-intl.org/resources/translation-standards/.)

Chapter 20

Steps 8 to 10: The Later Stages of the Translation Process

Continuing the review of "A Ten-Step Procedure in Translation," we now focus on finalising translations and preparing them for publication.

Step 8: Reviewing and more testing – focus on reviewing

Different ways of testing the translation were described in chapter 17, Step 5. The process of reviewing was also described in that chapter. Testing and reviewing activities continue throughout a translation project.

Reviewing is especially important in the later stages of the project. As more books are drafted, team checked, tested, and consultant checked, they become identified as "draft translations." Draft translations are distributed to the reviewers. Reviewers read, study, and use the translation by sharing it with others. Sometimes reviewers meet together to read through the draft translations. They send their feedback to the translation team, noting any possible errors or corrections needed, also making suggestions for improvement.

Sometimes reviewers may meet with the translators to read through passages together and discuss translation issues. Major changes resulting from the reviewing process should be reviewed with the consultant.

Each book should be reviewed by several reviewers. This process helps to ensure that there is opportunity for input from different parts of the community, including different church denominations.

A reminder: What is the difference between "testing" and "reviewing"?

Testing and reviewing are complementary activities, both having the goal of helping to check the accuracy of the translation and improve its communicative effectiveness. The following chart summarises these differences:

Community testing	Reviewing
When the translation team works on community testing, a wide cross-section of people is involved. Some may help only on one occasion, others may help many times, but usually there is no long-term commitment.	Reviewers are chosen by the translation committee and churches. They are chosen to represent different denominations, dialects, and other social groups. They commit themselves to serve regularly through the translation project.
Those who assist with testing come from many different backgrounds. They may or may not be church members. They may or may not be able to read. The only requirement is that they speak the language as their first language.	Reviewers are trained to read (and perhaps write) the receptor language. They are sympathetic to the translation project and are ready to give their help.
Those who assist with the testing process are not trained.	Reviewers are trained to understand basic principles of translation and to give feedback on the translation. Reviewers may also assist in testing the translation with others.
Testing starts early in the translation process, as soon as first draft translations have been prepared, and continues through the project.	Reviewing mostly takes place when the draft of the translation is more advanced, usually after the consultant check.
Testing is usually done orally, with face-to-face interaction.	Reviewers are given written copies of the translation to study. Interaction between translators and reviewers may be oral, face-to-face, or sometimes also in writing. Reviewers may work in groups or individually. Face-to-face interaction and discussion is very helpful.

Step 9: Final editing and consistency checking, preparing for publication

When preparing for publication of a New Testament or Bible, project leaders should be in discussion with the appropriate department of the Bible translation organisation to which the project is affiliated. For the publication of New Testaments and Bibles it is recommended to start planning and seek assistance at least one year before the consultant checking is expected to be completed.

The team should anticipate that considerable time will be needed for final editing and consistency checking. The Paratext program provides excellent tools to help in this final editing process, especially checking for consistency of the translation.

The following are some of the issues that need to be addressed:

- ☐ Comparison of parallel passages in the Gospels, and other parallel texts, for appropriate consistency in the translation
- ☐ Consistent use of key biblical terms, while allowing for variation of meaning depending on the context

- ☐ Final choice of illustrations, entering references in the text appropriately to indicate where they are to be placed
- ☐ Consistent spelling of proper names
- ☐ Checks for consistency of format, layout, spelling, and punctuation (including checks for consistency in the punctuation of direct and indirect quotations)
- ☐ Review of long and short sentences
- ☐ Preparing the glossary, if one is to be included, also reviewing other supplementary information to be included, such as a preface and book introductions

Step 10: Final reading for approval by receptor-language church and community representatives

When preparing to send the translation for publication, in addition to other checks, it is important to plan for the translation to be formally approved by the Translation Committee and other leaders who are partnering locally in the project.

It is recommended that when it seems that the translation is ready for publication, formal arrangements should be made, inviting representative church and community leaders, and other interested persons, to meet to read selected portions of the translation, hearing these read aloud while also viewing the text, with opportunity for discussion. They should also have opportunity to take portions of the translation and read them through with others in their church or community.

How many meetings will be needed for this interaction will depend on the situation. If the appointed reviewers have been giving regular feedback, and draft versions of sample books have been in circulation, then agreement on approval may be achieved in one or two meetings. In other situations, a series of meetings may be needed to give opportunity for interaction.

When everyone is agreed that the translation is ready, it can be sent for publication, in print and as an audio recording!

Additional resources on "The Later Stages of the Translation Process"

BT4 online materials

20_Final_editing.pptx
20_Punctuating_speech_quotations.pdf

Part 3

Studying Words and How They Are Used (Lexical Meaning)

Chapter 21

Exploring the Meanings of Words

The technical term used to refer to the meaning of words is *lexical meaning*.

The chapters in part 3 of this manual illustrate how words may have different meanings depending on the context in which they occur. We review the fact that the areas of meaning and the different senses of words in one language do not match up with those of another language and discuss the implications this has for translation.

We also review ways to translate concepts that are unknown in the receptor language culture, with specific application to the translation of key terms that occur in the Bible.

Translators are encouraged to use an English dictionary to explore the different senses that an English word may have, depending on the context. The *Oxford Advanced Learner's Dictionary* (*OALD*) is recommended for this purpose. See further information at the end of this chapter.

> A technical term that may be used when discussing the meaning of words is the term *morpheme*. A morpheme is the smallest unit in a language that has meaning. Every word is comprised of one or more morphemes.
>
> A word is a unit of language that can stand alone. A word may be comprised of one or more morphemes.
>
> The difference between a word and a morpheme is that some morphemes do not stand alone. For example, the English word "cats" consists of two morphemes: the root "cat" and the plural suffix "-s" – the plural suffix "s" cannot stand alone.

21.1 One word may have more than one meaning, depending on its context

Within one language, the same word may have several different meanings, sometimes referred to as different "senses." The context in which a word occurs shows which sense is being used.

Examples from English

- A "nail" is a pointed piece of metal used for carpentry work; a "finger nail" is the hard substance at the tip of a finger.
- A "foot" is a part of the body, the lower end of the leg; the "foot" of a mountain means the lower part of the mountain; and a "foot" is also a measurement, twelve inches in length.
- A "board" is a long, thin, flat piece of wood; the "board" of a school means the "governing committee" of the school.

Exercise 1

How would you translate each of these words into your own language?

a. "nail" as in, "He hammered the nail into the wall."
   "nail" as in, "I need to trim my finger nails."

b. "foot" as in, "He stamped on my foot."
   "foot" as in, "We reached the foot of the mountain."
   "foot" as in, "This stick is a foot long."

c. "board" as in, "I used the board to make a table."
   "board" as in, "He is the president of the school board."

Remember

Always translate a word according to its meaning in the context in which it occurs.

Exercise 2

Give three examples from your own language of words that have different senses. For example, in the Mbembe language,

ogbangbang can mean   1. 'zinc roof of a house'
                        2. 'an enamel basin'

fohno can mean   1. 'to wipe' (as i,n *ofohno okpokoro*, 'he wiped the table')
                        2. 'to iron' (as in, *ofohno ibara*, 'he ironed the cloth')
                        3. 'to sacrifice' (as in, *ofohno eja*, 'he made a sacrifice')

In many non-European languages, the tone on which a word is pronounced makes a difference to the meaning. For example, in Mbembe, *èfá* (low-high tone), means 'dog', while *éfà* (high-low tone), means 'power'. Such examples are not different senses of the same word, they are different words.

21.1 One word may have more than one meaning, depending on its context

> **Remember**
>
> Someone who is translating from a language that is not his first language may not be aware of all the different senses that a word has in the source language. He may think only of the most usual meaning of the word and may translate that meaning, without realising that this word has different meanings in different contexts.
>
> *Keep alert* to recognise the correct sense of each word in the context in which it occurs.

Exercise 3

In each of the following examples, check carefully the meaning of the word that is underlined. Use your *Advanced Learner's Dictionary* (or any other good English dictionary) for this purpose; also refer to different English Bible versions.

How would you translate the underlined words into your own language in each context?

- a. Acts 9:18 And immediately something like <u>scales</u> fell from his eyes, and he regained his sight.
- b. Revelation 6:5 And its rider had a pair of <u>scales</u> in his hand.
- c. Acts 7:35 by the hand of the angel that appeared to [Moses] in the <u>bush</u> (Compare with Exodus 3:2)
- d. Matthew 6:34 <u>Take</u> therefore no thought for the morrow. (*KJV*)
- e. Acts 23:11 <u>Take</u> courage.
- f. Hebrews 11:7 Noah…constructed an <u>ark</u> for the saving of his household.
- g. Hebrews 9:4 the <u>ark</u> of the covenant covered on all sides with gold
- h. Isaiah 56:10 They are all silent dogs; they cannot <u>bark.</u>
- i. Joel 1:7 It has laid waste my vine and splintered my fig tree; it has stripped off their <u>bark</u> and thrown it down.

Exercise 4

Complete the following study of the word "house" (Greek *oikos*; Hebrew *bayit*).

(1) The *KJV* uses the word "house" in all the references listed below. Look up each verse in the *English Standard Version* (*ESV*) and the *Good News Translation* (*GNT*) and compare how these versions have translated the meaning in each context.

(2) Think carefully about the meaning that the word has in each passage, then note the word or phrase you would use in translating its meaning in that context into your own language.

	KJV	ESV	GNT	Your own language
Matthew 7:24	a wise man, which built his house upon a rock			
Matthew 9:7	(he) departed to his house			

Luke 1:27	a man whose name was Joseph, of the house of David			
Acts 2:36	all the house of Israel			
Acts 7:20	in his father's house			
Acts 16:31	thou shalt be saved, and thy house			
1 Tim. 3:15	in the house of God			
Ruth 4:11	like Rachel and Leah, which two did build the house of Israel			

21.2 Meanings of words do not match across languages

Example

Here are three sentences in the Mbembe language of Nigeria, with an English translation:

ochi	**eten**			'he eats **meat**'
he-eats	eten			
ọwa	**eten**			'he catches a **fish**'
he-catches	eten			
eten	ndo	kk'ẹrọbha	z'ẹgba	'that **animal** has run off into the bush'
eten	that	has-run	to bush	

How should *eten* be translated into English?

- In the first sentence, it refers to "meat"
- In the second sentence, it refers to "fish"
- In the third sentence, it refers to a living "animal"

The area of meaning that is covered by one Mbembe word, *eten*, is covered by three words in English: 'meat,' 'fish,' 'animal.' Someone translating from Mbembe into English would need to use different words to translate *eten* in order to give the correct meaning in each context.

> The meaning of words in one language often do not match up, one-to-one, with words in another language!

Other examples

a. In English there is one word, 'cloth'; in Hausa there are three words:

   zane 'a cloth that one ties round the waist'
   yadi 'cloth bought by the yard'
   kyalle 'a small piece of cloth'

b. In English there are three words, 'grass,' 'flowers,' 'plants.' In the Mundu language of South Sudan, this area of meaning is covered by one Mundu word, the word *go*.

c. English has one basic word for "to carry." The Tzeltal language of Mexico has more than ten different words for "to carry," distinguishing "to carry on the shoulder," "to carry in the palm of the hand," "to carry in a bag," "to carry on the head," "to carry under the arm," "to carry in the arms," and more.
d. In Sudanese Arabic one word, *mara*, covers the area of meaning that is covered by two words in English, depending on the context: 'wife' or 'mother.'
e. In Sudanese Arabic, one word, *asma*, covers the area of meaning that is covered by three words in English, depending on the context: 'hear,' 'understand,' or 'obey.'
f. In Mbembe there is one word, *okora*; in English there are three words: 'red,' 'orange,' and 'yellow.' All three English words could be translated by *okora* in Mbembe. Similarly, in Mbembe there is one word, *obina*; in English there are three words: 'green,' 'blue,' and 'black.'

Some languages have more words to distinguish different colours than others do, and they divide up the range of colours differently.

Remember

Because the meaning of words in different languages do not match each other, the same word in the source language must sometimes be translated by different words in the receptor language.

A word must always be translated according to the meaning it has in the context in which it occurs.

21.3 Re-expressing the meaning of a word

In a dictionary, the meaning of a word can sometimes be defined by stating the different parts of the meaning of that word.

Examples

　　to dawdle　"to walk slowly, to do something slowly"
　　fragrant　"giving off a pleasant smell"
　　stink　　"giving off an unpleasant smell"

Here are some sample definitions of words, taken from an English dictionary. Look up these words in your own dictionary and compare the definitions:

　　bungalow　"house with one storey"
　　cardigan　"warm woolly jersey, with sleeves, opening at the front"
　　to burn　　"to be consumed by fire"
　　adder　　"a kind of small poisonous snake"
　　to dance　"to move with rhythmic steps, usually to music"

The technical name for the parts of meaning of a word is "components of meaning." Sometimes it seems there is no word in the receptor language directly equivalent to the word you are trying to translate. When this happens, consider expressing the meaning by breaking it down into parts.

In defining a word, it is helpful to compare that word with other words in the same area of meaning. For example, "bungalow" might be compared with: house, hut, cottage, flat, palace, mansion. These words share the component of meaning, "a building lived in by human beings." For further examples, see point 4 below.

One of the ways suggested for translating unknown ideas is to use a "descriptive phrase." A descriptive phrase involves breaking down the meaning of the word, expressing those components of its meaning that are important in the context. This method can also be used to translate a word for an idea that is known but for which there is no one-word equivalent in the receptor language. See further in section 22.2.

21.4 A method for comparing the meaning of words

It is often helpful to study and compare several words with similar meaning in a language. Comparing these words with each other helps to show the exact meaning of each word, and how that word differs in meaning from other words. It shows which parts of the meaning are the same and which are different. Here is a procedure to follow:

- Make a list of words that have meanings that are similar. List them down the side of a piece of paper, leaving two or three lines for each word.

  For example, words for describing something that is written: book, booklet, pamphlet, paper, letter, note.

  Or, list words for places where people live: house, hut, cottage, flat, palace, mansion.

- Write a definition for each word, breaking down the parts of meaning. Compare the words with other words in the group to make sure that you have defined precisely in what way the meaning of each word is different.

- Check that you have listed all the facts that are relevant for showing the difference in meaning between the words. If no difference can be found between any two words, it means that they are synonyms, at least in some contexts.

Example

In English, there are several words for different places where water is found. These include the following words: "river," "stream," "lake," "pond," "well," "sea."

A <u>river</u> is a large body of fresh water that flows.

A <u>stream</u> is a small body of fresh water that flows.

A <u>lake</u> is a large body of fresh water that does not flow.

A <u>pond</u> is a small body of fresh water that does not flow.

A <u>well</u> is a deep, man-made hole, from which water can be drawn.

A <u>sea</u> is a very, very large body of salt water.

A similar study of words with overlapping meaning should be made in the receptor language. For example, in the Mbembe language there are three words for water:

epe refers to any body of non-flowing water;

ekeka refers to a small body of flowing water;

ǫraanga refers to a large body of flowing water; whether the water is salt or not does not make any difference in the Mbembe system. "Sea" is expressed in Mbembe as *ǫraanga kwiden* 'big river'.

It is clear that the Mbembe words do not match one-on-one with English words for bodies of water. Someone translating from English into Mbembe must choose the appropriate word in each context.

Exercise 5

(1) In English there are words for different ways of cooking:

    to roast   "to cook something in an oven or over a fire, using fat or oil"

    to bake   "to cook something in an oven (without using fat or oil)"

    to fry   "to cook something in fat in a pan"

    to boil   "to cook something in water in a pan"

    to toast   "to cook bread or something similar, by holding it to the heat of a fire"

(2) List as many words as you can in your own language for different ways of cooking. Show how the words differ in meaning from each other. Compare the meaning of these words with the English words listed above.

Exercise 6

(1) Discuss the meaning of the following words in English:

    he was surprised

    he was amazed

    he was astounded

    he was shocked

    he was puzzled

(2) List as many words or expressions as you can in your own language for the idea of surprise or amazement. Consider how the words differ in meaning.

For discussion

Discuss the following sets of English words and compare them with sets of words in the same areas of meaning in your own language.

    a. error, crime, sin, fault, misdemeanour

    b. proverb, parable, story, riddle, allegory, fable

    c. to shout, to cry out, to scream

21.5 Words that go together

Many words have a natural "partner"; they "collocate," or "go together with" certain other words.

For example, in English, it is idiomatic to say, "he suffers" or "he has had a lot of suffering." In some languages, it is natural to say, "he <u>sees</u> suffering" or "he <u>drinks</u> suffering."

In each language, the natural collocation of a word is the other word or words with which it commonly occurs. For example, the words "to ask a question" form a common collocation in English. Other natural collocations are:

  "to sing a song"

  "to keep a law"

  "to drive a car"

Sometimes the meaning of a word changes depending on the collocation.

Example

In the Mbembe language, the verb *chi* 'to eat' can be used in a number of collocations:

chi ọdaang   'eat foufou'
eat foufou

chi akpuka   'embezzle money'
eat money

chi eden   'go first'
eat path

chi ngwo   'take a bribe'
eat bribe

chi akpen   'live it up (high life)'
eat life

chi ọnọng   'cheat someone'
eat person

Exercise 7

(1) What is the verb for "eat" in your own language?
(2) Make a list of phrases in which this word collocates with different objects. Give
   - a word-for-word key in English, and
   - a natural English phrase with the same meaning.

> **Remember**
>
> A common mistake that translators make is to translate too literally, carrying over the collocation of words from the source language. The result is an unnatural and often confusing translation.
>
> Remember to use collocations that are natural in the receptor language.

Further examples of collocations that do not match across languages:

Mark 1:6

   English: John…ate locusts and wild honey.

   Jukun (literally translated): John…ate locusts and drank wild honey.

   In some languages you "suck" or "lick" honey.

Mark 1:19

   English: mending the nets

   Jukun (literally translated): tying their nets

Mark 2:22

    Greek   *oudeis ballei oinon neon eis askous palaious*
                    no one casts/throws wine new into wineskins old

    ESV   No one puts new wine into old wineskins.

    GNT   nor does anyone pour new wine into used wineskins

Mark 3:6

    Greek   *hoi Pharisaioi sumboulion edidoun kat' autou*
                    the Pharisees … counsel/plan gave about him

    Greek (literally translated): The Pharisees…*gave* plan about him.

    ESV   held counsel…against him

    KJV   took counsel…against him

    GNT   They made plans.

    NIV   began to plot

Revelation 11:1b

    Greek   *Egeire kai metrēson ton naon tou theou kai*
                    rise and measure the shrine of God and

                    to thusiastērion kai tous proskunountas en autō
                    the altar and the ones-worshipping in it

    ESV   Rise and measure the temple of God and the altar and those who worship there.

    GNT   Go and measure the temple of God and the altar, and count those who are worshiping in the temple.

Exercise 8

Translate the following sentences into your own language. Note any places where the natural collocation of words is different from English.

    a. He ate an orange.
    b. He ate some sugarcane.
    c. He put up an umbrella.
    d. He built a shelter.
    e. He smoked a cigarette.
    f. He loaded his gun.
    g. He has a cold.
    h. He is cold.
    i. He is hungry.
    j. He made a sacrifice.
    k. He made an idol.
    l. He gave the children his advice.
    m. He gave way to his brother's appeal.
    n. She gave birth to a son.

Exercise 9

Translate the underlined phrases into your own language. Be careful to use natural collocations. Please give a word-for-word key in English.

a. Matthew 3:4   His food was locusts and <u>wild honey</u>.

                         Compare with Genesis 16:12 your son will live like a wild donkey. (GNT)

b. Matthew 26:75   And he went out and <u>wept bitterly</u>.

c. John 2:10   Everyone serves the <u>good wine</u> first, and when people have drunk freely, then the <u>poor wine</u>. But you have kept the good wine until now.

d. Acts 15:39   There was a <u>sharp argument</u>. (*GNT*)

e. Titus 1:13   You must <u>rebuke them sharply</u>. (*GNT*)

f. Jude 13   in the <u>deepest darkness</u> (*GNT*)

g. Revelation 11:19   There were flashes of lightning, rumblings, peals of thunder, an earthquake, and <u>heavy hail</u>.

Exercise 10

In the examples below, identify any collocations that may need adjustment when translating into your own language.

a. Matthew 27:48   And one of them at once ran and took a sponge, filled it with sour wine, and put it on a reed and gave it to him to drink.

b. Matthew 27:54   They were filled with awe.

c. Matthew 28:8   The women hurried away from the tomb, afraid yet filled with joy. (*NIV*)

d. Luke 3:4   Prepare the way of the Lord, make his paths straight.

e. John 3:8   The wind blows where it wishes.

                         Compare, Revelation 8:7 with The first angel blew his trumpet.

f. Hebrews 8:5   for when Moses was about to erect the tent

g. Hebrews 8:8   I will establish a new covenant with the house of Israel.

Remember

Check that each word is used in its natural collocation. Avoid carrying over collocations from the source text that are not natural in the receptor language.

21.6 The natural order of words

In most languages there are words that are often used together in a fixed order.

For example, English speakers say, "ladies and gentlemen," never "gentlemen and ladies." But in some languages, the natural order of the equivalent phrase is "gentlemen and ladies." Some East African languages say, "men and mothers."

For another example, English speakers say, "to go back and forth." The equivalent phrase in the Kamasau language of Papua New Guinea uses the order, more logically, "to go forth and back." (Example contributed by Arden Sanders, personal communication.)

More examples from English

sons and daughters	not "daughters and sons"
bread and butter	never "butter and bread"
black and white	not "white and black"
heaven and earth	not "earth and heaven"

How would you express the equivalent phrases in your language?

Exercise 11

What is the natural order for the following pairs of words in your language?

a. Genesis 2:24   That is why a man leaves his father and mother.
b. Acts 7:2   Brothers and fathers, hear me!
                  (Consider the context – also see the explanatory note in the UBS Translator's Handbook.)
c. 2 Kings 9:25   When you and I rode side by side
                  (Hebrew has the order "I and you." KJV follows the Hebrew order.)

Remember

The natural order of words in the receptor language may be different from the order in the original Hebrew or Greek text or in the intermediary source language. Adjust the order for naturalness.

21.7 Words that include a component "say"

There are some English words that include the meaning of something being said or thought. Depending on the context, these may sometimes be expressed by using the form of a speech quotation.

Examples

I <u>wondered</u> whether this was true.
⇒ I said to myself, "Is this true?"

He <u>asked</u> whether the man had come.
⇒ He said, "Has the man come?"

She <u>exclaimed</u> in surprise.
⇒ She said, "Ashe!"

("Ashe" is an exclamation of surprise in the Hausa language.)
Mark 5:13   So he gave them permission.
⇒ So he said to them, "Go."   (Compare with Matthew 8:31–32)

Mark 14:31 But he said emphatically, "If I must die with you, I will not deny you."

⇒ ". . . If I must die with you, I will not say that I do not know you."

1 Corinthians 11:22   What shall I say to you? Shall I commend you in this?

⇒ What shall I say to you? Shall I say that you did well?

Remember

When studying the meaning of a word in any language, you need to research the following topics:

1) The different senses of the word; does it have different meanings in different contexts?

2) Other words with similar meanings; how do these words differ from each other in meaning?

3) With which other words does this word occur? What are the natural collocations of this word?

Additional resources on "Exploring the Meanings of Words"

For further reading

Oxford Advanced Learner's Dictionary (*OALD*). 2014. Ninth edition. Oxford: Oxford University Press.
(Recent editions include a CD and links to online resources with audio facilities designed to help those learning English explore the different senses that a word may have, depending on the context.)

Chapter 22

Translating Unknown Concepts

22.1 Recognising unknown concepts (also referred to as "unknown ideas")

Think again about the differences between the culture and way of life in the times when the Bible was written, and the culture and way of life in the country where you live. There are differences of *geography* and *weather*, for example.

Because of these differences, there are many concepts and actions mentioned in the Bible that are not known by the people in the area where the receptor language is spoken:

For people in Alaska, sheep and locusts are unknown.
For many people in Africa, snow is unknown.

There will also be many *unknown customs*; for example, the custom of resting on a housetop, or of washing the feet of a visitor.

Some common groups of unknown ideas are:

names of animals	such as bear, camel
names of plants and trees	such as grapevine, fig, sycamore, oak, hyssop, cumin, dill
features of geography	such as desert, sea, mountain
weather differences	such as snow, ice, summer, winter
money and measurements	such as denarius, pound, bushel, mile
things that people wear	such as crown, helmet, breastplate
housing and household objects	such as cornerstone, upper room, millstone, scales

Two other important groups of unknown concepts are the following:

Unfamiliar names of places and people: If someone hears a name that is unknown to him (for example, "Ataparo"), he will not know if it is the name of a town or a country or perhaps even a person. See chapter 23, point 2.

Key biblical terms referring to the religion of the Jews; for example, "temple," "synagogue," "priest," "scribe." See further discussion in chapter 24.

What is unknown will depend on each location. For example, camels are well known in northern Nigeria, but unknown in southern Nigeria, or in Papua New Guinea. By contrast, the sea is well known in the Solomon Islands, but unknown in northern Nigeria. Many things and customs that are unknown in Europe are known in Africa.

When an idea is known to the people of the area, your task as a translator is to choose the right word or expression to refer to that idea. But when the idea is unknown to the people, then your task is harder. You must find a way to communicate a completely new idea. You must help people understand something that is previously outside their experience.

22.2 Ways to translate unknown concepts

In chapters 14 and 15, we considered ways of providing the reader with essential background information that he needs to understand the message correctly. Some of the information about unknown ideas can be provided outside the text. For example, by illustrations, glossary entries, and footnotes.

It is recommended that such helps be included in the translated Bible. But this is not a substitute for meaningful translation in the text itself. You must still aim to make the translation itself as meaningful as possible.

How then can you communicate the meaning of these unknown concepts? Follow the step-by-step procedure for translation. First, discover the exact meaning of the idea you are translating. Then, look for a way to re-express that meaning in the receptor language.

Remember

First, *discover the meaning*. You cannot translate until you know the meaning of the original word or phrase accurately. Use a dictionary or Bible "Bible dictionary, *Translator's Notes* and other appropriate online resources, to find the meaning of the original idea. See also the resources described in the Appendix.

Then, re-express the meaning.

There are five main methods by which the meaning of an unknown idea can be communicated. Each method has certain advantages and disadvantages.

1) Use a descriptive phrase.
2) Substitute something similar that is known to the receptor language speakers.
3) Use a word that is more general in meaning.
4) Use a word that is more specific in meaning.
5) Use a foreign word from another language, with explanatory information.

Sometimes a combination of more than one method may be used.

> An important point to keep in mind when translating unknown ideas is that *historical facts must not be changed*. It may be possible to substitute a similar form for a teaching illustration, but not for a historical reference.

Method 1: Use a descriptive phrase

Instead of a single word, it may be possible to use a phrase to describe the concept that is being talked about. Identify the part of the meaning that is most relevant in the passage that is being translated.

Examples

- a. pen ⇒ "a thing/stick for writing with"
- b. clock ⇒ "a thing for measuring how the sun goes"
- c. aeroplane ⇒ "a canoe that travels in the sky"

    An example from Mbembe (literally translated): "canoe for up"
- d. altar ⇒ "place/table where people sacrifice to God" (Matthew 5:23)
- e. wolf ⇒ "fierce wild animal" – not "animal with a long tail that resembles a dog" (John 10:12)

    There are many things that could be said to describe a wolf, but what is important in this passage is that the wolf is a fierce animal that frightened not only the sheep but the person looking after them too.
- f. gardener ⇒ "person who looks after the garden/farm" (John 20:15)
- g. They weighed anchor. ⇒ "They lifted the heavy weight that they used to keep the boat still." (Acts 27:13)

    Here it is not the shape of the anchor that is important but what it was used for.
- h. jewels and pearls ⇒ "different kinds of beautiful stones/rocks that are used to decorate/adorn things" (Revelation 17:4)

One disadvantage of using a descriptive phrase is that the phrase may be long. The translator must be careful to fit the descriptive phrase neatly into the passage so that it does not draw attention away from the main theme.

If the word is mentioned several times in a passage, it may not be necessary to use the full descriptive phrase each time it is mentioned. For example, "synagogue" might be translated "house where Jews met to worship God" in the first occurrence, and then, when mentioned again later in the passage, be referred to simply as "that meeting house."

Compound words

A compound word is a kind of descriptive phrase. In some languages, two or more words can be joined together to have a special meaning:

throne ⇒ "chieftaincy-seat"
bank ⇒ "money-house"
shepherd ⇒ "sheep-watcher"

Think of some compound words in English. Some compound words have been invented to refer to concepts that have recently come into the culture. For example, "passport," "football," and "tape-recorder."

For discussion

Think of some compound words in your own language. Are there compound words that have been used for many years and are well established? Are there any new compound words that are now being widely used?

Exercise 1

For each of the following passages, do the following:

(1) Mark any word that expresses an idea that is unknown to people of your own area.

(2) Re-express that word in English using a descriptive phrase.

Use your dictionary or Bible dictionary to check the meaning of words wherever necessary. Look up the context of the passage in your Bible and compare how the concept is translated in different Bible versions. Remember to focus on that part of the meaning of the word that is important in the context.

a.	Luke 1:63	And [Zechariah] asked for a writing tablet.
b.	Luke 7:2	A centurion had a servant who was sick and at the point of death, who was highly valued by him.
c.	Luke 7:14	And [Jesus] came up and touched the bier, and the bearers stood still.
d.	2 Chronicles 9:1	Now when the queen of Sheba heard of the fame of Solomon, she came to Jerusalem to test him with hard questions.

Note: The word "queen" has two primary senses in English. It may mean "a woman who rules a country" (like Queen Elizabeth, the queen of England, or the queen of Sheba in 1 Kings 10:1). Or it may mean "the wife of a king." Translate according to the correct sense in the context.

e.	Nehemiah 2:6	The king said to me (the queen sitting beside him), . . .
f.	Acts 10:6	He is lodging with one Simon, a tanner, whose house is by the seaside.
g.	Revelation 6:5	And its rider had a pair of scales in his hand.
h.	Revelation 9:16	The number of the troops of cavalry was twice ten thousand times ten thousand. (RSV)
i.	Revelation 9:17	They wore breastplates the color of fire and of sapphire and of sulfur.

Method 2: Substitute something similar

Sometimes the exact thing referred to in the text may be unknown to the people of the receptor language area, but there may be something similar that is known that can be used instead, perhaps with some added description.

This method should be used with caution, taking care not to change any historical information in the text. It may be considered when a comparison is being made, as in the following examples:

1 Peter 5:8   Your adversary the devil prowls around like a roaring lion seeking whom he may devour.

In this passage, the important idea is that the lion is a dangerous animal that prowls around looking for an animal to pounce on and eat. In an area where lions are unknown,

Method 2: Substitute something similar   145

> *but where leopards are found, consider substituting "leopard" for "lion." A leopard, like a lion, is a fierce beast that attacks and eats other animals, it also belongs to the same animal family.*

Revelation 1:14   The hairs of his head were white like wool, as white as snow.

> *In one language in Africa, this was translated "white as egrets' feathers." This translation communicates the relevant point, that is, the extreme whiteness. Some languages could use an "ideophone" – an expressive form used to refer to extreme whiteness.*

Remember

In deciding whether or not it is appropriate to substitute something from the receptor language culture, take the following points into account:

1) Choose something that is similar in form to the original idea, provided it also communicates the idea that is important for the context.

2) The idea must be something that fits in with the Bible culture, something that would have existed at that time, or which at least does not seem inappropriate in the context.

3) This solution is good where a teaching illustration is being given, or where a figure of speech, such as a comparison, is being used. But it should not be used where a historical event is referred to. For example, in Mark 11:13, Jesus cursed a tree and that tree was a fig tree. To substitute any other kind of tree would be untrue to a historical fact.

4) Certain concepts are referred to through the Bible and have symbolic meaning in the New Testament because of Old Testament references. For example, in some passages, the vine and the vineyard symbolise Israel (Isaiah 5:7). References to a fig tree, and to a shepherd and his sheep, also have strong Old Testament associations. Care should be taken to translate such references in the same way, wherever possible, so that this connection of thought is not lost.

Exercise 2

In the following examples, which of the underlined words refer to things that happened at a specific time in history? And which are illustrations or comparisons for the purpose of teaching?

Examples are given from the *ESV* translation unless otherwise indicated. You are encouraged to look at the translation of the verse in other Bible versions.

  a. John 12:3   Mary…took a <u>pound of expensive ointment</u> made from <u>pure nard</u> and anointed the feet of Jesus.
  b. John 12:13   So they took <u>branches of palm trees</u> and went out to meet him.
  c. Luke 6:44   For <u>figs</u> are not gathered from <u>thorns</u>, nor are <u>grapes</u> picked from a <u>bramble bush</u>. (*RSV*)
  d. Mark 13:28   From the <u>fig tree</u> learn its lesson: as soon as its branch becomes tender and puts out its leaves, you know that summer is near.
  e. Mark 15:17   And they clothed him in a purple <u>cloak</u>, and plaiting a <u>crown of thorns</u> they put it on him. (*RSV*)

f.	Mark 4:31	It is like a grain of <u>mustard seed</u>, which, when sown on the ground, is the smallest of all the seeds on earth.
g.	2 Kings 13:15	And Elisha said to him, "Take a <u>bow</u> and <u>arrows</u>." So he took a bow and arrows.
h.	Psalm 150:3	Praise God with <u>trumpet</u> sound; praise him with <u>lute</u> and <u>harp</u>!

Exercise 3

In the passages below, first mark any words or phrases that refer to ideas that are unknown in your language area. Look up each passage and compare how the concept is translated in different Bible versions. How might you translate each of the concepts you have marked into your own language?

a.	Matthew 3:7	You brood of vipers! Who warned you to flee from the wrath to come?
b.	Matthew 5:15	Nor do men light a lamp and put it under a bushel, but on a stand, and it gives light to all in the house. (*RSV*)
c.	Matthew 5:40	And if anyone would sue you and take your tunic, let him have your cloak as well.
d.	Mark 9:42	It would be better for him if a great millstone were hung around his neck and he were thrown into the sea.
e.	Luke 10:19	I have given you authority to tread on serpents and scorpions.
f.	Revelation 18:22	And the sound of harpists and musicians, of flute players and trumpeters, will be heard in you no more.

Exercise 4

For each of the following passages, do the following:

(1) First, mark any words that refer to ideas that may be unknown to people in your own language area.

(2) Then, note down how you might translate each idea, using a word for something similar in your own culture.

a.	Song of Solomon 2:2	As a lily among brambles, so is my love among the young women.
b.	Song of Solomon 2:3	As an apple tree among the trees of the forest, so is my beloved among the young men.
c.	Song of Solomon 2:15	Catch the foxes for us, the little foxes that spoil the vineyards, for our vineyards are in blossom.

Method 3: Use a word that is more general in meaning

What is meant by a word that is more general than another word?

- Compare the two words "cat" and "animal." A cat is one kind of animal; there are also other kinds of animals, like "dog" and "horse." So the word "animal" is *more general* than the word "cat," because it includes other kinds of animals besides cats. All cats are animals, but not all animals are cats!

- Similarly, the word "furniture" is more general than the word "table" because a table is one example of a piece of furniture. There are also other kinds of furniture, like "chair," "cupboard," or "bed."

Method 4: Use a word or phrase that is more specific in meaning 147

- The word "building" is more general than the word "house" because a house is a kind of building. There are other kinds of buildings, like "school" or "mosque."
- The word "to kill" is more general than the word "to strangle" because strangling is just one way of killing a person.

Exercise 5

For each of the following words, give an example of a word that would be more general than that word (in English):

a. shirt
b. sparrow
c. car
d. gun
e. to devour

In some passages where there is an unknown idea, a more general word can be used without the meaning of the message being lost.

Matthew 6:28   Consider the <u>lilies of the field</u>, how they grow: they neither toil nor spin.

⇒   Consider the flowers in the bush, how they grow.

"Flowers" is a more general word than "lilies." In this passage, the exact kind of flower is not in focus.

Luke 12:18   There I will store all my grain and my goods.

In any area where the main thing grown on the farms is not a cereal crop, a more general word or phrase could be used, such as "crops" or "things/harvest of my farm."

Acts 3:6   I have no silver and gold.
⇒   I have no money.

Method 4: Use a word or phrase that is more specific in meaning

Sometimes where it seems there is no word in the receptor language to express a concept, the idea can be translated by giving specific examples of the thing referred to.

Genesis 1:16   And God made the two great lights.

If there is no word for "lights" in this sense, it may be possible simply to say "the sun and the moon," using the specific words.

Matthew 5:29   It is better that you lose one of your members than that your whole body be thrown into hell.

A possible translation might be, "It is better for you to lose an eye or an ear than that your whole body be thrown into hell."

Mark 4:4   Some seed fell along the path.

It is not stated in this passage what kind of seed was sown. However, from background knowledge it was almost certainly wheat. To use a general word for seed may be possible in some languages, but in other languages it would be confusing. In that case, the translator might translate this teaching illustration by using a more specific word for whatever cereal crop is best known in the receptor language area. In West Africa, this might be "guinea corn seed" (the nearest equivalent to wheat). In some languages of Northern Nigeria, "acha" would be preferred, because that is sown by scattering the seed, while guinea corn seeds are planted individually.

Acts 5:1 A man named Ananias, with his wife Sapphira, sold a piece of property.

It is clear from the following context (verse 3) that this was a piece of land. So if there is no general word for "property" in the language (or if the more general word would not usually include land) then this might be translated more specifically "sold a piece of land (or a farm)" without losing accuracy.

Remember

Consider the whole passage carefully. A word should be translated according to its meaning and significance in the passage in which it occurs.

Method 5: Use a foreign word from another language

Distinguish between a foreign word and an adopted word as follows:

A *foreign word* is a word taken from another language. Foreign words are words that are not already in use by speakers of the receptor language.

An *adopted word* is a word, originally taken from one language, that has become a part of another language. All languages adopt words from other languages in this way. Usually words are adopted from major languages that are spoken in the area, referring to things or ideas that have recently become known. For example, through the years English has taken many words from Latin, Greek, and French. Adopted words are also sometimes called "borrowed words" or "loan words."

Words are adopted gradually. At first the word is not often used. Then people start to use it more and more and so everybody comes to know its meaning. Then everybody uses it, even those people who do not know the language that it comes from. The pronunciation changes so that the word is pronounced using the common sounds of the language that has adopted it. Words that have been adopted into a language in this way are no longer foreign words.

The following two exercises are designed to help the translator distinguish between adopted words and foreign words.

Exercise 6

In this passage, do the following:

(1) Mark three examples of words that have been adopted into English.

(2) Put a circle around three examples of words that seem like foreign words to you.

John went into the hotel and sat down. He took up the menu and began to choose what he would eat. The choice was between tim-sam and salad, or laksa, or gado-gado, or something called "escargots." He had decided to order laksa with a cup of coffee when he saw Kim Sai enter the restaurant. She was wearing a cheongsam and holding a wok in her hand.

In this exercise, you may find it difficult to recognise the words that have been adopted into English. This is because words that have been adopted have become just like other words of

Method 5: Use a foreign word from another language 149

the language. Unless you happen to know something about the history of the language, it is not possible to tell that they have been adopted. It will be easier to recognise the foreign words.

Exercise 7

List five examples of adopted words in

    (1) your own language

    (2) a language of wider communication spoken in your home area

The use of foreign words in translations

The following is a translation of Mark 1:1–4 in a very early Bible version in an African language. (The spelling has been slightly modified.) Mark any foreign words that you recognise in the translation. What problem would these words give to the reader?

> 1 Eritono gospel Jesus Christ Eyen Abasi. 2 Kpa nte ewetde ke nwed prophet Isaiah, ete,
>   Sese, mmodon isunutom mi ebem Fi iso,
>   Emi edinamde usun Fo;
> 3 Uyo andifiori ke desert, ete, Mbufo edion usun Jehovah,
>   Eneng ere okpousung Esie;
> 4 John oto edi edinim owo baptism ke desert, edinyun okworo baptism erikabare esit, man efen mme idiok-knpo.

The disadvantage of using foreign words in a translation is that the receptor language speakers may not know what the words mean. The words are probably unfamiliar to them, and so they mean nothing. The use of foreign words should, therefore, be used with caution.

There are, however, some places where it does seem best to use a foreign word, especially where the reference is to a historical event. In these cases, the foreign word should be introduced in a way that gives the reader an idea of its meaning:

1) Use the foreign word together with a descriptive phrase that explains its meaning.
2) Use the foreign word together with a more general word that helps the reader to understand the meaning.
3) Provide an explanatory footnote.
4) Place a picture near the text, to illustrate what an unknown object looked like and how it was used historically, as relevant to the context (if this would be appropriate).

Examples

Mark 1:6   John was clothed with camel's hair.

> *In a language spoken in an area where camels are unknown, this might be translated as "John was clothed with a garment made with the hair of an animal called 'camel'." The more general word "animal" provides the information that a camel is a kind of animal. As camels are mentioned several times in the Bible text, it would be good to consider including a picture of a camel at an appropriate place.*

Mark 14:1   It was now two days before the Passover.
        It was now two days before the Festival of Passover. (*GNT*)

> *The inclusion of the more general word "festival" in GNT shows that the foreign word "Passover" is the name of a specific festival. In this way, some of the meaning is communicated.*

It is essential to consider carefully what aspect of the meaning is relevant and important for each context. Compare, for example, the following suggested translations for three references to myrrh.

Mark 15:23	And they offered him wine mingled with a medicine called "myrrh."
Matthew 2:11	They offered him costly gifts: gold and frankincense and myrrh.
Song of Solomon 1:13	My beloved is to me like a bag of sweet-smelling myrrh that lies between my breasts.

In Mark 15:23, it is the property of myrrh as a medicine, relieving pain, that is most important. In Matthew 2:11, it is the fact that myrrh was a costly gift such as kings would give and receive (there may also be further symbolism). And in the Song of Solomon 1:13, it is the fact that myrrh smells sweet that is relevant.

Exercise 8

In each of the following passages, do the following:

(1) Mark any idea that might be unknown to people of your own area.

(2) Consider how you might translate using a foreign word together with either a descriptive phrase or a more general word that communicates the most relevant part of the meaning.

a.	Numbers 11:5–6	We remember the fish we ate in Egypt that cost nothing, the cucumbers, the melons, the leeks, the onions, and the garlic. But now our strength is dried up, and there is nothing at all but this manna to look at.
b.	Numbers 11:31	Then a wind from the LORD sprang up, and it brought quail from the sea, and let them fall beside the camp.
c.	Numbers 13:23	And they came to the Valley of Eshcol and cut down from there a branch with a single cluster of grapes, and they carried it on a pole between two of them; they also brought some pomegranates and figs.
d.	Isaiah 41:19	I will put in the wilderness the cedar, the acacia, the myrtle, and the olive. I will set in the desert the cypress, the plane, and the pine together.
e.	Matthew 23:23	Woe to you, scribes and Pharisees, hypocrites! For you tithe mint and dill and cumin, and have neglected the weightier matters of the law: justice and mercy and faithfulness.

22.3 Practice in recognising and translating unknown concepts

Exercise 9

Each of the following passages includes one or more ideas that may be unknown in the receptor language area (or that is not readily expressed by a single word in that language).

(1) Mark all the unknown ideas.

(2) Note down how you might re-express the meaning of the word or phrase you have marked in your language. Consider whether each example is a teaching illustration or a

reference to a historical fact. For each example, note which of the methods for translating an unknown idea you have used.

- a. Matthew 10:29   Are not two sparrows sold for a penny?
- b. Matthew 21:33   Hear another parable. There was a householder who planted a vineyard, and set a hedge around it, and dug a wine press in it, and built a tower. (*RSV*)
- c. Mark 1:12–13   The Spirit immediately drove him out into the wilderness. ¹³ And he was in the wilderness forty days.
- d. Mark 11:13   And seeing in the distance a fig tree in leaf, [Jesus] went to see if he could find anything on it.
- e. Mark 13:18   Pray that it may not happen in winter.
- f. Mark 14:44   The one I will kiss is the man.

Exercise 10

For each of the following examples, re-express the meaning of each underlined term, in English, using the method that seems most appropriate for the context.

- a. Matthew 20:1   For the kingdom of heaven is like a master of a house who went out early in the morning to hire labourers for his <u>vineyard</u>.
- b. Luke 11:3   Give us each day our daily <u>bread</u>.
- c. 1 Samuel 2:13–14 The custom of the priests with the people was that when any man offered sacrifice, the priest's servant would come, while the meat was boiling, with <u>a three-pronged fork</u> in his hand, ¹⁴ and he would thrust it into the <u>pan</u> or <u>kettle</u> or <u>cauldron</u> or <u>pot</u>. All that the <u>fork</u> brought up, the priest would take for himself.
- d. Proverbs 15:17 Better is a dinner of <u>herbs</u> where love is than a <u>fattened ox</u> and hatred with it.

Exercise 11

Each of the following passages includes one or more ideas that may be unknown in the receptor language area. There may also be some ideas that, though known, may not be easily expressed in the receptor language by a single word.

(1) Mark all the unknown ideas or problem words for which there seems to be no direct single word equivalent.

(2) Write down how you might re-express the meaning of the word or phrase you have marked in a way that could be readily translated into your language. State which of the five possible methods for translating an unknown idea you have used.

- a. Luke 1:27   a virgin betrothed to a man whose name was Joseph
- b. Luke 9:58   Foxes have holes, and birds of the air have nests.
- c. Luke 9:62   No one who puts his hand to the plough and looks back is fit for the kingdom of God.
- d. Luke 12:33   where no thief approaches and no moth destroys

e.	Luke 19:4	[Zacchaeus] ran on ahead and climbed up into a sycamore tree to see him.
		(See the explanatory note concerning this tree in the *UBS Translator's Handbook* and *Translator's Notes*, both available in Paratext.)
f.	Acts 2:1	when the day of Pentecost arrived
g.	Acts 3:15	To this we are witnesses.
h.	Acts 16:24	[The jailer] fastened their feet in the stocks.
i.	Acts 19:29	They rushed together into the theatre.
j.	Acts 27:5	when we had sailed across the open sea along the coast of Cilicia and Pamphylia
k.	Acts 27:28a	So they took a sounding and found twenty fathoms.

Exercise 12 (Old Testament examples)

Instructions, as for exercise 11.

a.	Genesis 6:14	Make yourself an ark of gopher wood; make rooms in the ark, and cover it inside and out with pitch.
b.	Genesis 8:8–11	Then [Noah] sent forth a dove from him…. ¹¹ And the dove came back to him in the evening, and behold, in her mouth was a freshly plucked olive leaf.
c.	Genesis 37:7	Behold, we were binding sheaves in the field, and behold, my sheaf arose and stood upright. And behold, your sheaves gathered around it and bowed down to my sheaf.
d.	Genesis 37:25	Then they sat down to eat. And looking up they saw a caravan of Ishmaelites coming from Gilead, with their camels bearing gum, balm, and myrrh, on their way to carry it down to Egypt.
e.	Genesis 43:11	Then their father Israel said to them, "If it must be so, then do this: take some of the choice fruits of the land in your bags, and carry a present down to the man, a little balm and a little honey, gum, myrrh, pistachio nuts, and almonds."
f.	Genesis 50:2	So the physicians embalmed Israel.
g.	Exodus 2:3	When she could hide him no longer, she took for him a basket made of bulrushes, and daubed it with bitumen and pitch; and she put the child in it and placed it among the reeds by the river bank.
h.	Exodus 8:16	Then the LORD said to Moses, "Say to Aaron, 'Stretch out your staff and strike the dust of the earth, so that it may become gnats in all the land of Egypt.'"
i.	Exodus 9:8	And the LORD said to Moses and Aaron, "Take handfuls of soot from the kiln, and let Moses throw them in the air in the sight of Pharaoh."
j.	Exodus 12:22	Take a bunch of hyssop and dip it in the blood that is in the basin, and touch the lintel and the two doorposts with the blood that is in the basin.
k.	Exodus 16:13–14	In the evening quail came up and covered the camp, and in the morning dew lay around the camp. ¹⁴ And when the dew had gone up, there was on the face of the wilderness a fine, flake-like thing, fine as frost on the ground.

Exercise 13 (advanced)

Instructions, as for exercise 11.

 a. Matthew 3:12 His winnowing fork is in his hand, and he will clear his threshing floor and gather his wheat into the barn, but the chaff he will burn with unquenchable fire.

 b. Matthew 9:17 Neither is new wine put into old wineskins. If it is, the skins burst, and the wine is spilled and the skins are destroyed. But new wine is put into fresh wineskins, and so both are preserved.

 c. Matthew 11:21 For if the mighty works done in you had been done in Tyre and Sidon, they would have repented long ago in sackcloth and ashes.

 d. Matthew 11:29 Take my yoke upon you, and learn from me, for I am gentle and lowly in heart, and you will find rest for your souls.

 e. John 15:1 I am the true vine, and my Father is the vinedresser.

 f. James 3:3 If we put bits into the mouths of horses so that they obey us, we guide their whole bodies as well.

 g. James 3:4 Look at the ships also: though they are so large and are driven by strong winds, they are guided by a very small rudder wherever the will of the pilot directs.

 h. Revelation 1:12 I saw seven golden lampstands.

 i. Revelation 4:7 the first living creature like a lion, the second living creature like an ox, the third living creature with the face of a man, and the fourth living creature like an eagle in flight

 j. Revelation 8:3 And another angel came and stood at the altar with a golden censer, and he was given much incense to offer with the prayers of all the saints upon the golden altar before the throne.

Exercise 14

(1) Translate Acts 8:26–28 into your own language. Pay particular attention to the translation of any ideas that may be unknown to your people.

(2) Make a back translation to your translation, in English. Discuss with your advisor or consultant the advantages and disadvantages of the ways in which you have translated these unknown ideas.

Exercise 15

Esther 1:5–7: Instructions, as for exercise 14.

Additional resources on "Translating Unknown Concepts"

BT4 online materials

22_Unknown_ideas_1.pptx
22_Unknown_ideas_2.pptx
22_Unknown_ideas_in_Luke-Exercise.pptx

Chapter 23

More on Translating Unknown Concepts

In this chapter, the translation of measurements, weights, and amounts is discussed. These are challenging to translate because the original biblical terms refer to historical systems that do not correspond directly to modern systems. The biblical terms are often not as precise as modern measurements.

The transliteration and introduction of foreign names will also be discussed.

23.1 Translating measurements, weights, and amounts of money

Different systems of measurements are currently used in the English-speaking world. Most countries use the Metric (or decimal) System, based on multiples of ten, including units such as "metre/meter" and "kilometre/kilometer," also "gram" and "kilogram." A few countries use the older Imperial measurement system or similar, with units such as "feet," "yards," and "miles," also "ounces" and "pounds."

All these modern systems are different from the various systems used in the original biblical texts. When preparing to translate, it is important to research the meaning of the original terms, using the available helps for translators (see resources listed in the text box below).

When re-expressing the meaning in a translation, consider carefully what system is most familiar to those for whom the translation is being prepared. Consider whether a change in the terms being used is in progress or is likely to happen. Some English versions use footnotes to give alternative forms. *NIV* often uses a modern equivalent in the text, with a footnote quoting the form in the original language, and sometimes also an alternative modern equivalent.

Major English Bible versions are published in more than one edition, depending on the area of distribution, for example, USA or UK. Different modern equivalents may be used in different editions, depending on the intended area of distribution.

Each translation project needs to decide on the system they are going to use and then be consistent. Possibilities need to be carefully considered and tested. Once a decision has been made on the system to be used in that translation project, all translators on the team, and others involved, need to follow the agreed system consistently. It is important to keep a record of the terms that have been translated, and how each one has been translated. The Paratext program has checklists that help you check for consistency.

> There is a useful table of weights and measures at the back of the *New International Version Study Bible*. Notes in the *NET Bible* are also a helpful source of information on the original measurements, weights, and terms used to refer to amounts of money. The *UBS Translator's Handbooks* and *Translator's Notes* also provide information for each verse on equivalent measurements in different systems.

23.1.1 Distance and liquid measurements

Genesis 6:15		This is how you are to make it: the length of the ark three hundred cubits, its breadth fifty cubits, and its height thirty cubits.
	GNT	Make it 450 feet long, 75 feet wide, and 45 feet high.
	NIV	This is how you are to build it: The ark is to be three hundred cubits long, fifty cubits wide and thirty cubits high. [with footnote: That is, about 450 feet long, 75 feet wide and 45 feet high or about 135 meters long, 23 meters wide and 14 meters high.]
John 11:18		Bethany was near Jerusalem, about two miles off.
	KJV	About fifteen furlongs off
	NIV	Bethany was less than two miles from Jerusalem. [with footnote: Greek *fifteen stadia* (about three kilometers)]
Acts 1:12		Then they returned to Jerusalem from the mount called Olivet, which is near Jerusalem, a Sabbath day's journey away.
	GNT	Then the apostles went back to Jerusalem from the Mount of Olives, which is about half a mile away from the city.
	GNTUK	Then the apostles went back to Jerusalem from the Mount of Olives, which is about a kilometre away from the city.
	NIV	Then they returned to Jerusalem from the hill called the Mount of Olives, a Sabbath day's walk from the city. [with footnote: That is, about 3/4 mile (about 1,100 meters)]
Luke 16:6		A hundred measures of oil
	NIV	Eight hundred gallons of olive oil [with footnote: Greek *one hundred batous* (probably about 3,000 liters)]
	GNT	One hundred barrels of olive oil
	NLT	800 gallons of olive oil
John 2:6		There were six stone water jars there, for the Jewish rites of purification, each holding twenty or thirty gallons.
	NIV	Nearby stood six stone water jars, the kind used by the Jews for ceremonial washing, each holding from twenty to thirty gallons. [with footnote: Greek *two to three metretes* (probably about 75 to 115 liters)]
	KJV	And there were set there six waterpots of stone, after the manner of the purifying of the Jews, containing two or three firkins apiece.

23.1.2 Weights

John 19:39b	Nicodemus also…came bringing a mixture of myrrh and aloes, about seventy-five pounds in weight.
NIV	Nicodemus brought a mixture of myrrh and aloes, about seventy-five pounds. [with footnote: about 34 kilograms]
REB	a mixture of myrrh and aloes, more than half a hundredweight
GNT	taking with him about one hundred pounds of spices, a mixture of myrrh and aloes

Some African languages translate using the equivalent of "about a salt-sack weight, nearly a salt-sack weight." The weight of a "salt-sack" is a standard one hundred pounds in some areas, and is widely used as a measurement in trading. There may be other local weights or measurements that could be considered.

23.1.3 Amounts of money

Genesis 23:16	Abraham listened to Ephron, and Abraham weighed out for Ephron the silver that he had named in the hearing of the Hittites, four hundred shekels of silver, according to the weights current among the merchants.
Hebrew	silver shekels
GNT	pieces of silver (also *NLT* and *CEV*)

Before coins came into use, the price was measured by weight.

Matthew 20:9	And when those hired about the eleventh hour came, each of them received a denarius.
Greek	*dēnarion*
GNT	a silver coin
NLT	a full day's wage
REB	the full day's wages [with footnote: "one denarius each"]
KJV	a penny
Mark 14:5	For this ointment could have been sold for more than three hundred denarii and given to the poor.
GNT	three hundred silver coins
NIV	for more than a year's wages [with footnote: *three hundred denarii*]
KJV	three hundred pence
Some African languages:	three money bags

In many areas of West Africa, the term "money bag" means one hundred pounds. This term is widely used for a very large amount of money being referred to in a general way.

Matthew 18:24, 28	one was brought to him who owed him ten thousand talents…. ²⁸ one of his fellow servants who owed him a hundred denarii
NIV	A man who owed him ten thousand bags of gold was brought to him…. [with footnote: Greek ten thousand talents; a talent was worth about 20 years of a day laborer's wages.] ²⁸ he found one of his fellow servants who owed him a hundred silver coins [with footnote: Greek a

hundred denarii; a denarius was the usual daily wage of a day laborer (see 20:2).]

The footnote to the UK edition of NIV has [24 That is, millions of pounds 28. That is, a few pounds].

GNT who owed him millions of dollars.... ²⁸ he found one of his fellow servants who owed him a few dollars

NLT who owed him millions of dollars.... ²⁸ he went to a fellow servant who owed him a few thousand dollars

The NLT translation recognises that the amount the fellow servant owed was still large, although very small compared with the amount of the debt that was forgiven.

Mark 12:42 And a poor widow came and put in two small copper coins, which make a penny.

NIV two very small copper coins, worth only a fraction of a penny [with footnote: Greek *two lepta*]

GNT two little copper coins, worth about a penny

NLT two small coins

Summary

From the examples given above, we see that there are several ways of translating measurements, weights, and money amounts:

- Re-express the actual amount using modern currency or a modern system of measuring: For example, "twenty dollars," "a penny."

    This method helps people understand the actual meaning. Be cautious in using this system for money amounts because systems and values may change. Inflation can quickly make the figures inaccurate, and currencies may change.

- Re-express to show the equivalent value, but avoiding the use of specific modern terms.

    For example, "a full day's wages" is the actual value of a denarius. It communicates the amount meaningfully and accurately.

- For measuring length, some languages may have an equivalent measurement in their traditional system that is very similar to the original. The Hebrew word translated into English as a "cubit" is about eighteen inches, the length of a man's arm from elbow to fingertip. If the receptor language has a term for this length, then this is a good solution in some contexts.

- Keep the original term or a literal translation of it: For example, denarius, cubit.

    The disadvantage of this method is that those who read the translation will not know what amount or size was meant. The translation will not be meaningful. A footnote can be added to explain this. Footnotes, however, are often overlooked, and are not heard when the Scripture is read aloud. It may be better to put the meaningful form in the text, and the original term, with explanation, in a footnote.

Study each passage to find the solution that is most appropriate. Remember that a good translation should be each of the following:

Accurate – it should communicate the correct meaning that the original author intended;

Clear – the meaning that the original author intended should be understood by the new audience, not only the physical measurement or amount, but also the point that was being taught in the context;

Natural – it should sound natural in the language, and be appropriate to the situation; and

Acceptable – when examples are tested in the community, the system used should be accepted and agreed.

Exercise

For each of the examples listed under point 23.1.3 above, write down how you might translate the amount into your own language.

23.2 Transliterating and introducing unfamiliar names

"Proper names" are names that refer to specific places or people. Proper names that are unfamiliar to the speakers of the receptor language may cause difficulties for several reasons:

- The name may be hard to pronounce. For this reason, in most translations proper names are adapted to a form that is easy to pronounce in the receptor language. They are then spelled according to the spelling system of the receptor language.
- Readers or hearers may not know to what they refer. For example, a name might refer to a region or a town, or to a river or a mountain. In some contexts it may even not be clear whether a place or a person is referred to.
- It can happen that a transliterated proper name can be an offensive term in the receptor language. Where that happens, a slight adjustment in the pronunciation and spelling of the name is permissible.

Wherever necessary, the translator should provide information that the hearer needs to understand the reference correctly. This may be done by including a general word that indicates the kind of place referred to, as illustrated in the examples below. The translator should be careful to check all unfamiliar place names on a map to make sure that he himself knows what is referred to.

In contexts where the name of a person is significant, the meaning of the original name should be provided in a footnote. For an example, see Genesis 17:5.

Paratext has a system for recording the spelling of proper names. This helps translators to achieve consistency.

Numbers 25:1		While Israel dwelt in Shittim the people began to whore with the daughters of Moab.
	⇒	While the Israelites were living in the region of Shittim, the men began to indulge in sexual immorality with the Moabite women (that is, women of the country of Moab).
Matthew 4:25		And great crowds followed him from Galilee and the Decapolis, and from Jerusalem and Judea, and from beyond the Jordan.
	⇒	Large crowds followed him from the regions of Galilee and Decapolis and from the town of Jerusalem and the whole region of Judea, and from the other side of the River Jordan.

The name Decapolis means "Ten towns," hence GNT and NLT translate as, "the Ten Towns."

Acts 27:7   We sailed slowly for a number of days and arrived with difficulty off Cnidus, and as the wind did not allow us to go farther, we sailed under the lee of Crete off Salmone.

GNT   We sailed slowly for several days and with great difficulty finally arrived off the town of Cnidus. The wind would not let us go any farther in that direction, so we sailed down the sheltered side of the island of Crete, passing by Cape Salmone.

Chapter 24

Translating Key Biblical Terms

There are many words in the Bible that need careful attention in translation because they refer to Jewish or Christian ideas and customs, or because they are used in special ways in the Bible. They often introduce an idea that may be previously unknown, or not well understood, in the area for which the translation is being made.

Translators need to recognise such key biblical terms, and to give careful attention to studying the meaning of each term in the original text.

24.1 Verses from chapter 1 of the Gospel of Mark

The following verses are taken from the first chapter of Mark's Gospel in the *ESV*. In these verses, mark every example of words or phrases that refer to Jewish or Christian beliefs and religious systems:

> [1] The beginning of the gospel of Jesus Christ, the Son of God.
> [2] As it is written in Isaiah the prophet,
>
> > "Behold, I send my messenger before your face,
> > who will prepare your way,
>
> [3] The voice of one crying in the wilderness:
> > 'Prepare the way of the Lord,
> > make his paths straight.'"
>
> [4] John appeared, baptizing in the wilderness and proclaiming a baptism of repentance for the forgiveness of sins.
>
> [9] In those days Jesus came from Nazareth of Galilee and was baptized by John in the Jordan. [10] And when he came up out of the water, immediately he saw the heavens opening and the Spirit descending on him like a dove. [11] And a voice came from heaven, "You are my beloved Son; with you I am well pleased."
>
> [12] The Spirit immediately drove him out into the wilderness. [13] And he was in the wilderness forty days, being tempted by Satan. And he was with the wild animals, and the angels were ministering to him.

²¹ And they went into Capernaum; and immediately on the Sabbath he entered the synagogue and was teaching. ²² And they were astonished at his teaching, for he taught them as one who had authority, and not as the scribes.

Many of the words that you have marked refer to things that were unknown in the receptor language area before the introduction of Christianity. This will depend on the local situation. In areas where Islam is established, some of these ideas will already be known.

The words you have marked may include the following:

verses 1–4: gospel
             Christ
             prophet
             Lord
             baptize
             preach
             possibly also: sins and forgive

verses 9–12: heaven
             Spirit
             Satan
             angel

verses 21–22: Sabbath
              synagogue
              scribes

These are all examples of key biblical terms, sometimes referred to as special biblical terms. They are a special kind of unknown concept.

The translation of these terms is important for the full communication of the biblical message. The wrong choice of words, or inconsistent translation, will result in misunderstanding.

For each translation project, the situation will be different:

- In some areas, there may be as yet no Christians, or very few, and no terms are yet in use for these key biblical ideas.
- In other areas, Christianity may have been established for some time, and certain terms are already in common use. These terms will need to be reviewed and carefully evaluated to check whether they are the best terms to communicate accurately the original meaning.

Where some terms are already in common use, these may be some problems:

- There may be several words in use for a certain idea. Sometimes people living in one town or region may use one word, while people living in a different place or dialect area use a different word. Sometimes different denominations use different words. The translators will need to discuss with all concerned and decide together which of these words should be used in the translation.
- It may sometimes happen that the word that is already in general use in the church has some wrong meaning.

People may feel strongly about the choice of key biblical terms. If certain terms are already in use, they may be reluctant to change. Decisions should be made in careful consultation with church leaders of all denominations in the area.

24.2 Two groups of key biblical terms

There are two groups of key biblical terms:

1) Those words that (with very few exceptions) have the same meaning in every context in which they occur. Examples are: "Sabbath," "apostle," "Holy Spirit." Sections 24.3 and 24.4 focus on terms with one sense.

2) Words that have several different senses according to the context in which they occur. Examples are: "believe," "flesh," "spirit," "grace," "law." Such words may need to be translated in different ways in different contexts, in order to give the correct sense in each context. See the examples in section 24.5.

24.3 Procedure for translating key biblical terms

Four steps should be followed in deciding how to translate key biblical terms.

Step 1 Study the meaning of the original term.

The first step in translating is always to discover the meaning.

> For New Testament terms, look up the term in *Key Biblical Terms in the New Testament: An Aid for Bible Translators,* a collection of word studies prepared to help translators, available on *Translator's Workplace.*
>
> For Old Testament terms, see the list of words discussed in *Old Testament Glossary,* compiled by David Gray. This is available in *Translator's Workplace* and, for those who have registered with Academia.edu, this can also be viewed at https://www.academia.edu/2907731/Old_Testament_Glossary. Further research is in progress.
>
> Study the entry for the term in a Bible dictionary. The following excellent Bible dictionaries are accessible to view in *Translator's Workplace*:
>
> *New Bible Dictionary*, published by InterVarsity Press
>
> *Lexham Bible Dictionary*, published online by Lexham Press
>
> *Zondervan Illustrated Bible Backgrounds Commentary: Old Testament* (5 vols.)
>
> *Zondervan Illustrated Bible Backgrounds Commentary: New Testament* (4 vols.)

If you see from this study that the term you are focusing on has more than one sense, then you need to do the three further steps listed below for each sense of the term separately.

Step 2 Compare the term with other biblical terms that have similar meaning.

In section 24.4, terms that have similar meaning are compared. Comparing these terms shows more clearly the exact differences in meaning between them (the contrastive components), and so helps you to understand the meaning of each term more precisely.

Step 3 Make a list of possible solutions for re-expressing the idea and tentatively choose the most appropriate.

Review the ways in which unknown concepts can be translated (see chapters 22 and 23). Make a list of different possibilities for translating the idea, considering alternative solutions.

To evaluate these possibilities, consider the following points:
- Is the proposed word or phrase communicating the meaning? How will it be understood by non-Christians and people who have not had any Christian teaching?
- Does the proposed term focus on the most relevant part of the meaning of the original term? It may not be possible to communicate the whole meaning of the original term, but that part which is most central to the meaning should be communicated.
- Does the proposed term include any meaning that is *contrary* to the meaning of the original term? Even if the term does not at first have the full meaning of the original term, the meaning will gradually be built up through teaching in the churches. But do not choose a word that has any sense that is contrary to, or incompatible with, the meaning of the original term. It is possible to develop and expand the meaning of a word, but it is not possible to wipe out or remove meanings that the speakers of the language already consider part of that word.
- Consider writing an explanation of the term in the receptor language. This exercise may help you, as translator, think through the full meaning of the term, and may also serve as a base for a glossary entry.
- Other factors also need to be taken into account.
    a. How has the term been translated in other versions of the Bible that are in use in the area, such as versions in the national or trade language?
    b. Are there differing denominational feelings? The translator must translate accurately, but when there is room for different opinions, avoid using any word that would offend readers in any of the denominations in the area.
    c. Do church leaders and others have opinions on the term? The translator must listen carefully to views expressed.
    d. Have the terms been tested in the community? Tentative decisions on key terms should be widely tested in the language community, checked with the consultant, and then presented for review by the Language and Translation Committee.

Step 4 When a choice has been made, as translation of further books continues, continue to review how the term fits in the further contexts in which it occurs.

Do not make final decisions on the translation of key terms too quickly. Give people an opportunity to express their views. Prayer and reasoned discussion will result in agreement and a right decision.

Once tentative choices have been made, it is helpful to prepare a list of terms that can be shared with reviewers. In this way people will have an opportunity to make suggestions. When agreement has been reached, the list can be distributed to preachers, teachers, and interpreters in the language in order that everyone will begin to use the term consistently.

Look up the list of key biblical terms that occur in the Gospels. You will find this in the introduction to the book *Key Biblical Terms in the New Testament: An Aid for Bible Translators* on *Translator's Workplace*. Start to fill this in with some tentative proposals for ways to translate these terms in your own language.

> **Remember**
>
> When deciding how to translate key biblical terms, do the following:
>
> 1) First, *study the meaning* of the original term.
>
> 2) Compare the *term* with other biblical terms that have similar meaning.
>
> 3) Think about possible solutions for re-expressing the idea in the receptor language, discuss with other speakers, and tentatively choose the most appropriate term.
>
> 4) As translation work continues, observe to see how the term you have tentatively chosen fits in further contexts in which it occurs.

Exercise 1

For each of the words listed below, make a study of the meaning of that word in the New Testament. Refer to the following resources:

- *Key Biblical Terms in the New Testament: An Aid for Bible Translators* (available on *Translator's Workplace*)
- a Bible dictionary
- a Bible concordance

For each word, make a short list of the facts about the meaning of the word that you feel are most important to consider when translating. Study these words:

a. prophet
b. priest
c. cross
d. gospel
e. Sabbath
f. angel
g. Satan

24.4 Comparing words with similar meaning

Words that have similar meanings should be studied as a group. Comparing and contrasting them with each other helps to highlight more precisely

1) the ways in which the meanings of the words are the same; and
2) the ways in which the meanings of the words are different.

In making this comparison, it may be necessary to compare different senses of the word concerned with different groups of words. For example, in the New Testament, the word "synagogue" refers to a gathering of Jews who met regularly together to worship and pray. It also came to be used for the building in which the group regularly met. See the discussion of this term in PowerPoint 24_Key_Terms_1.pptx.

Exercise 2

The words "synagogue" (when referring to a building), "temple," and "tabernacle" are similar in that they all refer to a building or shelter that is used for religious purposes. The differences in meaning between the three words can be compared as follows:

Tabernacle	Temple	Synagogue
place used by the Jewish people for religious purposes		
place where God was present in a special way	place where God was present in a special way	place where Jewish people regularly met for worship
temporary shelter	permanent building	permanent building
only one existed	only one temple existed at any given time (this was in Jerusalem)	there were many; each town or village had its own synagogue
people went there to take animals to be sacrificed	people went there to take animals to be sacrificed, also to pray, to teach and learn, to burn incense	people went there for the reading of the Laws of Moses and for prayer (sacrifices were not made there)

In view of this comparative study, list three possible ways in which you might translate these three terms into your own language, arranging them in order of preference.

Exercise 3

The words "angel," "evil spirit," "demon," and "Satan," all refer to spiritual beings. These are all personal beings; they have the power to speak and act. The following chart shows some of the differences and similarities between the words.

Angel	Evil spirit or unclean spirit	Demon	Satan/the devil/the evil one
messenger from God, serves God	serves Satan	serves Satan	Satan was originally an angel, but he rebelled against God. Now he is the leader of the spirits who rebelled with him.
brings messages from God, acts under God's direction	acts against God	acts against God	tries to make people disobey God
Cannot enter a person	Can enter a person and control him	Can enter a person and control him	Can enter a person and control him
good	bad	bad	bad, cunning, fierce, dangerous

Angel	Evil spirit or unclean spirit	Demon	Satan/the devil/the evil one
can take a visible form	not usually visible	not usually visible	can take visible form
they are many and have different ranks and kinds	they are many and have different ranks and kinds (causing madness, dumbness, etc.)	they are many and have different ranks and kinds (causing madness, dumbness, etc.)	he is only one, unique

A comparison of these words shows that there are in fact no contrastive differences between "evil spirit" and "demon." These two terms are alternative names for the same beings. In the receptor language, the same term can be used to translate both words. (This is a topic that needs further study and research.)

Exercise 4

Apply steps 1, 2, and 3 to the groups of words listed below: Look up each of these words in *Key Biblical Terms in the New Testament* -- available on *Translator's Workplace*.

  a. Levite, priest, high priest, scribe
     (See especially the chart that compares the meaning of these words in *Key Biblical Terms in the New Testament* under "priest.")
  b. apostle, disciple, believer
     (See the comparative chart in *Key Biblical Terms* under "disciple.")
  c. prophet, angel, apostle, messenger
  d. gospel, Scriptures, epistle/letter
  e. (for more advanced translators) Christ, Messiah, Lord, LORD, Son of Man
  f. covenant, oath, vow, promise

24.5 Key biblical terms that have more than one sense

We have already seen that words may have several different senses, according to the context in which they occur. Since the meanings of words in one language do not match up with those of another language, the different senses often need to be translated by different words.

Example 1

The Greek word *pneuma* has many different senses. Most of them can be translated in English by the word "spirit":

  a. "demon, evil spirit"   And the unclean spirits came out, and entered the pigs. (Mark 5:13)
  b. "angel, good spirit"   Are they not all ministering spirits sent out to serve…? (Hebrews 1:14)

c.	"Spirit of God, Holy Spirit"	And they were all filled with the Holy Spirit and began to speak in other tongues as the Spirit gave them utterance. (Acts 2:4)
d.	"part of the human personality"	The spirit indeed is willing, but the flesh is weak. (Matthew 26:41)
e.	"ghost, spirit of a dead person"	They were startled and frightened, and thought they saw a spirit.... A spirit does not have flesh and bones as you see that I have. (Luke 24:37,39)

There are some senses of Greek word *pneuma* that cannot be translated by the English word "spirit." A different word is needed:

f.	"wind"	The wind blows where it wishes. (John 3:8)
g.	"breath"	Whom the Lord Jesus will kill with the breath of his mouth. (2 Thessalonians 2:8)

Exercise 5

The Greek word translated as "flesh" has several different senses in the Bible. Three of the most common of these senses include the following:

(1) the physical substance that covers the bones of the body (muscle)

- Luke 24:39   A spirit does not have flesh and bones as you see that I have.
- John 6:52   How can this man give us his flesh to eat?

(2) human beings, people in general, especially when used in the phrase "flesh and blood"

- Luke 3:6   And all flesh shall see the salvation of God.
- Galatians 1:16   I did not confer with flesh and blood. (*RSV*)

Compare NIV "I did not consult any man" or NLT "consult with any human being."

(3) fallen human nature, human nature apart from God

For each of the verses listed below, compare translations in different English versions. Then write down how you might translate the word "flesh" into your own language. Would you be able to use the same word in each context?

a.	Matthew 16:17	And Jesus answered him, "Blessed are you, Simon Bar-Jonah! For flesh and blood has not revealed this to you, but my Father who is in heaven."
b.	Matthew 26:41	Watch and pray that you may not enter into temptation. The spirit indeed is willing, but the flesh is weak.
c.	John 8:15	You judge according to the flesh; I judge no one.
d.	Romans 1:3	concerning his Son, who was descended from David according to the flesh
e.	Romans 4:1	Abraham, our forefather according to the flesh
f.	Romans 7:18	For I know that nothing good dwells in me, that is, in my flesh.

g. 1 Peter 1:24–25   All flesh is like grass and all its glory like the flower of grass. The grass withers, and the flower falls, ²⁵ but the word of the Lord remains forever.

Further examples of terms that have more than one sense

Look up the words listed below in *Key Biblical Terms in the New Testament* on *Translator's Workplace*. Each of these words has several different senses, depending on the context.

a. believe
b. grace
c. glory

Exercise 6

(1) Study the entry for the word "bless" in *Key Biblical Terms in the New Testament*.
(2) Below are listed some verses that contain the word "bless." They illustrate three or four different senses of the original word. Compare the translation in different English versions.
(3) In the light of the study you have just made, for each of the verses, write down how you might translate the word "bless" into your own language. Would you be able to use the same word in each context?

a. Genesis 17:16   [God said to Abraham] "I will bless her [Sarah] and she shall be a mother of nations." (*RSV*)
b. Mark 10:16   [Jesus] took [the children] in his arms and blessed them.
c. Luke 1:64   [Zechariah] spoke, blessing God.
d. Luke 1:68   Blessed be the Lord God of Israel.
e. Luke 2:28   [Simeon] took [the child Jesus] up in his arms and blessed God and said . . .
f. Luke 2:34   And Simeon blessed them [the father and mother of Jesus] and said to Mary, his mother . . .
g. Luke 6:27–28   But I say to you who hear, Love your enemies, do good to those who hate you, ²⁸ bless those who curse you, pray for those who abuse you.
h. Luke 24:50   And lifting up his hands he [Jesus] blessed them [the disciples].
i. Luke 24:52–53   And they [disciples of Jesus] worshiped him and returned to Jerusalem with great joy, ⁵³ and were continually in the temple blessing God.
j. Acts 3:25–26   "[God said] to Abraham, 'And in your offspring shall all the families of the earth be blessed.' ²⁶ God, having raised up his servant, sent him to you first, to bless you by turning every one of you from your wickedness."
k. Revelation 5:13   To him who sits on the throne and to the Lamb be blessing and honour and glory and might forever and ever!

Exercise 7

Below are listed some verses that contain the word "church." Study the entry for "church" in *Key Biblical Terms in the New Testament*. Then, for each verse, write down how you might translate the word "church" into your own language. Would you be able to use the same word in each context?

a. Acts 8:1 — And there arose on that day a great persecution against the church in Jerusalem; and they were all scattered.

b. Acts 11:26 — For a whole year they met with the church, and taught a great many people. And in Antioch the disciples were first called Christians.

c. 1 Corinthians 7:17 — Only let each person lead the life that the Lord has assigned to him, and to which God has called him. This is my rule in all the churches.

d. 1 Corinthians 14:19 — Nevertheless, in church I would rather speak five words with my mind in order to instruct others, than ten thousand words in a tongue.

e. 1 Corinthians 16:19 — The churches of Asia send greetings. Aquila and Priscilla, together with the church in their house, send you hearty greetings in the Lord.

f. Galatians 1:13 — I persecuted the church of God violently and tried to destroy it.

g. Ephesians 5:23 — For the husband is the head of the wife even as Christ is the head of the church, his body, and is himself its Saviour.

h. Hebrews 2:12 — "I will declare thy name unto my brethren, in the midst of the church will I sing praise unto thee." (*KJV*)

This is a quotation from Psalm 22:22. Compare the translation in other Bible versions.

i. Acts 7:38 — This is he [Moses], that was in the church in the wilderness with the angel who spoke to him in the mount Sinai, and with our fathers. (*KJV*)

Compare the translation in other Bible versions.

j. Revelation 2:1 — To the angel of the church in Ephesus write . . .

24.6 Summary list for consistency checking

Here is a list of some key biblical terms that have relatively constant meaning in all contexts and should, with occasional exceptions, be translated by the same expression in each occurrence:

God, Christ/Messiah (when used as a title), Son of Man
Holy Spirit
priest, chief priests, High Priest
prophet, scribe, apostle, disciple
angel, evil spirit/demon
baptism/to baptise
Sabbath

Key biblical terms that have different senses in different contexts include the following. The different senses should be translated consistently according to context.

> grace, glory, holy, bless, law
> to believe/to have faith
> to repent/repentance
> to save/salvation

Translators must study the different senses of the underlying Hebrew, Aramaic, or Greek terms.

It is important to compare how terms in the Old Testament correspond with comparable New Testament terms. For example, compare the use of the Hebrew term *nabi* 'prophet' in the Old Testament with the use of the Greek *prophētēs* in the New Testament. It is also very important to study the meaning and use of the names and titles for God in the Old and New Testaments.

Reference helps for both Old Testament and New Testament terms are listed below.

Additional resources on "Translating Key Biblical Terms"

BT4 online materials

24_Key_Terms_1.pptx
24_Key_Terms_2.pptx
24_Key_Terms_in_gospels-Review.pptx
24_Key_Terms_in_gospels-Chart_to_record_translations.pdf

Bible Dictionaries available in Logos Bible software

New Bible Dictionary, published by InterVarsity Press.
Lexham Bible Dictionary, published online by Lexham Press.
Zondervan Illustrated Bible Backgrounds Commentary: Old Testament (5 vols.).
Zondervan Illustrated Bible Backgrounds Commentary: New Testament (4 vols.).

Concordance and other online resources

Logos Bible software provides a way to generate a concordance, enabling the user to find all examples of any word or phrase for any Bible in the system.

Other resources on key biblical terms, available on *Translator's Workplace*

Barnwell, Katharine, Paul Dancy, and Anthony Pope. 2015. *Key biblical terms in the New Testament: An aid for Bible translators*. Dallas: SIL International.
Daams, Nico. 2005. Translating YHWH. *Journal of Translation* 1:47–55. https://www.sil.org/resources/publications/jot/1.1.
Gray, David, comp. 2011. *Old Testament glossary*.
 (This is available in *Translator's Workplace* and, for those who have registered with Academia.edu, this can also be viewed at: https://www.academia.edu/2907731/Old_Testament_Glossary.)
Persson, Janet. 2018. Translating Old Testament key terms for African languages. Ms.
Harris, R. Laird, Gleason L. Archer Jr., and Bruce K. Waltke, eds. 1980. *Theological wordbook of the Old Testament*. Chicago: Moody Press.

Louw, Johannes P., and Eugene A. Nida. 1989. *Greek-English Lexicon of the New Testament based on semantic domains*. New York: United Bible Societies.

"Key Terms in the Old Testament." Forthcoming, 2020.

(This is an SIL project involving translation consultants and exegetical researchers from SIL International, UBS, the Seed Company, and others. It is designed to make essential information relating to the translation of Old Testament key terms accessible to translators and consultants, including those who have a minimal knowledge of biblical Hebrew. The information will be included as a source-language dictionary in Paratext, and connected with *Translator's Workplace* [Logos Version].)

Chapter 25

Exploring Terms Referring to the Supernatural World

When translating terms referring to the supernatural world, it is necessary to study both (1) the terms used in the original Scripture texts, in both the Old and New Testaments, and (2) terms used in the receptor language that reflect the traditional beliefs of the receptor community.

25.1 Why study the receptor language culture?

- Bible translators are educated people. You have learnt other languages and have been exposed to other cultures besides your own. You may have spent some years outside your own language area. For this reason, you may need to go back and sit with people in your home area in order to be aware of assumptions and presuppositions that may affect the way that they interpret and understand any new message.

- Sometimes, as a translator, you may think you have found a good way to translate a key biblical term. But when you test the proposed translation, you discover that people understand something different from the meaning that you wanted to communicate.

For example, when preparing to translate the term "Christ" into one of the languages of Nigeria, the translator studied carefully the meaning of the original word. He learnt that it means literally "an anointed person." In this language, there is an expression for "someone who has been anointed." So the translator decided to use that term for "Christ." But when he studied the term further, he discovered that, in that culture, the "anointed one" referred to a new bride on whom oil had been poured before marriage. So he realised that the term was quite unsuitable to translate "Christ." If he had not studied how this term was used in his own culture, he might have made a serious mistake.

Remember

Even when you are a fluent speaker of the receptor language and have grown up speaking that language, it is still necessary to study your own culture and the terminology that is used to refer to the spiritual world.

25.2 How to study the culture of your own people

- Spend time sitting with the older people of the area. Ask them to explain the meaning of words and phrases that refer to traditional beliefs and customs. Listen to their discussions. From their agreements and disagreements, you will learn a great deal. Often it will be helpful to make an audio recording of the discussion, so that you can study it in more detail later.

- In order to discover the exact meaning of a specific word in the receptor language, compare and contrast it with other words in the same area of meaning. Do this in the way that has been explained, with examples, in section 24.4.

Remember

Be ready to listen and learn.

25.3 What kinds of words need to be studied?

Words to do with the supernatural or spiritual world are especially important.
For example, the translator needs to study

- Words and phrases referring to the supreme being, God, in contrast to other things that are worshipped, such as idols.

- Words that refer to spiritual beings in the receptor language.

    Too often in the past, "evil spirit" has been translated by an expression that means something like "bad temper." This gives a wrong meaning, hiding the fact that in the biblical world, evil spirits are independent spiritual beings that can take possession of a person.

- Words used to refer to the non-physical parts of human beings. For example, "soul," "self," "life," "mind," "heart." In the receptor culture, how do people perceive and refer to the basic parts of a human being? What is the function of these parts? What remains after the body has died?

Keep alert to find ideas, customs, and terms that could serve as a bridge to help people understand biblical truths. For example, there may be something in the culture that reflects truths about forgiveness, cancelling of sin, or redemption. Use what people already know and believe to help them understand the full truth revealed in the Bible.

> Be careful to choose the right words to translate terms that refer to spiritual beings. This is essential if the full truth of the Bible message is to be communicated.

25.4 Other areas of meaning that should be studied

1) Make a study of words in the receptor language that refer to persons who have any kind of religious function in that culture. Investigate terms for the following:

   a. people who speak on behalf of the chief

      (This may help you to find a good expression to translate "prophet.")

   b. people who carry messages for the chief

      (This may help you to find an expression to translate "angel.")

c. people who represent the chief

   (This may help you to find an expression for "apostle.")

   d. people who make sacrifices or perform other rituals, or mediate between a deity and the people

   (This may help you to find an expression for "priest.")

   e. diviners (From whom do they get their insight?)

In choosing known terms from within the culture to translate key biblical terms, the translator should test the proposed words carefully, to find out whether they are suitable. Sometimes such terms are so closely associated with the worship of other gods or idols that they cannot be used to refer to Christian worship. But sometimes the terms can be successfully modified. It helps communication if you can build on an idea that is already known.

2) There are passages in the New Testament where different kinds of sins are listed. For example, see Matthew 15:19 and Romans 1:29–31. In preparation for translating such passages, list all the words for different sins or evil actions that are used in the receptor language, and compare them. These will not match up one-to-one with the English words. The important point in translating such passages is, of course, to convey the total meaning of the whole message, even if words do not match up one-to-one.

List and compare the words for different kinds of sexual sins. In English, common words in this area of meaning are: immorality, adultery, fornication. Compare the words in the receptor language with the English words. Do they match one-to-one? In what ways do they differ from the English words in meaning?

25.5 Same form, different significance

It may be that a custom or concept exists in the receptor language culture, but its significance and meaning in that culture is very different from its significance and meaning in the biblical culture.

Examples

Circumcision may be practised in the receptor culture, but its function in the receptor language culture is likely to be very different from its function in the biblical culture. For the Jewish people, circumcision identified someone as a member of God's chosen people.

If circumcision is practised in the receptor culture in the project you are involved with, write a description of the practice of circumcision in that culture, stating at what age this is done and what its significance is in the culture. Compare this with the practice and significance of circumcision in the Bible.

Leprosy (or a similar disease) may be known in the receptor language culture, but lepers may not be social outcasts as they were in biblical times, needing not only healing but cleansing from contamination in the sight of God.

Tax collectors may be known in the receptor language culture, but they may not be looked down on as were tax collectors in Israel in the time of Christ. Jewish tax collectors in the time of Christ were viewed as traitors to their own people because they served the hated Roman conquerors.

Translators need to study not only surface similarities of ideas and customs, but also their deeper significance and meaning within the culture. Consider preparing glossary entries for the terms concerned, explaining the cultural difference.

25.6 Continuing to listen and observe

Studies of cultural differences need to be done over a period of time. You may have to wait for the right opportunity to discuss the translation of terms that refer to the spiritual world with those who can help you best. Look for people who have a reputation for being good speakers of the language and who know the culture well.

Allow time for research, for proposed terms to be well tested and for new insights to emerge.

Additional resources on "Exploring Terms Referring to the Supernatural World"

BT4 online materials

25_Understanding_the_world_of_the_supernatural.pptx

For further reading

Several of the articles listed below refer to the translation of specific terms, such as the translation of "God" or "Holy Spirit." Are there any key biblical terms that are proving challenging to translate into your language? Look up and read articles in this list that might help on that topic.

Many of these articles are available to view in *Translator's Workplace*. The journal *The Bible Translator* is available for purchase at http://journals.sagepub.com/loi/tbt. The complete texts for vols. 1–51 (1950–2012) can also be viewed free of charge at http://www.ubs-translations.org/bt/archives_1950_2012/.

Arensen, Jonathan E. 1987. The God of the sky: The supreme God concept among the Eastern Sudanic peoples of southern Sudan. *Notes on Anthropology* 9:4–21.

Arichea, Daniel C. 1983. Translating breath and spirit. *The Bible Translator* 34:209–213.

Bratcher, Robert G. 1983. Biblical words describing man: breath, life, spirit. *The Bible Translator* 34:201–209.

Bunkowske, Eugene W. 1977. Religious words! Which and where? *The Bible Translator* 28:226–231.

Loewen, Jacob A. 1983. Clean air or bad breath? *The Bible Translator* 34:213–219.

Richardson, Don. 1974. *Peace child*. Glendale, CA: Regal Books.

SIL Africa Area Translation Department. 1986. Understanding the world of the supernatural. Africa Area Translation Aids 19. Nairobi: SIL International.
(Available in *Translator's Workplace*. This paper is adapted from an article by Dr Jacob A. Loewen in *Practical Anthropology* 12(4):183–187, July-August 1965. See also the article by Richard Mansen with the same title "Understanding the world of the supernatural," published in *Notes on Translation* 39:3–12, March 1971, a close adaptation of the work by Dr Loewen.)

Wiesemann, Ursula. 1978. Holy Spirit in Kaingang. *Notes on Translation* 69:32–35.

The issues of *The Bible Translator* for April and October 1984 and October 1985 include a number of articles on the names of God in the Bible.

Part 4

More on Discovering the Meaning

Chapter 26

Discovering the Meaning – Event Ideas

It has been suggested that all "ideas" or "concepts" belong to one of four classes:[1]

(1) The THING class includes all things and objects, whether things that are touchable or which cannot be touched. Typically, but not exclusively, "things" are referred to by grammatical nouns.

(2) The EVENT class includes all actions, processes, or happenings. This includes movements, whether voluntary or involuntary, and all mental processes. Typically, but not exclusively, "events" are referred to by grammatical verbs. However, they can also be expressed by other grammatical forms.

(3) The ATTRIBUTE class includes qualities and quantities or degree, referring to either things, events, or other attributes. Typically, but not exclusively, attributes are referred to by grammatical adjectives or adverbs.

The above three classes all refer to concepts that can be identified.

(4) The RELATION class, however, does not refer to concepts, but to functions; these are signals that show how the concepts mentioned are related together to form a meaningful discourse.

In studying a complex passage of Scripture, it is often helpful to identify the EVENT ideas, to re-express these as verbs, and to see how the other concepts mentioned relate to, or participate in, that event.

Grammatical terms

Grammatical terms used in the discussion below include "noun," "verb," "pronoun," and others. The presentations listed at the end of this chapter provide an explanation of these terms. If you are not familiar with using these grammatical terms, take time to work through the presentations.

---

[1] See detailed analysis in *The Theory and Practice of Translation* (Nida and Taber 1969:37–55).

26.1 Recognising EVENT ideas

As we saw above, event ideas are often expressed by verbs. However, in English, and in Hebrew and Greek, events (actions and processes) are sometimes expressed by nouns.

In each of the following examples, a noun in the first version expresses an event idea, an action, something that happened, or a process. In the second version, the noun is replaced by a verb.

Examples

let your <u>laughter</u> be turned to <u>mourning</u> (James 4:9)
⇒ don't laugh any more, instead begin to weep/mourn

and there is <u>salvation</u> in no one else (Acts 4:12)
⇒ there is no one else who can save (us)

that they may receive <u>forgiveness</u> of sins (Acts 26:18)
⇒ that (God) may forgive them for their sins

until the <u>coming</u> of the Lord (1 Thessalonians 4:15)
⇒ until the Lord comes

In each case, the underlined noun expresses an event idea; that is, something that someone does, or something that happens. In many languages, events are more naturally expressed by verbs. Many languages use a verb where English might use a noun.

Preparing to translate

When preparing to translate, it is helpful to look for any event ideas in the passage, especially those that are expressed by a grammatical form other than a verb. Re-express the meaning using a verb to express the event idea. This is useful for two reasons:

1) It helps to reveal more precisely the meaning of the source text. The meaning, especially the relationships between ideas, often appears more clearly when the event ideas are expressed as verbs.
2) Often this restructuring will help the translator to find an easier way to express the meaning in the receptor language.

Remember

When studying a complex passage in preparation for translation, do this:
- find all the event ideas and mark them; and
- wherever an event idea is expressed by a form other than a verb, re-express this event idea as a verb – this may help to make the meaning clearer.

Exercise 1

Each of the following nouns expresses an **event** idea (an action, a happening, or a process). Re-express the idea as a verb.

26.1 Recognising EVENT ideas

For example, death ⇒ to die
  a. punishment ⇒
  b. song ⇒
  c. knowledge ⇒
  d. student ⇒
  e. suggestion ⇒
  f. deliverance ⇒
  g. departure ⇒
  h. joy ⇒
  i. ignorance ⇒   (be careful!)
  j. faith ⇒

Exercise 2

In each of the examples below, the word underlined expresses an event idea. For each example, look at the context of the verse and compare translations in other English Bible versions. Then rewrite the meaning, in English, using a verb to express the event idea.

  a. Matthew 24:31   They will gather his <u>elect</u>.
  b. Matthew 26:66   He deserves <u>death</u>.
  c. Luke 8:48   Your <u>faith</u> has made you well.
  d. Luke 12:47   That servant...will receive a severe <u>beating</u>.
  e. Luke 12:58   As you go with your <u>accuser</u> before the magistrate . . .
  f. Acts 8:20   You thought you could obtain the <u>gift</u> of God with money!
  g. Colossians 1:8 He . . . has made known to us your <u>love</u> in the Spirit.
  h. Philemon 21   Having <u>confidence</u> in thy <u>obedience</u> (*KJV*)
  i. Romans 6:5   For if we have been united with him in a <u>death</u> like his, we shall certainly be united with him in a <u>resurrection</u> like his.
  j. Hebrews 13:1   Let brotherly <u>love</u> continue.

Exercise 3

For each of the examples listed below, do the following:

(1) Mark the nouns that express an event idea. Check the context of the passage carefully and compare different English Bible versions.
(2) Rewrite the meaning, in English, using a verb to express the event idea.

  a. Luke 1:44   When the sound of your greeting came to my ears, the baby in my womb leaped for joy.
  b. Luke 2:26   That he would not see death . . .
  c. Luke 2:47   All who heard him were amazed at his understanding and his answers.
  d. Luke 4:18b   He has sent me to proclaim liberty to the captives and recovering of sight to the blind.
  e. Acts 13:36   For David . . . fell asleep and was laid with his fathers and saw corruption.

f.	Acts 16:26	And suddenly there was a great earthquake.
g.	Romans 1:16	For I am not ashamed of the gospel, for it is the power of God for salvation to everyone who believes.
h.	2 Timothy 4:21	Eubulus sends greetings to you, as do Pudens and Linus and Claudia and all the brothers.
i.	Hebrews 4:6	Those who formerly received the good news failed to enter because of disobedience.
j.	Hebrews 9:6	These preparations having thus been made, the priests go regularly into the first section, performing their ritual duties.

Be alert for subtle differences of focus or emphasis in the source text. Try to re-express the same distinctions in the translation. The grammatical form of the expression may be different, but the meaning should be the same.

26.2 Participants in an event

The *participants* in an event are the people or things that take part in that event. When re-expressing an event idea as a verb, it is often necessary to state who or what are the participants in that event. For example, who did an action and who was affected by the action. Usually this will be clear from the context.

Examples

- The dog ate the meat.

    Event: to eat

    Participants in the event:

    The *dog* is the one who does the action, the subject of the verb.

    The *meat* is the object of the action.

- Eubulus sends greetings to you. (2 Timothy 4:21)

    Event: to greet

    Participants in the event:

    Eubulus, the one who does the action; Eubulus is the subject of the clause.

    you – the receiver of the greeting, the one Eubulus is greeting.

In grammatical terms, in the examples above, the actor (the person or thing who does the action) is labelled as the *subject* of the verb; the person or thing to whom the action is done, is labelled as the *object* of the verb. In English, however, there is a distinction between *active* and *passive* verb forms. In the active form, as in the examples above, the subject is the one who does the action. In the passive form, the subject is the person or thing to whom the action is done. Passive forms will be discussed in chapter 28.

Remember

The people or things that are involved in a certain event are called the *participants*.

Exercise 4

For each of the three examples listed below, do the following:

(1) Mark the event ideas.

(2) List the participants in that event.

(3) If any of these participants is implicit in the original form, state it explicitly and put brackets round it.
  a. John's death
  b. Mary's love for children
  c. There was much joy.

> Languages are different. Some languages use more noun forms, some use more verb forms. As you continue with your training as a translator, there will be opportunities to study narratives and other texts that have been spoken naturally in your language and to discover the typical features of your language. You will start to appreciate the unique patterns of the language. This is a very interesting and very important study.

Additional resources on "Discovering the Meaning – Event Ideas"

BT4 online materials

These presentations are intended to help translators recognise parts of speech in English in preparation for discovering the parts of speech in their own language.

26_Recognizing_word_classes_in_English.pptx
26_Recognizing_nouns_and_verbs.pptx
26_Reviewing_grammatical_terms.pptx
26_Practice_in_re-expressing_meaning.pptx
26_Kinds_of_clauses-Some_grammatical_terms_defined.pdf

Chapter 27

Discovering the Meaning –
"Of" Phrases in English (Genitive Constructions)

27.1 "Of" phrases in English

An "of" phrase in English is a phrase in which two nouns are closely related to each other, one being dependent on the other. This relationship is signalled in English by the word "of."

the house *of* my father

the tail *of* the dog

a bucket *of* water

the song *of* Miriam

the death *of* the child

the price *of* meat

One of the nouns may be expressing a verbal idea – it may refer to an event rather than to a thing. For example, "the song of Miriam" or "the death of the child."

English "of" phrases can be described as "genitive constructions" or "noun-noun phrases." The construction is used to express many different relationships between the concepts referred to.

English uses many "of" phrases and other genitive constructions. The Greek language, as used in the original text of the New Testament, uses the genitive construction even more than English does. Biblical Hebrew also uses the genitive construction frequently. A genitive construction in the *ESV* usually reflects a genitive construction in the original language text.

27.2 Recognising different underlying relationships

As you will see from the examples below, many quite different relationships are expressed by "of" phrases. This is especially true where one of the nouns expresses an event idea.

When you observe that a noun is expressing an event idea, follow the principle of re-expressing the event as a verb and identifying the participants in that event.

In re-expressing the meaning, some participants have been made explicit, based on the meaning in the context. Information that has been made explicit is enclosed in rounded brackets ( ).

Examples

Matthew 1:18	the birth of Jesus Christ
⇒	*Jesus Christ was born*
Matthew 13:35	since the foundation of the world
⇒	*since (God) founded/created the world*
Matthew 21:25	the baptism of John
⇒	*John baptises (people)*
Romans 5:10	by the death of his Son
⇒	*by the means that his Son died*
Ephesians 1:1	by the will of God
⇒	*because God willed it*
Ephesians 1:13	the word of truth
⇒	*the word/message that is true*
Ephesians 1:13	the gospel of your salvation
⇒	*the gospel/good news that (God) saves you*
Ephesians 1:13	the holy Spirit of promise (KJV)
⇒	*the Holy Spirit whom (God) promised (to send)*

At this point we are concerned primarily with discovering the relationship between the concepts referred to, that is, the parts of the "of" phrase. How the ideas may be expressed in translations in other languages is a different question, to be considered later.

Remember

"Of" phrases in English express many different relationships. Always study the phrase in its context to discover what the relationship is between the parts. To help in discovering this, re-express any event ideas as verbs.

Exercise 1

Study the "of" phrases in each of the examples listed below and do the following:

(1) Look at the translation of each phrase in *NIV*, *GNT*, and *NLT*. If possible, use the Paratext program to compare these versions.

(2) Re-express the meaning of the phrase in a way which makes the relationship between the parts clear.

a. Luke 2:4   from Galilee, from the town of Nazareth
b. Luke 2:4   to Judea, to the city of David, which is called Bethlehem
   (Compare the translations in GNT and NLT; see the explanatory notes on Luke 2:4 in Translator's Notes.*)*
c. Luke 2:11   in the city of David
d. Luke 4:31   to Capernaum, a city of Galilee
e. John 1:44   the city of Andrew and Peter
f. Acts 8:1   the regions of Judea and Samaria

In which of these examples does "of" mean "called" or "named"?
In which examples does it mean "in the region called"?
In which examples does it mean "where someone lived" or "where someone was born"?

27.3 The importance of context

Often when a noun-noun phrase stands alone, the relationship between the concepts is not expressed explicitly. The relationship could be understood in more than one way. For example, when an underlying event idea is present, the noun concept to which it relates may be either the subject or the object of that event. As you study the context in which the phrase occurs, the relationship becomes clear.

Example 1

Study the meaning of the phrase "the love of God" in the following passages. Compare the translation of these verses in *NLT, GNT,* and *CEV.*

Romans 8:39		Nor height nor depth, nor anything else in all creation, will be able to separate us from the love of God in Christ Jesus our Lord.
	NLT	Nothing in all creation will ever be able to separate us from the love of God that is revealed in Christ Jesus our Lord.
	CEV	Nothing in all creation can separate us from God's love for us in Christ Jesus our Lord!
John 5:42		But I know that you do not have the love of God within you.
	CEV	I do know that none of you love God.
1 John 5:3		For this is the love of God, that we keep his commandments. And his commandments are not burdensome.
	NLT	Loving God means keeping his commandments, and his commandments are not burdensome.

The phrase "love of God" occurs in each of these passages. When the contexts in which the phrase occurs are studied, it becomes clear that the relationships are different. Romans 8:39 refers to the love that God has for us. John 5:42 and 1 John 5:3 refer to the love that we have for God.

Example 2

Compare the relationships expressed in the underlined phrases:

Acts 2:38	And Peter said to them, "Repent and be baptized every one of you in the name of Jesus Christ for the forgiveness of your sins, and you will receive the gift of the Holy Spirit."
Ephesians 2:8	For by grace you have been saved through faith. And this is not your own doing; it is the gift of God

In Acts 2:38, it is the Holy Spirit himself who is given – someone (God) gives people the Holy Spirit. In Ephesians 2:8, the phrase "the gift of God" refers back to the beginning of the sentence: "you have been saved." The gift is salvation (God has caused us to be saved); God is the giver.

Exercise 2

Look up each of the underlined phrases in *NIV*, *GNT*, and *NLT*, and study the context in which each occurs. Rewrite the text, in English, making the relationships clear.

a. Luke 3:6 — And all flesh shall see the salvation of God.
b. Ephesians 1:13 — In him you also, when you heard the word of truth, the gospel of your salvation, and believed in him, were sealed with the promised Holy Spirit.
c. Matthew 16:12 — to beware…of the teaching of the Pharisees and Sadducees
d. Acts 13:12 — For he was astonished at the teaching of the Lord.
   Compare NIV "For he was amazed at the teaching about the Lord." Check the context carefully!
e. Revelation 2:15 — So also you have some who hold the teaching of the Nicolaitans.
f. Galatians 1:12 — For I did not receive it from any man, nor was I taught it, but I received it through a revelation of Jesus Christ.
g. 1 Corinthians 1:7 — so that you are not lacking in any spiritual gift, as you wait for the revealing of our Lord Jesus Christ
h. John 12:31 — Now is the judgment of this world.
i. Romans 2:2 — We know that the judgment of God rightly falls on those who practice such things.
j. Revelation 14:7 — Fear God and give him glory because the hour of his judgment has come.

27.4 More about genitive constructions: Other grammatical forms in English

In English, many of the noun-noun relationships that are expressed by "of-phrases" can also be expressed by using -'s (apostrophe s). For example,

"the house of my father"	⇒	"my father's house"
"the tail of the dog"	⇒	"the dog's tail"
"the song of Miriam"	⇒	"Miriam's song"
"the roof of the house"	⇒	"the house's roof" – to discuss

In English, in any given context, one form may be more natural than another. This may sometimes depend on whether one of the nouns concerned is animate or inanimate.

The same relationships can be expressed in English by a noun with a *possessive pronoun*, such as "his," "her," "its," "your," "my," "our," or "their." This is also a genitive construction, expressing a relationship between two concepts.

> his house
>
> its tail
>
> her song
>
> their song

The following exercises give practice in recognising the relationships between two concepts, whether expressed by two nouns or by a pronoun and a noun.

Exercise 3

Examples are from Acts chapter 5. Look up each of the following phrases in *NIV*, *GNT*, and *NLT*, and study the context in which each occurs. Rewrite the phrase in English, making the relationships clear, expressing the meaning more explicitly where necessary.

- a. 5:1   a piece of property
- b. 5:2   with his wife's knowledge
- c. 5:4   Was it not at your disposal?
- d. 5:7   after an interval of about three hours
- e. 5:12   in Solomon's Portico
- f. 5:19   an angel of the Lord
- g. 5:20   all the words of this Life
- h. 5:34   a teacher of the law
- i. 5:37   in the days of the census
- j. 5:39   They took his advice.

Exercise 4

Examples are from Acts chapter 8. Instructions, as for exercise 3.

- a. 8:5   to the city of Samaria
- b. 8:11   his magic
- c. 8:14   the word of God
- d. 8:18   through the laying on of the apostles' hands
- e. 8:20   the gift of God
- f. 8:25   many villages of the Samaritans
- g. 8:27   a court official of the Candace
- h. 8:27   queen of the Ethiopians
- i. 8:32   the passage of the Scripture
- j. 8:35   the good news of Jesus (*RSV*)

Exercise 5

Examples are from the Letter to the Hebrews. Instructions, as for exercise 3.

- a. 1:3   the word of his power
- b. 2:14   the one who has the power of death
- c. 2:15   through fear of death

d. 2:17   in the service of God
e. 2:17   the sins of the people
f. 3:3   the builder of a house
g. 3:8   on the day of testing
h. 3:9   where your fathers…saw my works
i. 3:13   by the deceitfulness of sin
j. 3:16   under the leadership of Moses (*RSV*)

Exercise 6

Examples are from the Old Testament (1 Samuel and Psalms). Instructions, as for exercise 3.

a. 1 Samuel 2:1   I rejoice in your salvation.
b. 1 Samuel 2:3   The LORD is a God of knowledge.
c. 1 Samuel 2:10   The adversaries of the LORD shall be broken in pieces.
d. 1 Samuel 2:17   the offering of the LORD
e. Psalm 1:1   Blessed is the man who walks not in the counsel of the wicked, nor stands in the way of sinners, nor sits in the seat of scoffers.
f. Psalm 3:3   But you, O LORD, are a shield about me, my glory, and the lifter of my head.
g. Psalm 118:28   You are my God, and I will give thanks to you.

Remember

Always study the meaning of a word or phrase in the context in which it occurs. Consider the possible relationships to determine which meaning is being used in this context.

27.5 Translating genitive phrases

In many languages, genitive constructions are not as frequent as they are in English, or in biblical Hebrew or Greek. Relationships that are expressed by "of" phrases in an English source text may be more naturally expressed in other ways in your language.

Study genitive constructions in your own language. In chapter 39 there are some guidelines on how to make this study and discover the grammar of your own language. An awareness of how these relationships are expressed in your language will alert you to places where you need to restructure the text in your translation.

Remember

- Keep alert to recognise "of" constructions in the source text.
- Study each "of" phrase to discover the underlying relationship.
- Re-express the meaning in the way that is most clear and natural in your language.

Exercise 7

(1) Study the "of" phrases in Luke 1:5–11 below.

(2) Re-express the meaning of each phrase in a way that makes the relationship between the parts clear, expressing event ideas as verbs.

(3) Make information explicit, where necessary, and enclose anything you have made explicit in brackets ( ).

(4) Translate these verses into your own language.

Luke 1:5–11

> ⁵ <u>In the days of Herod</u>, <u>king of Judea</u>, there was a priest named Zechariah, of the division of Abijah. And he had a wife from <u>the daughters of Aaron</u>, and her name was Elizabeth. ⁶ And they were both righteous before God, <u>walking blamelessly in all the commandments and statutes of the Lord</u>. ⁷ But they had no child, because Elizabeth was barren, and both were advanced in years.
>
> ⁸ Now while he was serving as priest before God when his division was on duty, ⁹ <u>according to the custom of the priesthood</u>, he was chosen by lot to enter the temple of the Lord and burn incense. ¹⁰ And <u>the whole multitude of the people</u> were praying outside <u>at the hour of incense</u>. ¹¹ And there appeared to him <u>an angel of the Lord</u> standing <u>on the right side of the altar of incense</u>.

Exercise 8

Consider the following example from Matthew 1:1–6, for discussion:

> ¹ The book of the genealogy of Jesus Christ, the son of David, the son of Abraham. ² Abraham was the father of Isaac, and Isaac the father of Jacob, and Jacob the father of Judah and his brothers, ³ and Judah the father of Perez and Zerah by Tamar, and Perez the father of Hezron, and Hezron the father of Ram, ⁴ and Ram the father of Amminadab, and Amminadab the father of Nahshon, and Nahshon the father of Salmon, ⁵ and Salmon the father of Boaz by Rahab, and Boaz the father of Obed by Ruth, and Obed the father of Jesse, ⁶ and Jesse the father of David the king.

Compare this translation from the *English Standard Version* (*ESV*) with other English translations. Compare how different versions use formatting to make the passage easier to follow and to read.

Also compare with the *King James Version* rendering of this passage:

> ¹ The book of the generation of Jesus Christ, the son of David, the son of Abraham. ² Abraham begat Isaac; and Isaac begat Jacob; and Jacob begat Judah and his brethren.

In verse 2 onwards, the *King James Version* follows the form of the Greek text, which uses a verb to express the idea "begat." Modern English translations have not followed this form, perhaps because the verb "to beget" is no longer in common use in English. Consider whether your language has a verb similar to the meaning of the Greek verb, which could be used to translate this passage.

Additional resources on "'Of' Phrases in English (Genitive Constructions)"

BT4 online materials

27_Genitive_constructions.pptx

Chapter 28

Discovering the Meaning – Active and Passive Voice

28.1 What is the difference between "active" and "passive" forms?

In English, it is possible to say

    John built the house.   (active form)

or, The house was built by John.   (passive form)

- In the *active* form, the <u>subject</u> of the sentence is *the person who does the action.*
- In the *passive* form, the <u>subject</u> of the sentence is *the person or thing to which the action is done.* Someone or something else, not necessarily named, does the action to that person or thing.

Exercise 1

For each of the following sentences, identify the event. Then identify who did the action. State whether the form is active or passive.

    a. The dog bit John.
    b. John was bitten by the dog.
    c. His bones have been buried in the compound.
    d. John is digging a deep hole.
    e. John caught ten fish yesterday.
    f. The truth is known by everyone.
    g. The paper had been torn into small pieces.
    h. The flag was carried by the leading soldier.
    i. The children had eaten all the oranges.

Many languages do not have a passive form; only an active form exists. Therefore, in translating from English, it may be necessary to turn a sentence from the passive form into the active form.

Examples

In the following verses, the underlined form is passive.

    Mark 1:13   He was in the wilderness forty days, <u>being tempted by Satan</u>.

"He was tempted by Satan" can be re-expressed in the active form as, "Satan tempted him."

    Mark 1:14   Now <u>after John was arrested</u>, Jesus came into Galilee, preaching the gospel of God.

In this passage, who arrested John is not in focus. A possible rendering in the active form would be, "After people arrested John" or "After people put John in prison."

    Mark 1:15   <u>The time is fulfilled</u>.

        NIV: "The time has come."   GNT: "The right time has come."

Exercise 2

Each of the following sentences is expressed in the passive form in English. How would you translate each example into your own language? Use a form that is natural in your language.

    a.   Acts 4:11   This Jesus is the stone that was rejected by you, the builders.
    b.   Acts 12:23   He was eaten by worms and breathed his last.
    c.   Acts 16:2   He was well spoken of by the brothers at Lystra and Iconium.
    d.   Acts 22:11   I was led by the hand by those who were with me.
    e.   Acts 24:26   He hoped that money would be given him by Paul.

28.2 Implicit participants

In the active form, the person who does the action is always mentioned.

In the passive form, the person who does the action is not always mentioned.

In turning a passive form into an active form, therefore, it is sometimes necessary to make explicit (that is, to state openly) who did the action.

> *Implicit* information is information that is implied and intended to be understood, but that is not stated in words.
>
> *Explicit* information is information that is clearly stated in words.

Examples

    Matthew 3:16   and when Jesus was baptised   [passive form]
    ⇒   *and when (John) baptised Jesus*   [corresponding active form]

    Luke 8:5   Some [seed] fell along the path and was trampled under foot.
    ⇒   *And people trampled on them.*

28.2 Implicit participants 195

When it is necessary to mention the person who does the action explicitly, how do you know who the actor is? Usually this is clear from

1) the context of the passage; or
2) other related passages in the Bible; or
3) general knowledge.

Exercise 3

Imagine that you are translating into a language that does not have a passive form. Re-express each of the following passages in a form in which they might be expressed in such a language. Study each context carefully.

    a. Mark 1:14   Now after John was arrested.
    b. Mark 13:9   You will be beaten in synagogues.
    c. Mark 14:4   Why was the ointment wasted like that?
    d. Mark 14:5   This ointment could have been sold for more than three hundred denarii and given to the poor.
    e. Acts 10:29   So when I was sent for, I came without objection. I ask then why you sent for me.

Sometimes the subject "God" has to be supplied. For example,

    Colossians 1:11   May you be strengthened with all power.
    ⇒   May (God) strengthen you with all power.

Exercise 4

Instructions, as for exercise 3 above.

    a. Acts 10:31   Cornelius, your prayer has been heard and your alms have been remembered before God.
    b. Acts 10:33   Now therefore we are all here in the presence of God to hear all that you have been commanded by the Lord.
    c. 1 Corinthians 11:15   Her hair is given to her for a covering.
    d. Ephesians 2:5   By grace you have been saved.
    e. 2 Thessalonians 3:1–2   Finally, brothers, pray for us, that the word of the Lord may speed ahead and be honoured, as happened among you, ²and that we may be delivered from wicked and evil men.

Exercise 5

Instructions, as for exercise 3 above.

    a. Matthew 3:3   For this is he who was spoken of by the prophet Isaiah.
    b. Matthew 4:1   Then Jesus was led up by the Spirit into the wilderness to be tempted by the devil.
    c. Matthew 4:12   Now when he heard that John had been arrested . . .
    d. Matthew 7:1   Judge not, that you be not judged. For with the judgment you pronounce you will be judged, and with the measure you use it will be measured to you.

e.	Matthew 28:18	All authority in heaven and on earth has been given to me.
f.	Mark 6:14	John the Baptist has been raised from the dead.
g.	Mark 10:45	For even the Son of Man also came not to be served but to serve.
h.	Luke 1:15	For he will be filled with the Holy Spirit, even from his mother's womb.
i.	John 19:20	the place where Jesus was crucified
j.	Acts 1:5	You will be baptized with the Holy Spirit. (Compare with Acts 1:4 and 2:17.)

28.3 The use of the passive form in the source text

English, like biblical Hebrew and biblical Greek, has both passive and active forms. So we need to ask, "Why, in certain contexts, does an author choose to use the passive rather than the active?"

There are several reasons why the passive is used. It is important to recognise these, so that you can understand the author's intention in the source text, and be faithful to it.

- The author may use the passive form in order to bring into focus the person (or thing) to whom (or which) the action was done. This draws attention away from the subject and places it on the object. For example,

    The Son of Man will be delivered over to the chief priests and to the scribes, and they will condemn him to death. (Mark 10:33)

    Why was the ointment wasted like that? ⁵ For this ointment could have been sold for more than three hundred denarii, and given to the poor. (Mark 14:4–5)

    There will not be left here one stone upon another that will not be thrown down. (Matthew 24:2)

- In English, the author may use the passive because the person who does the action is unknown. For example, "My car was stolen last night."
- The author may use the passive for stylistic effect, in order to make a short and memorable saying, focusing on one particular idea, leaving less important ideas out of focus. 1 Timothy 3:16 is a good example of this.

Exercise 6

(1) Study 1 Timothy 3:16, looking at different versions.

(2) In English, without changing the meaning, turn each passive form into an active form.

(3) Then translate this verse into your own language, using whatever form best expresses the correct meaning.

1 Timothy 3:16

> Great indeed, we confess, is the mystery of godliness:
> He was manifested in the flesh,
>> vindicated by the Spirit,
>> seen by angels,
>> proclaimed among the nations,
>> believed on in the world,
>> taken up in glory.

When translating a passive form in the source text, consider why the passive was used in that context. There will be ways of achieving the same effect in the translation.

28.4 Re-expressing the passive meaning

Some languages have "non-specific" forms of pronouns. This might be translated approximately "they did something" or "one did something," where "they" or "one" does not refer to anyone in particular; the subject is left indefinite. This form may sometimes be used to translate the English passive, especially in places where there is a reason why the person who did the action should not be openly stated.

Do you have a form of this kind in your language? If so, study natural texts in the language to find out (a) how frequently it is used, and (b) under what circumstances it is used. See also part 6 of this manual "Discovering Your Language."

Beware of using an indefinite form if the implied subject is God. If the implied subject is God, it may be best to make the reference to God explicit.

Some languages have both active and passive forms, but they may not use these in the same way as in English. Again, observe natural texts to find out how the passive is used. Do not use a passive every time there is a passive in English without carefully considering the pattern of use in the receptor language.

Exercise 7 (for advanced translators)

Study Hebrews 11:1–3 in the *ESV*, *NIV*, and *GNT* translations. In English, without changing the meaning, turn each passive form in the passage into an active form.

Additional resources on "Discovering the Meaning – Active and Passive Voice"

BT4 online materials

28_Verbs-Active_and_passive.pptx

Chapter 29

Discovering the Meaning – Shortcuts

Every language has ways of taking shortcuts. The technical name for this is *ellipsis*. Example of a shortcut:

Question: "Where are you going?"
Answer: "To market."

Everyone understands that the answer means, "I am going to market." In English, the words "I am going" can be left out. They are understood because of the question that has just been asked. Thus, because of the grammatical form, some information is implicit – it is not stated in words, but it is well understood by the hearers.

Examples

In each of the examples below, some information was left implicit. The implicit information has been marked with parentheses ( ).

Mark 14:17   And when it was evening he came with the twelve (disciples).

John 1:21   And they asked him, "What then? Are you Elijah?" He said, "I am not (Elijah)." "Are you the Prophet?" And he answered, "No (I am not the Prophet)."

John 2:10   Everyone serves the good wine first, and when men have drunk freely, then (they serve) the poor wine.

It seems all languages take shortcuts, but they do it in different ways. In translation, it may sometimes be necessary to make the implicit meaning explicit, in order to communicate the correct meaning in a natural way.

In doing this, nothing is added to the meaning. What was already implicit, and was understood by the original hearers, is stated in words.

Exercise

Each of the following passages includes a grammatical shortcut (ellipsis). Rewrite each passage making the implicit meaning explicit.

a. John 4:12   Are you greater than our father Jacob? He gave us the well, and drank from it himself, as did his sons, and his livestock.
b. John 7:46   No one ever spoke like this man!
c. 1 Corinthians 2:8   None of the rulers of this age understood this; for if they had, they would not have crucified the Lord of glory.
d. 1 Corinthians 7:19   For neither circumcision counts for anything nor uncircumcision, but keeping the commandments of God.
e. 1 Corinthians 11:25   In the same way also the cup, after supper, saying . . . (*RSV*) *Check the context.*

Chapter 30

Discovering the Meaning – Complex Passages

A "complex passage" is defined as a passage where several events are described in sequence, sometimes with different logical relationships between the events, and where there may be some embedding of ideas. The sequence of events may not always be clear in the source text. The following method will help you

- to discover the meaning of a complex passage, and
- to re-express the message in a way that will make it easier to translate in some languages.

A procedure to follow

Stage 1: Find all the event ideas in the passage. List these event ideas, expressing them all as verbs.

Stage 2: Fill in the participants in each event, stating who did what.

Also observe any "of" phrases in the passage and study the relationship between the parts. Make explicit any participants, or information, that is implicit in the message and that is essential for a full understanding of the passage.
Re-express any passive verbs in the active form. Study the way in which the events fit together in relation to each other.

Stage 3: Rewrite the passage in a way that expresses this relationship clearly.
As you do this, begin to think about how the ideas will be expressed in the translation in your language.

These three stages are all part of the process of discovering the meaning of the original text, Step 1 in the procedures for translation.

Example 1

Acts 8:1–2

> ¹ And Saul approved of his execution. And there arose on that day a great persecution against the church in Jerusalem, and they were all scattered throughout the regions of Judea and Samaria, except the apostles. ² Devout men buried Stephen and made great lamentation over him.

STAGE 1: List the event ideas

    APPROVE/CONSENT/AGREE
    EXECUTE/PUT-TO-DEATH
    PERSECUTE
    SCATTER
    WORSHIP/HONOUR
    BURY
    LAMENT/WEEP

> *In the ESV translation, "arose" is not a real event. "A great persecution arose" means, "people began to persecute very much."*
> *Similarly, "made" is not a real event. "People made lamentation" means, "people lamented."*
> *"Devout" has the meaning "people who worship God."*
> *In this context, the verb "scatter" means, "cause to scatter" or "cause to flee."*

STAGE 2: Fill in the participants

    Saul CONSENTED/AGREED
  (people) PUT TO DEATH (Stephen)
  (people) PERSECUTED the church (the believers/followers) in Jerusalem
  (people) CAUSED TO SCATTER the believers/followers throughout the region of Judea and Samaria
the apostles (STAYED in Jerusalem)
    people who WORSHIPPED/HONOURED (God)
    people BURIED Stephen
    people LAMENTED/WEPT very much over him

> *The event idea "stayed" has now been included in the list of events. This idea was implicit – it could have been expressed as "did not scatter."*
>
> *The event "worship, honour" is not part of the main line of events. It is an embedded description of the people who buried Stephen.*
>
> *Some events have been re-ordered in the list, so that they are listed in the order in which they happened.*

STAGE 3: Rewrite showing the relationships

      Saul CONSENTED/AGREED
that (people) PUT Stephen TO DEATH

Event ideas, participants, and relationships

    (people) PERSECUTED the church (the believers/Christians) in Jerusalem
    (people) CAUSED the believers to SCATTER throughout the region of Judea and Samaria
the apostles (STAYED in Jerusalem)
People who WORSHIPPED/HONOURED (God)
        BURIED (the body of) Stephen
   and LAMENTED/WEPT very much for (his absence)

Consider this restatement reflecting the probable order in which the events happened:
> Saul consented that people put Stephen to death. People who worshipped God buried (the body of) Stephen, and lamented greatly. At that time people began to persecute the believers in Jerusalem, and caused them to scatter throughout the regions of Judea and Samaria. Only the apostles remained in Jerusalem.

> *The burial of Stephen's body would have happened very soon after his death. The event of the believers scattering throughout Judea and Samaria must have taken a period of time.*

> *This statement introduces the account of how the gospel spread to other regions. CEV reflects this by combining the mention of Stephen's burial (part of verse 2) with verse 1, and placing the rest of verse 2, referring to persecution and scattering, at the beginning of a new section. NLT does not change the order, but indicates a break in the order of events by placing brackets around the statement about Stephen's burial.*

Example 2

Luke 1:76–77

> 76 And you, child, will be called the prophet of the Most High; for you will go before the Lord to prepare his ways, 77 to give knowledge of salvation to his people in the forgiveness of their sins.

STAGE 1: List the event ideas

    CALL
    PROPHESY
    GO BEFORE
    PREPARE
    CAUSE TO KNOW
    SAVE
    FORGIVE
    SIN/DO EVIL THINGS

STAGE 2: Fill in the participants

  (people) will CALL you (something)
    (you) will PROPHESY (that is, proclaim a message from God)
    (God) (RULES/IS ABOVE) all
     you will GO BEFORE the Lord
     you will PREPARE the way for the Lord
    (you) will CAUSE the people of the Lord TO KNOW (something)

```
        (God)  SAVES his people
   (the Lord)  FORGIVES (his people)
(his people)  have SINNED/DONE evil things
```

STAGE 3: Rewrite showing the relationships

```
                    You, child,  people will CALL you
                                   "the person who SPEAKS OUT the message from (God)
                                       (God) who RULES/IS HIGH ABOVE all"
because                  you  WILL GO BEFORE the Lord
in order that            you  PREPARE the way for the Lord.
                    You  WILL CAUSE his people TO KNOW
                             how (God) SAVES (his people)
                             by means that he FORGIVES (them) for their sins.
```

"The Most High" is a title identifying the participant God, the one on whose behalf the child will speak.

Study the translation of Luke 1:76–77 in the *GNT* (below). Compare this with the *ESV*. What differences of form do you notice in the *GNT*?

⁷⁶ "You, my child, will be called a prophet of the Most High God.

You will go ahead of the Lord

    to prepare his road for him,

⁷⁷ to tell his people that they will be saved

    by having their sins forgiven.

Remember

When studying the meaning of a complex passage, follow these three steps:
1) List the *event* ideas and express them as verbs.
2) Fill in the *participants*.
3) Rewrite the passage in a way that shows the *relationships*, making these connections clear.

Exercise

For each of the following passages, follow the three steps illustrated above. Compare the translations in different Bible versions.

    a. Luke 24:46–47

    b. Acts 4:34–35

    c. Ephesians 1:7 (for advanced translators)

Additional resource on "Discovering the Meaning – Complex Passages"

BT4 online materials

30_Analysing_complex_passages.pptx

For further reading

Ettien, Koffi Nda. 1996. Translating the term "but" – unsuspected challenges. *The Bible Translator* 47(2):218–226. http://www.ubs-translations.org/tbt/1996/02/TBT199602.html?num=218&x=0&y=0&num1=.

Chapter 31

Discovering the Meaning – Order of Events

Events are not always told in the order in which they happened. Sometimes the writer doubles back to mention something that happened at an earlier time in the story. To show this change of time, the English language sometimes uses

- different verb tenses; or
- time words or phrases, such as "yesterday," "last year," or "before that."

In some languages it is clearer to tell the events of a story in the order in which they happen. Otherwise confusion may arise.

Example 1

Luke 10:34

[The Samaritan] went to him and bound up his wounds, pouring on oil and wine.

> *The oil and wine were poured onto the wounds before the wounds were bound, not afterwards! It may therefore be necessary to rearrange the order in translation: The Samaritan went to him, he took oil and wine, poured (them) on his wounds, then he bound the wounds.*
>
> *Alternatively, the order of events could be made clear by using connecting words: "went to him and bound the wounds, after pouring oil and wine on them."*

Example 2

Revelation 5:2

    ESV   Who is worthy to open the scroll and break its seals?
    GNT   Who is worthy to break the seals and open the scroll?
            The seals had to be broken before the scroll could be opened.

> **Remember**
>
> When events in the source text are not described in the order in which they happened, take special care. As you translate, it may sometimes be helpful to either
>
> 1) re-order to follow the actual order in which the events happened; or
> 2) check that there are other signals, such as connecting words, that make the order clear.

Exercise

In each of the following passages there is a possibility of misunderstanding. What adjustments would you suggest to avoid confusion?

a. Mark 1:43–44 – compare with Luke 5:14

And Jesus sternly charged him and sent him away at once, ⁴⁴ and said to him, "See that you say nothing to anyone, but go, show yourself to the priest and offer for your cleansing what Moses commanded, for a proof to them."

> *It is clear that Jesus spoke the words in verse 44 before he sent the healed leper away. NIV and NLT make this clear in the translation of verse 43:* Then Jesus sent him on his way with a stern warning.

b. Luke 8:37–38 – compare with Mark 5:18

Then all the people of the surrounding country of the Gerasenes asked him to depart from them, for they were seized with great fear. So he got into the boat and returned. ³⁸ The man from whom the demons had gone begged that he might be with him, but Jesus sent him away, saying. . . .

> *The parallel passage in Mark 5:18 makes it clear that the action described in Luke 8:38 happened as Jesus was getting into the boat, preparing to depart.*

c. Luke 19:12–13 – compare *ESV* and *GNT* versions

d. Acts 28:14–16 – compare *ESV* and *CEV* versions

Is it appropriate to reorder verses?

In some English versions, you will see that occasionally two verses are combined and the content re-arranged within them. For an example, see *GNT* Acts 13:32–33. You will see that the verse numbers 32 and 33 are written together because the two verses have been combined and rearranged in the translation. Compare this with the *ESV* and notice the differences.

Other passages where two or more verses have been rearranged or combined in the *GNT* are Numbers 14:36–37 and Joshua 6:12–13.

It is permissible to combine verses in this way if the re-ordering helps achieve a clearer and more accurate translation. Combine or re-order verses only occasionally, when this is necessary to avoid wrong meaning or confusion. Any re-ordering of longer passages should be done with caution. Discuss this with your translation consultant.

Example

Mark 6:17–18

> ¹⁷ For it was Herod who had sent and seized John and bound him in prison for the sake of Herodias, his brother Philip's wife, because he had married her. ¹⁸ For John had been saying to Herod, "It is not lawful for you to have your brother's wife."

> ¹⁷⁻¹⁸ Herod had earlier married Herodias, the wife of his brother Philip. But John had told him, "It isn't right for you to take your brother's wife!" So, in order to please Herodias, Herod arrested John and put him in prison. (*CEV*)

Study Mark 6:17–18 in its context. Mark 6:17-29 is an account of the death of John the Baptist, which happened before Jesus began his ministry in Galilee (see Mark 1:14). In this passage, there is doubling back in the order of the events of the story. The translator can gain a clearer understanding of what happened by listing the events in the order in which they happened.

In the *ESV*, the events are told in the following order:

1. Herod sent (men)
2. (men) seized John
3. (men) tied up John
4. (men) put (John) in prison
5. Herodias caused/incited (Herod) ["for the sake of Herodias"]
6. Herodias was the wife of (Philip)
7. Philip was the brother of King Herod
8. (Herod) married (Herodias)
9. John said to Herod
10. "It is not right
11. that you took/snatched the wife of your brother."

In the following rearrangement of the verses, background information is stated first. The events of the story are then arranged in the order in which they happened. (The numbers refer to the original order above):

7. the brother of King Herod was Philip
6. the wife of (Philip) was (Herodias)

THEN

8. (Herod) married (Herodias) – he took his brother's wife and married her

BECAUSE OF THIS

9. John said to Herod:
11. "You took/snatched the wife of your brother.
10. That is not right."

THEREFORE

5. Herodias caused/incited (Herod):

SO THAT

1. Herod sent (men)
2. (men) seized John

4. (men) put (John) in prison
3. (men) tied up (John)

Notice the order of the last two events. The meaning is probably that, after being put in prison, John was chained to the wall. This was the custom at that time.

CEV has reflected this chronological order of the events, combining verses 17 and 18:

> Herod had earlier married Herodias, the wife of his brother Philip. But John had told him, "It isn't right for you to take your brother's wife!" So, in order to please Herodias, Herod arrested John and put him in prison.

Chapter 32

Discovering the Meaning – Long and Short Sentences

The Greek text sometimes has long sentences. The *ESV* follows the Greek structure closely and keeps these long sentences in the English translation.

In many languages, it is good style to have shorter sentences, or, when sentences are longer, to simplify the structure. In re-expressing the meaning in the receptor language, it is sometimes helpful to break up some of the original long sentences into several shorter sentences.

Some modern English translations, like the *GNT* and *NLT*, have broken some of the long sentences into shorter sentences, as the examples below show.

Exercise

Compare the translation of the following passages in *ESV* and *GNT*: For each passage, what do you notice about the following:

(1) the number of sentences?

(2) the length of the sentences?

(3) the grammatical patterns of the sentences in the two versions?

    a. Luke 1:1–4

    b. Luke 15:3–4

    c. Romans 1:1–7 (for advanced translators)

    d. 2 Kings 23:16; 25:18–19

    e. Jeremiah 40:7–8

Take time to study the natural sentence structures of the receptor language. Observe different patterns used in different kinds of text. There may also be different patterns – sometimes shorter sentences – at the climax of a text. Follow these natural patterns of the receptor language as you translate. Chapters 38 and 40 give suggestions on how to make this study.

> Keep observing natural sentence patterns in texts in your own language. Keep a notebook or a named computer file to record what you observe.

Part 5

Figures of Speech and Other Challenges

Chapter 33

Figures of Speech – Comparisons

A *figure of speech* is a special way of saying something with an implied meaning beyond the literal meaning of the words. What is said is not intended to be taken literally but to catch the attention of the hearer, to emphasise or clarify a point, and to stimulate a response.

There are many different types of figures of speech in the Bible. In this chapter we will focus on metaphors and similes, which involve comparisons. In chapter 34, other types of figures of speech will be illustrated and discussed.

33.1 Introducing simile and metaphor

A *simile* is a figure of speech that involves a comparison.

> His car rattles like a sack of tin cans.
> *"his car" is being compared to "a sack of tin cans." The similarity is in the noise it makes.*
> Sugar is sweet, and so are you.
> *"you" are being compared to "sugar," something that is good to experience.*
> I'm as hungry as a horse.
> *"my hunger" (implied) is being compared to that of a horse.*
> My feet are colder than ice.
> *"my feet" are being compared to "ice."*
> He ran like the wind.
> *"his running" is being compared to "the wind."*

A *metaphor* is also a comparison. The difference between a simile and a metaphor is that *in a simile it is explicitly stated that it is a comparison*, usually by words such as "like" or "as," while *in a metaphor the comparison is implied*.

Genesis 49:27	Benjamin is a ravenous wolf; in the morning devouring the prey, and at evening dividing the spoil.
NIV	Benjamin is a ravenous wolf; in the morning he devours the prey, in the evening he divides the plunder.

> *ESV and NIV use the form of a metaphor, as in the original Hebrew text, to compare Benjamin with a wolf.*
>
> GNT   Benjamin is like a vicious wolf. Morning and evening he kills and devours.
>
> *GNT uses the form of a simile, making it explicit that this is a comparison.*

More examples of metaphor:

> My feet are blocks of ice!
>
> John is a tower of strength to me.
>
> That child really is a greedy little pig!
>
> Fear not, you worm Jacob, you men of Israel! (Isaiah 41:14)
>
> You brood of vipers! Who warned you to flee from the wrath to come? (Matthew 3:7)

Exercise 1

Mark all examples of comparisons, both simile and metaphor, in the following passage:

> John wandered aimlessly along the road. The sun was as hot as fire, and the sharp stones seemed to cut through his thin shoes like knives. His throat was as dry as the dust which covered everything, and he longed for a drink of cool fresh water. Suddenly, he saw Atamba coming towards him, the man whom everyone called, "The Lion of the Desert."

Exercise 2

In your own language, give examples of three similes and/or metaphors that are commonly used in everyday speech.

33.2 For what purpose are metaphors (and other comparisons) used?

Metaphors and other comparisons are used

1) as illustrations, to clarify or explain an idea by comparing it with something;
2) to catch the attention of the hearer and make the message more vivid and memorable to him;
3) to give rise to implications and associations that can be expanded and discussed, encouraging people to think creatively;
4) to involve the hearer in interpreting the meaning – the hearer uses the memory of his past experiences to recall possible implications; and
5) to arouse a response in the hearers.

Metaphors are often used for poetic effect. The more appropriate and original the metaphor, the more powerful its impact will be.

33.3 How to discover the meaning of a metaphor or simile

Metaphors and similes have three parts:

1) The "topic" (what is being talked about),
2) The "illustration" (the concept to which the topic is compared)

3) The "point of similarity" (the way or ways in which the topic and the illustration are similar).

For example, in the example mentioned above from Genesis 49:27, *Benjamin is a ravenous wolf,*

the topic is *Benjamin*. It is Benjamin who is being talked about.
the illustration is *a hungry wolf*. Benjamin is being compared to a hungry wolf.
the point of similarity is that both Benjamin and a hungry wolf are *fierce and destructive.*

Examples

1. For the simile, "the sun was as hot as fire"
   the topic is   *the sun*
   the illustration is   *fire*
   the point of similarity is   *hot* (both the sun and fire are hot)

2. For the metaphor, "that child really is a greedy pig"
   the topic is   *that child*
   the illustration is   *a pig*
   the point of similarity is   *greedy* (both the child and a pig are greedy)

3. For the simile, "swift as an arrow from the bow the child darted into the house"
   the topic is   *the way that the child moved*
   the illustration is   *the way that an arrow comes from a bow*
   the point of similarity is   *speed, fast, and in a straight line*

The three parts of a metaphor or simile can be expressed in a sentence:

The *topic* is like the *illustration*
    because they both share a certain quality that is known as the *point of similarity.*
The *sun* is like *fire*
    because both are *hot.*
That *child* is like a *pig*
    because both are *greedy.*

At this point our focus is on how to discover the meaning of a metaphor or simile. How to translate metaphors and similes will be discussed later.

These examples show the three parts; topic, illustration, and point of similarity:

The child is as clever as a monkey.
    The child is like a monkey, because both are clever.
Fast as lightning, the train sped through the night.
    The train speeding through the night is like lightning, because both move fast.
The water shone in the sunlight like glass.
    The water in the sunlight is like glass, because both reflect the light brightly.
The food tasted bitter like medicine.
    The food tastes like medicine, because both are bitter.

Exercise 3

For each of the following comparisons, compare the translations in different English Bible versions, studying the context. Identify the three parts: topic, illustration, and point of similarity.

a. For you are my rock and my fortress. (Psalm 71:3b)
b. The righteous flourish like the palm tree
   and grow like a cedar in Lebanon. (Psalm 92:12)
c. Blessed be the LORD, my rock,
   who trains my hands for war,
   and my fingers for battle;
   ² he is my steadfast love and my fortress,
   my stronghold and my deliverer,
   my shield and he in whom I take refuge,
   who subdues peoples under me. (Psalm 144:1–2)
d. For the heavens vanish like smoke. (Isaiah 51:6)
e. All we like sheep have gone astray. (Isaiah 53:6)
f. descendants as many as the stars of heaven (Hebrews 11:12)
g. For you are a mist that appears for a little time and then vanishes. (James 4:14)
h. The hairs of his head were white like wool, as white as snow. (Revelation 1:14)

Remember

Every metaphor and simile has three parts:
1) The *topic* – what is being talked about;
2) The *illustration* – the concept to which the topic is compared; and
3) The *point of similarity* – the way or ways in which the topic and the illustration are similar.

33.4 One of the three parts may not be stated explicitly

Examples

Consider examples of comparisons where one of the three parts is not stated explicitly.

Psalm 25:15	My eyes are ever toward the LORD, for he will pluck my feet out of the net.
GNT	I look to the LORD for help at all times, and he rescues me from danger.
CEV	I always look to you, because you rescue me from every trap.

The topic is the danger in which the speaker finds himself. The illustration is of a person whose feet are entangled in a net, and he is unable to free himself. The point of similarity is the impossibility of escape – except through action of the LORD as saviour.

Luke 17:6   And the Lord said, "If you had faith like a grain of mustard seed, you could say to this mulberry tree, 'Be uprooted and planted in the sea,' and it would obey you."

GNT   The Lord answered, "If you had faith as big as a mustard seed, you could say to this mulberry tree, 'Pull yourself up by the roots and plant yourself in the sea!' and it would obey you."

NLT   The Lord answered, "If you had faith even as small as a mustard seed, you could say to this mulberry tree, 'May you be uprooted and thrown into the sea!' and it would obey you!"

In passages where mustard seed is mentioned as an illustration of how something small can grow large (Matthew 13:31–32, Mark 4: 30–32, Luke 13:18–19) the point of similarity is explicit in the original text. Here in Luke 17:6 the teaching point is different. Jesus is encouraging the apostles to increase their faith by assuring them that even a small amount of faith can have huge results. NIV, NLT, and GNT all make the point of similarity explicit in Luke 17:6, perhaps because the translators were aware that many English speakers do not know that mustard seed is small. Compare GNT "as big as" and NLT "even as small as."

1 Peter 1:22–25   Having purified your souls by your obedience to the truth for a sincere brotherly love, love one another earnestly from a pure heart, [23] since you have been born again, not of perishable seed but of imperishable, through the living and abiding word of God; [24] for
"All flesh is like grass and all its glory like the flower of grass.
The grass withers, and the flower falls,
[25] but the word of the Lord remains forever."
And this word is the good news that was preached to you.

The point of similarity between "flesh," referring to human beings, and "grass" and "wild flowers" is that all die. This is clearly understood from (a) the context and (b) the hearer's knowledge about grass and wild flowers.

Sometimes all three parts of the simile or metaphor are openly stated in the text. Sometimes one part (or even two) is left implicit. Quite often the point of similarity is left implicit.

Exercise 4

For each of the following comparisons, find the three parts, topic, illustration, and point of similarity, and re-express the meaning in English. If any of the three parts is not explicit in the source text, state it explicitly in your answer, indicating that you have made it explicit by putting brackets [ ] around that part. Look up the context in your Bible, comparing different Bible versions.

a. Your word is a lamp to my feet and a light to my path. (Psalm 119:105)
b. Like a gold ring in a pig's snout is a beautiful woman without discretion. (Proverbs 11:22)
c. A word fitly spoken is like apples of gold in a setting of silver. (Proverbs 25:11)
d. I have blotted out your transgressions like a cloud and your sins like mist. (Isaiah 44:22) *Compare with Job 7:9.*
e. But now, O LORD, you are our Father; we are the clay, and you are our potter; we are all the work of your hand. (Isaiah 64:8)
f. You are the salt of the earth, but if salt has lost its taste, how shall its saltiness be restored? (Matthew 5:13)

g. if you have faith like a grain of mustard seed (Matthew 17:20)
h. I will make you become fishers of men. (Mark 1:17)
i. Jesus said to them, "I am the bread of life; whoever comes to me shall not hunger, and whoever believes in me shall not thirst." (John 6:35)
j. And the tongue is a fire, a world of unrighteousness. (James 3:6)

33.5 How to find the correct point(s) of similarity

The correct understanding of any metaphor or simile depends on finding the *point of similarity* between the *topic* and the *illustration*. The topic and the illustration are not similar in all parts of their meaning, but only in a particular part (or component) of their meaning, or in a certain set of components.

In different contexts, different components of meaning may be in focus. For example, in each of the passages quoted below, the illustration is "sheep," but the point of similarity is different in each passage.

Psalm 95:7   For he is our God, and we are the people of his pasture, and the <u>sheep</u> of his hand.

NIV   and we are the people of his pasture, the flock under his care.

Point of similarity: God looks after us just as a shepherd looks after his sheep.

Isaiah 53:6   All we like <u>sheep</u> have gone astray; we have turned—every one—to his own way.

Point of similarity: We leave the path we should be following and we get lost, just as sheep ignore the shepherd's guidance and get lost.

Isaiah 53:7   Like a <u>sheep</u> that before its shearers is silent, so he opened not his mouth.

Point of similarity: The Lord did not protest or speak loudly against those who came against him.

Jeremiah 12:3   Pull them out like <u>sheep</u> for the slaughter, and set them apart for the day of slaughter.

Point of similarity: Take control (of those who do evil), remove them and set them apart until the time when they will be killed.

Micah 2:12   I will set them together like <u>sheep</u> in a fold, like a flock in its pasture, a noisy multitude of men.

Point of similarity: The people of Israel will be brought back into the land, they will be many, crowded together, making a noise.
Like a pasture full of sheep, your land will once again be filled with many people. (GNT)

Matthew 10:16   Behold, I am sending you out like <u>sheep</u> in the midst of wolves.

Point of similarity: you will be weak and defenceless, in a dangerous situation.
Listen! I am sending you out just like sheep to a pack of wolves. (GNT)

Clearly, there is danger of misunderstanding, sometimes serious misunderstanding, if the hearer focuses on the wrong component of meaning.

> Revelation 3:3   I will come like a thief, and you will not know at what hour I will come against you.
>
> *The meaning is that Jesus will come unexpectedly. His coming is not like the coming of a thief in other ways.*
>
> Matthew 28:3   His appearance was like lightning.
>
> *In English, we tend to associate "lightning" with speed, as in the expression "as quick as lightning"; in the context of Matthew 28:3, however, it is the brightness of lightning that is in focus. The context makes this clear, and the parallel passage in Luke 24:4 confirms it.*
>
> John 1:29   Behold, the Lamb of God, who takes away the sin of the world!
>
> *The point of similarity between Jesus and the lamb is that, in the religion of the Jews, the lamb was the animal sacrificed to atone for sins, the sacrificial lamb itself being without any blemish. Compare with 1 Peter 1:18–19: "you were ransomed…with the precious blood of Christ, like that of a lamb without blemish or spot." The significance of John's statement is often missed.*

An author may use the same metaphor in different ways in different contexts, to teach different points. For example, Paul uses the metaphor of the church as the body of Christ in several passages: In Colossians 1:18 and 2:19, the "head" of the body is Christ. But in 1 Corinthians 12:21, the head is listed as one of the parts of the body. An author develops his illustration according to the specific point that he wants to teach in that passage.

33.6 More about the point of similarity

Sometimes the *point of similarity* is itself expressed as a metaphor. In this case it may be necessary to make the comparison more explicit.

Examples

> Mark 1:17   I will make you become fishers of men.
>
> ⇒   *you will seek people to bring them to follow me (Jesus Christ), like fishermen going out to catch fish.*
>
> CEV   I will teach you how to bring in people instead of fish.
>
> Hebrews 4:12   For the word of God is…sharper than any two-edged sword, piercing to the division of soul and spirit, of joints and of marrow, and discerning the thoughts and intentions of the heart.
>
> ⇒   *The word of God penetrates the lives of people, revealing spiritual truths at the deepest level, just as a sharp two-edged sword cuts cleanly and deeply.*

33.7 How to translate metaphors and similes

So far this discussion of metaphors and similes has been concerned with how to discover the meaning correctly. In translating metaphors and similes, follow these guidelines:

1) The illustration should be kept, if at all possible.
2) Make sure that it is clear to the reader that a comparison is being made. In the case of a metaphor it may sometimes be necessary to express the comparison in the form of a simile, making the fact that it is a comparison clear.

    Genesis 49:17   Dan shall be a serpent in the way.
    ⇒   *Dan shall be like a serpent in the way.*

3) Make sure that the full meaning of the three parts is clear. When the reader of the original text read the text, he was able to understand that a comparison was being made and to recognise the point of the comparison. This was true even where one part of the three parts was left implicit. In the translation the same information should be communicated to the receptor language hearer. If it is necessary for accurate and clear communication, information that was implicit in the original text may be made explicit in the translation.
4) Keep alert for concepts that may be unknown to the receptor language audience.
5) Certain illustrations are used multiple times in Scripture, including places where illustrations in the Old Testament are quoted or echoed in the New Testament. Check cross references to make sure the illustration is translated consistently, wherever possible.

33.8 Cross-cultural challenges in translating comparisons

As we have already seen, the point of similarity between the topic and illustration is sometimes left implicit. The clues to correct interpretation are found in

a) the immediate context; or
b) the shared background knowledge of the speaker and the hearer.

When the message is translated, however, it is then being received by people whose cultural background is different from that of the original giver of the message. There are some background facts that the receivers of the translated message do not know, or that they understand in a different way. This is particularly true where the illustration is an unknown idea in the receptor language area. If the illustration is unknown, special care is needed to make sure that the receptor language audience understands the point of similarity that the original author intended.

Examples

The first three examples below illustrate passages where the illustration may be an unknown idea in the receptor language culture.

Matthew 18:17   And if [your brother] refuses to listen even to the church, let him be to you as a Gentile and a tax collector.

The point here is that Gentiles and tax collectors were both avoided by the Jews. The Jews avoided the Gentiles because they were not members of God's chosen people. And they avoided the tax collectors because, though Jews, they cooperated with the hated Romans who had occupied Palestine. This point of similarity might need to be made explicit in the translation: If your brother refuses to listen even to the church, avoid him as you would avoid a Gentile or a tax collector.

Acts 26:14 It is hard for you to kick against the goads.

In Palestine, people used a stick with a sharp point at the end to drive cows or oxen along. If the animal resisted, it would, of course, hurt itself more against the sharp point. For areas where such a custom is unknown, some information needs to be made explicit: You are hurting yourself by hitting back, like an ox kicking against its owner's stick. (GNT)

1 Peter 2:6 Behold, I am laying in Zion a stone, a cornerstone chosen and precious.

The idea of a "cornerstone" may be unknown to people who build their houses using materials other than stone. Ephesians 2:19–20 explains something of the function of the cornerstone: "Christ Jesus himself being the cornerstone, in whom the whole structure is joined together." The cornerstone was the most important stone in the building, with which the other stones were interlocked, and which therefore held the building together.

In translating this verse, it is necessary to consider the way in which houses in the receptor language area are built. Try these possibilities:

1) Substitute whatever might be the equivalent key part of the structure of a house, for example, the central pole of a round house. (This solution might have some problems because of other references to Christ as the "stone," as for example in Ephesians 2:19–20 and following verses.)

2) Make explicit the function of the cornerstone; for example, the most important stone, or a stone in relation to which all the other stones are fitted firmly in their place.

The following examples illustrate passages where the translator may need to make it clear that a comparison is being made:

2 Corinthians 11:8 I robbed other churches by accepting support from them in order to serve you.

NLT I "robbed" other churches by accepting their contributions so I could serve you at no cost.

GNT While I was working among you, I was paid by other churches. I was robbing them, so to speak, in order to help you.

NLT signals that "robbing" is not meant to be taken literally by the use of quotation marks. The quotation marks may be overlooked, however, and will not be heard when the translation is read aloud. GNT uses the phrase "so to speak" to make it clear that this does not refer to literal robbery.

Romans 3:13 The venom of asps is under their lips.

GNT And dangerous threats, like snake's poison, roll from their lips.

The GNT translation is still figurative. An alternative might be:
The words they speak are like the poison of deadly snakes, bringing death.

The following examples illustrate passages where information may need to be made explicit to express the message clearly:

Acts 2:20 The moon [shall be turned] into blood.

GNT The moon will turn red as blood.

Compare also Revelation 6:12: "The moon turned blood red."

1 Corinthians 15:54	Death is swallowed up in victory.
GNT	Death is destroyed; victory is complete.
⇒	*People won't die anymore; they will live forever.*
Colossians 1:18	And he is the head of the body, the church.
⇒	*The relationship between Christ and his church is like that of the head to the body.*

In the following examples the illustration has sometimes been dropped in the translation, and the point of similarity made explicit. Compare the following translations:

Matthew 5:6	Blessed are those who hunger and thirst for righteousness.
GNT	Happy are those whose greatest desire is to do what God requires.

One language: Blessed are those who have a burning desire to do what pleases God. This version uses a different metaphor to express the same meaning.

Matthew 12:39	An evil and adulterous generation
GNT	How evil and godless are the people of this day!

For the original hearers, the mention of "adultery" would call to mind the Old Testament comparison of God's people being like a wife who commits adultery because they leave God and follow other gods.

33.9 A warning

It is not always best to make the point of similarity explicit. Sometimes making the point explicit would lessen its impact. It may also limit the meaning – often there are several points of similarity and to make only one explicit would communicate only part of the total meaning.

In some passages there is repetition of an idea using more than one metaphor to illustrate the point. Beware of lessening, or destroying, this impact through clumsy translation.

Feed my lambs.... Tend my sheep.... Feed my sheep. (John 21:15, 16, 17)

Who makes his angels winds, and his servants flames of fire. (Hebrews 1:7)

It may be unhelpful, or indeed impossible, to make explicit in what ways angels are similar to "winds" and to "flames of fire." Try to retain the stylistic and emotional impact of the original figure of speech. Be sensitive to what is appropriate in each context.

In some contexts, the obscurity of the original metaphor should be retained because it was obscure to the original hearers:

Beware of the leaven of the Pharisees and the leaven of Herod. (Mark 8:15)

It is clear from the following discussion that the disciples did not understand what Jesus meant. A similar misunderstanding occurs in John 11:11–12:

After saying these things, he said to them, "Our friend Lazarus has fallen asleep, but I go to awaken him." [12] The disciples said to him, "Lord, if he has fallen asleep, he will recover." (John 11:11)

Exercise 5

For each of the passages below, do the following:

(1) Find the three parts: topic, illustration, and point of similarity. Look up each passage in its context.

(2) Translate the passage (just the part quoted below) into your own language in a way that makes the meaning clear. Give a back translation in English.

  a. But you, O LORD, are a shield about me. (Psalm 3:3)

  b. Save me from all my pursuers, and deliver me, ² lest like a lion they tear my soul apart. (Psalm 7:1–2)

  c. [The nations] surrounded me like bees. (Psalm 118:12)

  d. A continual dripping on a rainy day and a quarrelsome wife are alike. (Proverbs 27:15)

  e. [John] was a burning and shining lamp. (John 5:35)

  f. [Jesus said], "I am the door. If anyone enters by me, he will be saved and will go in and out and find pasture." (John 10:9)

  g. [Jesus again said to them,] "I am the good shepherd. The good shepherd lays down his life for the sheep." (John 10:11)

  h. I know that after my departure fierce wolves will come in among you, not sparing the flock. (Acts 20:29)

33.10 Dead metaphors

A "dead metaphor" is a phrase that may have once been a metaphor, but in which there is now no comparison intended. Metaphors become dead through being used very commonly, so that they become fixed forms. A dead metaphor is a kind of idiom. For example,

  a leg of a chair

  a key to the problem

  a smooth-tongued person

  a flaming temper

In a dead metaphor no comparison is intended. Such phrases can be translated as idioms, with no attempt to retain a comparison.

33.11 Extended metaphors

Metaphors are sometimes extended and developed. Consider, for example, Ephesians 6:13–17. The same principle of analysing the three parts can be applied.

Topic	Illustration	Point of similarity
what God gives us to protect us and for us to fight with	armour	for protection and for fighting
truth	fastened on the belt of truth	a person preparing himself for action
righteousness	breastplate	protects (the soul and spirit)

gospel (which causes) peace	putting on shoes	a person preparing himself to travel with a message
faith	shield	protects (the soul and spirit)
attacks of Satan	fiery darts	are dangerous
salvation	helmet	protects (a person's spiritual life)
word of God	sword	for attacking the spiritual enemy

Parables are also a kind of extended metaphor. Study, for example, the parable of The Sower in Mark 4:3–8, and the explanation of the meaning in 4:13–20.

Exercise 6 (for advanced translators)

Identify the three parts, topic, illustration, and point of similarity, in the following extended metaphors:

John 15:1–8

1 Corinthians 12:12–27

2 Timothy 2:3–6

33.12 Translation practice exercise

Identify the figurative language of this psalm. Think through the meaning, comparing different Bible versions. Then translate the psalm into your own language.

Psalm 1:1–6

> Blessed is the man who walks not in the counsel of the wicked,
>> nor stands in the way of sinners,
>> nor sits in the seat of scoffers;
> ² but his delight is in the law of the LORD,
>> and on his law he meditates day and night.
> ³ He is like a tree planted by streams of water
>> that yields its fruit in its season,
>> and its leaf does not wither.
>> In all that he does, he prospers.
> ⁴ The wicked are not so, but are like chaff that the wind drives away.
> ⁵ Therefore the wicked will not stand in the judgment,
>> nor sinners in the congregation of the righteous;
> ⁶ for the LORD knows the way of the righteous,
>> but the way of the wicked will perish.

> **Remember**
>
> When translating comparisons, do the following:
> 1) First find the three parts: *topic, illustration,* and *point of similarity*.
>   a) the *topic* – what is being talked about
>   b) the *illustration* – the concept to which the topic is compared
>   c) the *point of similarity* – the way or ways in which both the topic and the illustration are the same
> 2) Translate in a way that enables the new audience to understand both the picture that the author paints, and the point of comparison that the author aims to communicate.

Additional resources on "Figures of Speech – Comparisons"

BT4 online materials

33_Figures_of_speech_1-Introduction.pptx
33_Figures_of_speech_2-Metaphor_and_simile.pptx

For further reading

Kroneman, Dick. 2004. The LORD is my shepherd: An exploration into the theory and practice of translating biblical metaphor 2 vols. PhD dissertation. Amsterdam: Free University. Highly recommended for in-depth study on the translation of metaphors.

Chapter 34

Other Figures of Speech

34.1 Different types of figures of speech

In chapter 33, we looked at metaphors and similes, which are figures of speech that involve a comparison. Metaphors and similes are often used to illustrate and clarify an idea and to catch the attention of the audience.

Here are a few examples of other kinds of figures of speech:

> The whole world came to the meeting.
>
> I was shattered!
>
> He closed his ears to what I was saying.
>
> The wind moaned in the trees.

Some of the purposes for which such figures of speech are used:

- For emphasis
- To indicate a certain attitude that the speaker has
- To catch the attention of the hearer
- To arouse an emotional response in the hearer, for example, surprise, disapproval, or sympathy
- For stylistic variation

Every language and culture has different kinds of figures of speech. The seven kinds of figures of speech that are described in this chapter are found in the original Hebrew and Greek texts of the Bible. The receptor language may not have the same kinds of figures of speech.

In the discussion below, the technical name for each kind of figure of speech is given. It is not essential for the translator to remember the different technical names, although it may be useful to do so.

What is important is that the translator can (1) recognise that a figure of speech is being used, (2) recognise its purpose, and (3) understand the meaning and impact that the original author intended to communicate.

34.2 Euphemism

A *euphemism* is the use of a mild or indirect expression instead of words or phrases that would seem harsh or embarrassing to the hearers.

The *purpose* of using a euphemism is to avoid being offensive or disrespectful. For example,

> David…fell asleep and was laid with his fathers. (Acts 13:36)

"Fell asleep" is an indirect way of saying "he died."

Each language has its own euphemisms, the meanings of which are quite clear to a first-language speaker of the language. But someone who is learning the language may be very puzzled, especially if he does not recognise that a figure of speech is being used.

If euphemisms are translated word-for-word into another language, they may be quite meaningless, or may communicate wrong meaning. Or they may be highly offensive.

Different cultures have their own customs about what can be mentioned directly without giving offense or embarrassment, and what can only be mentioned indirectly. One culture may use euphemisms to refer to something that another culture speaks about directly.

Euphemisms may be either *positive* – something is considered too holy or too respected to be mentioned directly. Or they may be *negative* – something is not mentioned directly because it is either frightening or embarrassing.

Examples

In Jewish culture, many different titles were used *to refer to God*, focusing on different aspects of his wonderful nature. In the following examples the underlined words are all euphemisms referring to God.

a.	Matthew 26:64	Jesus said to him, "You have said so. But I tell you, from now on you will see the Son of Man seated at the right hand of <u>Power</u> and coming on the clouds of heaven."
	NIV	at the right hand of <u>the Mighty One</u> and coming on the clouds of heaven.
	GNT	at the right side of <u>the Almighty</u>
b.	Mark 14:61	But he remained silent and made no answer. Again the high priest asked him, "Are you the Christ, the Son of <u>the Blessed</u>?"
	GNT	the Son of <u>the Blessed God</u>
	CEV	the Son of <u>the glorious God</u>
c.	Luke 15:18	I will arise and go to my father, and I will say to him, "Father, I have sinned against <u>heaven</u> and before you."
	GNT	against <u>God</u> and against you

Also in Jewish culture, as in many other cultures, *sexual relations* are referred to by euphemisms. The following examples are quoted first from the *ESV*, which follows closely the original text form:

d.	Genesis 4:1	Now Adam <u>knew</u> Eve his wife.
	NIV	Adam <u>made love to</u> his wife Eve.
	GNT	Adam <u>had intercourse</u> with his wife.

e. Matthew 1:24–25 [Joseph] When Joseph woke from sleep, he did as the angel of the Lord commanded him: he took his wife, ²⁵ but <u>knew her not</u> until she had given birth to a son.

    NIV   He <u>did not consummate their marriage</u> until she gave birth to a son.

    GNT   He <u>had no sexual relations</u> with her before she gave birth to her son.

In English culture, as well as in many other cultures, euphemisms are used *to refer to death*. Some examples are "to pass away," "to be taken," "to be no more," "to go to a better world," "to sleep one's last sleep," "to be deceased."

Euphemisms are also used to refer to *physical/bodily functions*. Some of these examples would only be used in informal conversation:

    Going to the restroom

    Going to pay a call

    Going to the loo

    Going to the john

    Going to be excused

When he had gone, the servants came, and when they saw that the doors of the roof chamber were locked, they thought, "Surely he is <u>relieving himself</u> in the closet of the cool chamber." (Judges 3:24)

In some African cultures, euphemisms are used *to refer to a chief*. An example from Twi (Ghana): *Nana ko akuraa* 'grandfather (referring to the chief) has gone to the village'.

Exercise 1

List and explain five euphemisms from your own language.

How to translate euphemisms

1) Keep alert to recognise when a euphemism is being used in the source text. Make sure that you have understood the actual meaning.
2) Be sensitive to what is acceptable in the receptor language culture.
   - Sometimes a euphemism in the source text should be translated by a direct form in the receptor language.
   - Sometimes a euphemism in the source text has to be translated by a euphemism in the receptor language that is different in form but has the same meaning in the receptor culture.
   - Sometimes something that is referred to directly in the source text may have to be translated by a euphemism in the receptor language in order to avoid causing offense in the receptor culture.

Exercise 2

In each of the following passages there is a euphemism.

(1) Mark the euphemism.

(2) Look up each passage in its context and compare translations in different Bible versions.

(3) Write down the expression you would use in your own language to translate this meaning, whether figurative (e.g., as a euphemism) or non-figurative.
   a. And you…will be called the prophet of the Most High. (Luke 1:76)
   b. Mary…who was with child. (Luke 2:5)
   c. a woman of the city, who was a sinner (Luke 7:37)
   d. And having said this he breathed his last. (Luke 23:46)
   e. And [Abram] went in to Hagar, and she conceived. (Genesis 16:4)
   f. Let not my lord be angry that I cannot rise before you, for the way of women is upon me. (Genesis 31:35)

34.3 Litotes

A *litotes* is an emphatic statement made by saying that the opposite idea is <u>not</u> true. The purpose of litotes is usually *emphasis*. For example,

> Acts 20:12   And they took the youth away alive, and were not a little comforted.
>
> NIV   The people took the young man home alive and were greatly comforted.

In some languages, it may be necessary to express the emphasis by using an emphatic positive form, rather than by using a negative.

Exercise 3

Each of the following passages contains an example of a litotes.

(1) Mark the litotes. Compare translations in *NIV*, *GNT*, *NLT*, and *CEV*.
(2) Imagine you are translating into a language that does not use litotes. Re-express the meaning in a direct way. Be careful to keep the emphasis.
   a. I will multiply them, and they shall not be few; I will make them honoured, and they shall not be small. (Jeremiah 30:19)
   b. You are not far from the kingdom of God. (Mark 12:34)
   c. For nothing will be impossible with God. (Luke 1:37)
   d. And they remained no little time with the disciples. (Acts 14:28)
   e. Many of them therefore believed, with not a few Greek women of high standing as well as men. (Acts 17:12)
   f. About that time there arose no little disturbance concerning the Way. (Acts 19:23)
   g. I am a Jew, from Tarsus in Cilicia, a citizen of no obscure city. (Acts 21:39)
   h. I was not disobedient to the heavenly vision. (Acts 26:19)
   i. They make much of you, but for no good purpose. (Galatians 4:17)
   j. I do not cease to give thanks for you. (Ephesians 1:16)

34.4 Hyperbole

Hyperbole is a deliberate exaggeration, an overstatement, used for *emphasis* and *dramatic effect*, not intended to be understood literally. For example,

> "I'm starving" commonly means, "I am very, very hungry."
>
> "I'm frozen to death" means, "I am very cold."

"For John came neither eating nor drinking." (Matthew 11:18)

Clearly, John the Baptist did in fact eat and drink. In Mark 1:6 it is mentioned that he ate locusts and wild honey. The point is that John ate very simply, often fasted, and drank no wine.

Some languages do not use this figure of speech. If a hyperbole is translated word-for-word into such a language, it may be understood to mean what it literally says. A translator would need to express the actual meaning, retaining the emphasis of the original.

In Jur Mödö (South Sudan) this was translated, "John came here fasting, and not drinking anything strong (that is, alcoholic)."

Exercise 4

Each of the following passages contains a hyperbole. Re-express the meaning of each passage avoiding the use of hyperbole but keeping the emphasis of the original. Check the context where necessary and compare translations in other English versions.

a. Numbers 13:27   They told (Moses), "We came to the land to which you sent us. It flows with milk and honey, and this is its fruit."

A reference to the promise God had given to Moses, quoted in Exodus 3:8 and other references.

b. 1 Samuel 18:7   And the women sang to one another as they celebrated, "Saul has struck down his thousands, and David his ten thousands."

c. Matthew 25:29   For to everyone who has will more be given, and he will have an abundance. But from the one who has not, even what he has will be taken away.

d. Luke 15:24   "For this son of mine was dead and is alive again; he was lost and is found." And they began to celebrate.

e. John 3:32–33   He bears witness to what he has seen and heard, yet no one receives his testimony. [33] Whoever receives his testimony sets his seal to this, that God is true.

f. John 12:19   So the Pharisees said to one another, "You see that you are gaining nothing. Look, the world has gone after him."

34.5 Sarcasm and irony

Sarcasm involves the expression of *strong feeling* on the part of the speaker, often in a taunting or insulting way. It may sometimes also involve saying one thing but meaning the opposite. It is used to rebuke or ridicule someone. For example,

Mark 7:9   And he said to them, "You have a fine way of rejecting the commandment of God, in order to keep your tradition!"

The context makes it clear that Jesus was rebuking the Pharisees and scribes strongly for what they were doing.

"Irony" involves openly *pretending to adopt someone else's point of view*, while in fact you hold the opposite opinion.

2 Samuel 6:20   But when David returned to bless his household, Michal the daughter of Saul came out to meet David and said, "How the king of Israel honored himself today, uncovering himself today in the eyes of his servants' female servants as one of the vulgar fellows shamelessly uncovers himself!"

1 Kings 18:27	And at noon Elijah mocked them, saying, "Cry aloud, for he is a god! Either he is musing, or he is relieving himself, or he is on a journey, or perhaps he is asleep and must be awakened."

In each language, there are subtle grammatical or lexical signals when sarcasm or irony is being used. For example, in Mark 7:9 (quoted above) the use of the word "fine" in this context makes it clear to native English speakers that the speaker is being ironic. Another signal used in English translations is the occurrence of the exclamation mark, signalling the need for appropriate intonation when reading aloud. These signals will be different in each language. The translator needs to make sure that the appropriate receptor language signals are used, so that the hearer knows the meaning is not to be interpreted literally.

In some languages, the meaning has to be expressed more directly, but in a way that retains the force of the original. Mark 7:9 might be re-expressed: "Surely it is a terrible thing that you do when you reject the commandment of God in order to keep your tradition!" The use of a rhetorical question might be appropriate: "Is it good that you reject the commandment of God in order to keep your own tradition?" (Rhetorical questions will be discussed in chapter 35.)

Other biblical examples of irony and sarcasm include the following:

- And they began to salute him, "Hail, King of the Jews!" ¹⁹ And they were striking his head with a reed and spitting on him and kneeling down in homage to him. ²⁰ And when they had mocked him, they stripped him of the purple cloak and put his own clothes on him. And they led him out to crucify him. (Mark 15:18–20)
- So also the chief priests with the scribes mocked him to one another, saying, "He saved others; he cannot save himself. ³² Let the Christ, the King of Israel, come down now from the cross that we may see and believe." Those who were crucified with him also reviled him. (Mark 15:31–32)
- Already you have all you want! Already you have become rich! Without us you have become kings! And would that you did reign, so that we might share the rule with you! (1 Corinthians 4:8)
- For in what were you less favored than the rest of the churches, except that I myself did not burden you? Forgive me this wrong! (2 Corinthians 12:13)

Exercise 5

Compare the translations of Job 26:1–4 quoted below. Study the context. Mark and discuss the specific lexical and grammatical forms that indicate the attitude of the speaker.

ESV	*The Message*
¹ Then Job answered and said: ² "How you have helped him who has no power! How you have saved the arm that has no strength! ³ How you have counseled him who has no wisdom, and plentifully declared sound knowledge! ⁴ With whose help have you uttered words, and whose breath has come out from you?"	¹⁻⁴ Job answered: "Well, you've certainly been a great help to a helpless man! You came to the rescue just in the nick of time! What wonderful advice you've given to a mixed-up man! What amazing insights you've provided! Where in the world did you learn all this? How did you become so inspired?"

34.6 Metonymy and synecdoche

Metonymy and *synecdoche* both involve *using one concept to refer to an associated concept.*

- The <u>pot</u> is boiling.   "Pot" stands in place of the <u>water</u> in the pot.
- The <u>pen</u> is mightier than the <u>sword</u>.   "Pen" stands for <u>writing</u> or <u>what is written</u>; "sword" stands for <u>fighting</u>.
- <u>My tongue</u> rejoices. (Acts 2:26)   "My tongue" stands for <u>"I,"</u> also indicating <u>spoken praise, praise expressed in words</u>.

Languages use this figure of speech in different ways. It may be used for poetic effect. Or it may function as an idiom, especially when the form is in common use.

The difference between metonymy and synecdoche is as follows:

- In *synecdoche*, the word used in the synecdoche is usually a part of the thing to which it refers. For example, in the Acts 2:6 example above, tongue represents the person to whom that tongue belongs; the tongue is a part of the person. Or sometimes it is the thing that is referred to that is a part of the word used in the synecdoche. For example, in "Brazil won the match," "Brazil" stands for "the team representing Brazil."
- In *metonymy*, on the other hand, the word used in the metonymy may be any idea that is somehow connected with the thing referred to, as in the example of "sword" for "fighting."

In either case, the translator's task is to understand and communicate the actual meaning.

Metonymy and synecdoche are different from metaphor. In metonymy and synecdoche no comparison is involved, and there is no point of similarity between the ideas. But in metaphor there is always a comparison.

In many instances, a word-for-word translation of these figures of speech would result in complete nonsense in the receptor language. The actual meaning should be translated in a clear and natural way.

Exercise 6

In each of the following passages, do the following:

(1) Mark any examples of metonymy or synecdoche. Compare the translation in other Bible versions.

(2) Explain the actual meaning in this context of the word you have marked.

    a. Do not think that I have come to bring peace to the earth. I have not come to bring peace, but a sword. (Matthew 10:34)

    b. The Lord God will give to him the throne of his father David. (Luke 1:32)

    c. Carry no moneybag. (Luke 10:4)

    d. But if it is by the finger of God that I cast out demons (Luke 11:20)

    e. Blessed is the womb that bore you, and the breasts at which you nursed! (Luke 11:27)

    f. And the hand of the Lord was with them. (Acts 11:21)

    g. The hand of the Lord is upon you. (Acts 13:11)

    h. Their feet are swift to shed blood. (Romans 3:15)

i. who risked their necks for my life (Romans 16:4)

j. whose bodies fell in the wilderness (Hebrews 3:17)

Exercise 7

Each of the following passages includes an example of either metonymy or synecdoche. For each example, do the following:
(1) Mark the figure of speech.
(2) Re-express to show the actual meaning in a direct way.

You are encouraged to look at other Bible versions and to look up the biblical context, but you are not asked to recast more than the parts quoted below.

a. Woe to him who builds a town with blood and founds a city on iniquity! (Habakkuk 2:12)

b. Then Jerusalem and all Judea and all the region about the Jordan were going out to him. (Matthew 3:5–6)

c. This people honors me with their lips, but their heart is far from me. (Matthew 15:8)

d. I have sinned by betraying innocent blood. (Matthew 27:4)

e. a man whose name was Joseph, of the house of David (Luke 1:27)

f. And all flesh shall see the salvation of God. (Luke 3:6)

g. For I will give you a mouth and wisdom. (Luke 21:15)

h. The feet of those who have buried your husband are at the door, and they will carry you out. (Acts 5:9)

i. Moses has had in every city those who proclaim him, for he is read every Sabbath in the synagogues. (Acts 15:21)

j. so that every mouth may be stopped (Romans 3:19)

k. as often as you eat this bread and drink the cup (1 Corinthians 11:26)

l. Thy throne, O God, is forever and ever, the righteous sceptre is the sceptre of thy kingdom. (Hebrews 1:8, *RSV*)

m. And let the marriage bed be undefiled. (Hebrews 13:4)

34.7 Personification

Personification is a figure of speech in which an *abstract idea,* or something that is not alive, is treated or *spoken of as though it were a person.* It may be used for special focus on the concept, or for dramatic effect. For example,

Mark 5:34　　Your faith has made you well.

　CEV　　　You are now well because of your faith.

　　Possibilities to consider:
　　　You have become well because you believed.
　　　Your sickness has finished because you believed/trusted.

Luke 7:35　　Yet wisdom is justified by all her children.

　GNT　　　God's wisdom, however, is shown to be true by all who accept it.

　　Possibility to consider:
　　　Those who follow the wisdom of God, find that indeed it is truly right.

Personification is not a natural figure of speech in all languages, or in all contexts, so it may sometimes be necessary to adjust the form.

Exercise 8

Imagine that you are translating into a language in which personification is not possible. Re-express each of the following passages, avoiding the use of personification.

    a. Surely goodness and mercy shall follow me all the days of my life. (Psalm 23:6)

    b. Then the moon will be confounded, and the sun ashamed. (Isaiah 24:23)

       Compare with GNT: The moon will grow dark, and the sun will no longer shine.

    c. The mountains and the hills before you shall break forth into singing, and all the trees of the field shall clap their hands. (Isaiah 55:12)

    d. For the law was given through Moses; grace and truth came through Jesus Christ. (John 1:17)

    e. I commend you to God and to the word of his grace, which is able to build you up and to give you the inheritance among all those who are sanctified. (Acts 20:32)

       Compare with CEV: I now place you in God's care. Remember the message about his gift of undeserved grace! This message can help you and give you what belongs to you as God's people.

    f. The anger of man does not work the righteousness of God. (James 1:20)

    g. I heard the altar cry. (Revelation 16:7)

    h. And every island fled away. (Revelation 16:20)

       See REB: Every island vanished, and not a mountain was to be seen.

34.8 Apostrophe

The term *apostrophe* refers to a form where a speaker interrupts what he is saying *to address some person or thing directly*. The address form may also occur at the beginning of a speech. Older English translations use the form "O." The apostrophe is used for poetic and dramatic effect.

If the speaker is addressing a thing, this involves personification as well, since he is talking to the thing as if it were a person.

Examples

Psalm 24:7	Lift up your heads, O gates! and be lifted up, O ancient doors, that the King of glory may come in!
Jeremiah 46:9	Advance, O horses, and rage, O chariots! Let the warriors go out.
Luke 13:34	O Jerusalem, Jerusalem, killing the prophets and stoning those who are sent to you! How often would I have gathered your children together as a hen gathers her brood under her wings, and you would not!
1 Corinthians 15:55	O death, where is thy victory? O death, where is thy sting?

    In 1 Corinthians 15:55 the use of apostrophe is combined with the use of rhetorical questions.

(Note: The term "apostrophe" can also be used to refer to a punctuation mark. This is a quite different sense of the word. See the note on the use of the punctuation mark *apostrophe* in section 37.7.)

34.9 A note on translating figures of speech

It is important to recognise when a figure of speech occurs. If you fail to recognise a figure of speech and translate it word-for-word, the meaning will probably be obscure or even totally wrong.

1) First, identify the *meaning* of the figure of speech.

    Remember that meaning includes these aspects:
    - The purpose of the figure of speech (for example, emphasis).
    - The attitude of the speaker and the response aroused in the hearer.
    - The prominence that the use of a figure of speech may bring to a certain idea within the whole passage.

2) Then consider how all these aspects of the meaning can *best be communicated in the receptor language*. Aim to achieve in the translation the same effect as the original message had for its hearers.

Study natural texts (recorded from normal speech) and listen to conversation in the receptor language in order to observe what figures of speech are natural in that language, and with what frequency they are used. There may be some figures of speech in the language that are not used in English or Hebrew or Greek but that could be used effectively in the translation to achieve a natural, varied, and interesting style. Sometimes a figure may be appropriate in a certain place in the translation even though there was no figure in this place in the original text. Keep alert and sensitive to what fits well in the receptor language!

Exercise 9 Different kinds of figures of speech

Each of the following passages includes a figure of speech of some kind.

(1) Mark the figure of speech.

(2) Recast each passage to express the meaning without using figurative language.

    a. Lord, I am not worthy to have you come under my roof, but only say the word, and my servant will be healed. (Matthew 8:8)

    b. Was the baptism of John from heaven or from men? (Mark 11:30)

    c. Fear fell upon him. (Luke 1:12)

    d. Blessed is the fruit of your womb. (Luke 1:42)

    e. The Jews then said to him, "You are not yet fifty years old, and have you seen Abraham?" (John 8:57)

    f. You intend to bring this man's blood upon us. (Acts 5:28)

    g. He was reading the prophet Isaiah. (Acts 8:28)

    h. These men who have turned the world upside down have come here also. (Acts 17:6)

    i. I persecuted this Way to the death. (Acts 22:4)

    j. But we would not have you ignorant, brethren, concerning those who are asleep. (1 Thessalonians 4:13)

Exercise 10

For discussion: Identify all the figures of speech in each of the following passages:
 a. Psalm 23
 b. Psalm 42
 c. Proverbs 31:10–14

Summary of the figures of speech

Metaphor and simile involve a comparison between a topic and an *illustration*. It is important to recognise the point of similarity between them.

Metaphor differs from simile in that in a simile it is openly stated that there is a comparison, whereas in metaphor this is not openly stated.

Euphemism is an indirect way of referring to something, either to express special respect or to avoid using a direct form that would be offensive in that culture.

Litotes is a deliberate understatement, using the negative of the opposite idea; litotes is used for emphasis.

Hyperbole is a deliberate exaggeration, used for emphasis and dramatic effect.

Sarcasm and irony often involve saying the opposite of what is meant, with a strong attitude on the part of the speaker; this is often used for rebuke or ridicule.

Metonymy and *synecdoche* involve the use of a word or phrase to represent another, closely related, idea; it may be used for stylistic variation and dramatic effect, or sometimes just as an idiomatic form in the language with no difference of meaning.

Personification is referring to an abstract idea, or something that is not alive, as if it were a person; personification may be used to introduce variety, or to make a condensed, attention-catching statement.

Apostrophe is the use of a phrase that interrupts the main text. This is usually a phrase directly addressed to a thing (rather than to a person); it is used to catch the attention and to heighten the emotional impact.

While it is good to be able to recognise the different kinds of figures of speech in the biblical text and be able to name them, what is important is to discern the actual meaning at each point, and to translate the meaning correctly, with equivalent impact and emotional effect. The aim is that the new receptor audience, those reading or hearing the translation, will understand the same message that the original biblical audience understood.

Additional resources on "Other Figures of Speech"

BT4 online materials

34_Figures_of_speech_3-Euphemism.pptx
34_Figures_of_speech_4-Different_kinds.pptx

For further reading

Carmichael, Alex. *What kinds of literary techniques are used in the Bible?* Christian Apologetics and Research Ministry (CARM). See https://carm.org/bible-literary-techniques.

Warren-Rothlin, Andy L. 2005. Body idioms and the Psalms. In Philip S. Johnston and David G. Firth (eds.), *Interpreting the Psalms: Issues and approaches*, 195–212. Leicester: IVP Apollos.
(For those who are registered with Academia.edu, this article can be viewed at https://www.academia.edu/2244960/Body_Idioms_and_the_Psalms.)

Wenger, Mark. 2014. *Irony in Scripture*.
(For those who have registered with Academia.edu, this article can be viewed at https://www.academia.edu/7114303/Irony_in_the_Bible.)

Website

See the website: https://literarydevices.net/apostrophe.

Chapter 35

Rhetorical Questions

35.1 Two kinds of questions

All languages use questions. But questions are used for different purposes. The most usual purpose for which a question is used is to ask for information. The person asking the question expects an answer.

> And he said to them, "How many loaves have you?" (Mark 6:38)
> Answer: "Five, and two fish."

This is an example of a "real" question. Real questions expect an answer (although they may not always receive one).

But sometimes questions are used for other purposes.

For what does it profit a man, to gain the whole world and forfeit his life? (Mark 8:36)

Here no answer is expected. The speaker is not asking for information; he is emphasising a point: It is no advantage at all to a man to gain possession of the whole world, if by doing so he loses his life. This is an example of a *rhetorical question*.

There is another example of a rhetorical question in Mark 5:35.

> There came from the ruler's house some who said, "Your daughter is dead. Why trouble the Teacher any further?"

Here the "question" is really an opinion, "It is useless to trouble the Teacher any longer." It could also be understood as an instruction, "Don't trouble the Teacher further."

Two kinds of questions

A *real* question asks for information; it is usually followed by an answer.
A *rhetorical* question does not ask for information. It has some other purpose.

Test yourself with exercise 1 to see whether you can tell the difference between a real question and a rhetorical question.

Exercise 1

Which of the following questions are real questions, and which are rhetorical questions? Check the context where necessary.

a. Then the disciples came and said to Jesus, "Why do you speak to them in parables?" (Matthew 13:10)

b. Master, did you not sow good seed in your field? How then does it have weeds? (Matthew 13:27)

c. Who touched my garments? (Mark 5:30)

d. And they were amazed and astonished, saying, "Are not all these who are speaking Galileans? And how is it that we hear, each of us in his own native language?" (Acts 2:7)

e. For if a man does not know how to manage his own household, how will he care for God's church? (1 Timothy 3:5)

f. God is treating you as sons. For what son is there whom his father does not discipline? (Hebrews 12:7)

35.2 Rhetorical questions in everyday speech

Rhetorical questions are often used in everyday English. Consider these examples:

- Would you mind opening the window?

    This is not a question that needs an answer, but rather a polite way of asking someone to open the window.

- Will you come and eat with us?

    This is an invitation. In some cultures, if a question form is used in this context, the hearer may not understand that he is being invited to come and eat; rather he will think the speaker is asking him whether it is his intention to eat with them. In such cultures, a command form should be used to give the correct implication: "Come and eat with us."

- Do you think I don't know that?

    This question expresses indignation on the part of the speaker.

- It's a beautiful day, isn't it?

    Although a question in grammatical form, this is an expression of the speaker's feelings.

- How are you?

    This is a greeting in question form. Whether or not an answer is expected will depend on the situation!

Exercise 2

Give three examples of rhetorical questions you have heard people use, either in English or in your own language. Discuss the purpose of each one.

35.3 The different purposes or functions of rhetorical questions in the Bible

When translating questions, you must first decide whether the question is a real question or a rhetorical question.

If it is a rhetorical question, then you need to consider carefully exactly what the meaning or purpose of the question is in this context. This is necessary in order to be sure of transferring the correct implications into the translation.

Rhetorical questions in the Bible can have many different meanings or purposes. Here are six of the most common uses.

35.3.1 To emphasise a fact that is obviously true

1 Samuel 4:8	Woe to us! Who can deliver us from the power of these mighty gods?
⇒	*No one can deliver us from the power of these mighty gods!*
1 Samuel 17:8	Am I not a Philistine, and are you not servants of Saul?
Matthew 7:22	On that day many will say to me, "Lord, Lord, did we not prophesy in your name, and cast out demons in your name, and do many mighty works in your name?"
Mark 3:23	How can Satan cast out Satan?
⇒	*It is impossible for Satan to cast out Satan.*

In English, a negative question form implies a positive statement, while a positive question form implies a negative statement. For example,

1 Samuel 17:8	Am I not a Philistine?	[Negative question]
⇒	"I am most certainly a Philistine."	[Positive statement]
John 18:35	Pilate answered, "Am I a Jew?"	[Positive question]
⇒	"I am certainly not a Jew."	[Negative statement]

35.3.2 To focus on a certain condition, especially where two or three possible conditions are listed one after each other

This type of rhetorical question can sometimes be transformed into an "if" clause without changing the meaning. For example,

James 5:13–14	Is any one among you suffering? Let him pray. Is any cheerful? Let him sing praise. Is any among you sick? Let him call for the elders of the church.
⇒	*If anyone is suffering, let him pray.*
Romans 13:3	Would you have no fear of him who is in authority? Then do what is good, and you will receive his approval.
⇒	*If you want to have no fear of him who is in authority, do what is good.*

35.3.3 To introduce a new topic, a new aspect of a topic, or to catch attention

Psalm 15:1–2 O LORD, who shall sojourn in your tent? Who shall dwell on your holy hill? He who walks blamelessly, and does what is right and speaks truth in his heart.

The two questions introduce the topic of the psalm, providing the setting for the answer.

Mark 13:1–2   One of his disciples said to him, "Look, Teacher, what wonderful stones and what wonderful buildings!" And Jesus said to him, "Do you see these great buildings? There will not be left here one stone upon another that will not be thrown down."

Here Jesus focuses on the topic of the destruction of Jerusalem and of the temple by using a question.

Luke 7:44   Then turning toward the woman he said to Simon, "Do you see this woman?"

Study the context of this passage (Luke 7:36–50). The question form is used to focus again on the woman, who has been mentioned earlier in the passage.

Romans 9:30   What shall we say, then? That Gentiles who did not pursue righteousness have attained it.

The expression, "What shall we say then?" is used to indicate the conclusion of one part of the argument and the beginning of a new point. Look for other places in the letter to the Romans where this expression, or a similar form, is used to show the beginning of a new point in the argument.

35.3.4 To express surprise

Mark 6:2–3   And many who heard him were astonished, saying, "Where did this man get these things? What is the wisdom given to him? How are such mighty works done by his hands? Is not this the carpenter, the son of Mary and brother of James and Joses and Judas and Simon? And are not his sisters here with us?" And they took offense at him.

The repetition of a series of questions expresses the emotional reaction of the speakers, their indignation as well as their surprise.

35.3.5 To rebuke or exhort someone

Questions are sometimes used to rebuke someone without offending them. Or they may be used instead of a direct command to instruct someone respectfully.

Genesis 20:9–10   Then Abimelek called Abraham in and said, "What have you done to us? How have I wronged you that you have brought such great guilt upon me and my kingdom? You have done things to me that should not be done." ¹⁰ And Abimelek asked Abraham, "What was your reason for doing this?" (*NIV*)

Abimelek's first two questions are rhetorical, expressing indignation and rebuke. Then he changes to ask a real question – notice the new speech-introducing clause.

Mark 4:40   Why are you so afraid? Have you still no faith?

Mark 5:35   Your daughter is dead. Why trouble the Teacher any further?

35.3.6 To express uncertainty

This kind of rhetorical question is often used by the speaker to address himself. It might be regarded as a real question addressed to oneself.

Luke 12:17   And he thought to himself, "What shall I do, for I have nowhere to store my crops?"

Luke 16:3   And the manager said to himself, "What shall I do, since my master is taking the management away from me?"

> **Remember**
>
> In summary, there are six common purposes or functions of *rhetorical questions*:
> 1) To emphasise a fact that is obviously true
> 2) To focus on a particular condition
> 3) To introduce a new topic, a new aspect of a topic, or to catch attention
> 4) To express surprise
> 5) To rebuke or exhort someone
> 6) To express uncertainty
>
> A rhetorical question may have more than one of these functions at the same time. There are also other purposes for which rhetorical questions may be used.

Exercise 3

What is the function of each of the rhetorical questions listed below? Check the context where necessary.

a. John would have prevented him, saying, "I need to be baptized by you, and do you come to me?" (Matthew 3:14)
b. But Jesus said, "Leave her alone; why do you trouble her?" (Mark 14:6)
c. And they woke him and said to him, "Teacher, do you not care that we are perishing?" (Mark 4:38)
d. Nathanael said to him, "Can anything good come out of Nazareth?" Philip said to him, "Come and see." (John 1:46)
e. Come, see a man who told me all that I ever did. Can this be the Christ? (John 4:29)
f. Again he asked, "What shall I compare the kingdom of God to? [21] It is like yeast that a woman took and mixed into about sixty pounds of flour until it worked all through the dough." (Luke 13:20–21, *NIV*)
g. Who shall separate us from the love of Christ? Shall tribulation, or distress, or persecution, or famine, or nakedness, or danger, or sword? (Romans 8:35)
h. Why do you pass judgment on your brother? Or you, why do you despise your brother? For we will all stand before the judgment seat of God. (Romans 14:10)
i. Are you bound to a wife? Do not seek to be free. Are you free from a wife? Do not seek a wife. (1 Corinthians 7:27)
j. For to which of the angels did God ever say, "You are my Son, today I have begotten you"? (Hebrews 1:5)
   Look up how NLT translates this verse.
k. Are they not all ministering spirits sent out to serve for the sake of those who will inherit salvation? (Hebrews 1:14)

35.4 Some implications for translation

Having analysed the actual meaning of each rhetorical question in its context, consider how best to transfer that meaning into the receptor language.

(1) Different languages use rhetorical questions in different ways. Most languages do have rhetorical questions, but these may not have the same functions as those illustrated above. A language may have some of these functions but not others. Some languages use rhetorical questions much more frequently than other languages do.

(2) Therefore, it is not possible to assume that a rhetorical question in the source text will necessarily be best translated by a rhetorical question in the receptor language. The question form may not always be appropriate. A meaning-based translation such as *NLT* quite often re-expresses rhetorical questions using a non-question form, which brings out the implications in the context more clearly. For example,

> 1 Samuel 6:6   Why should you harden your hearts as the Egyptians and Pharaoh hardened their hearts? After he had dealt severely with them, did they not send the people away, and they departed?
>
> *NLT*   Don't be stubborn and rebellious as Pharaoh and the Egyptians were. By the time God was finished with them, they were eager to let Israel go.

(3) Always check that the question form has the right implication. In one language, Luke 15:4 was translated as follows: "Do you think that a man who has a hundred sheep, if he loses one of them, will leave the ninety-nine and go after the one that is lost?" The form of the question implied that no one would do such a foolish thing! This, of course, makes nonsense of the story that follows!

(4) Sometimes, if this is required by the natural patterns of the receptor language, the implied answer to the question needs to be made explicit.

(5) It may be that the receptor language uses rhetorical questions for some functions for which the source language does not use them. Therefore it may sometimes be appropriate to use a rhetorical question in the translation even though the source text does not have a question form at that point.

(6) In the Doohyayo language of Cameroon, irony may be expressed by a rhetorical question. The literal back translation of Mark 7:9 in Doohyayo reads as follows: "You, you know how to throw away God's law terribly so that you may follow your customs then, don't you?"

(7) In Ebira (Nigeria) rhetorical question form is used in Mark 10:25 to avoid what might otherwise be a clumsy and awkward construction in the language. The literal back translation of this verse reads: "Do you think that a camel can enter into hole of needle go pass through? It is even harder than this for a rich man that he should be able to enter the kingdom of God."

35.5 Discovering how the receptor language uses rhetorical questions

Translators need to listen and observe how speakers of the receptor language use rhetorical questions in everyday speech. They also need to study longer texts that have been recorded in the receptor language. The aim is to investigate the following:

1) Whether that language uses rhetorical questions at all (most languages do), and if so, then, the functions that rhetorical questions have in that language.

2) Also, in what situations do speakers of the receptor language use rhetorical questions?
For example, are they used in both spoken and written language?
Are they used in both formal and informal (colloquial) speech?
In what kinds of discourse do they most commonly occur? Is it in conversation? Or in preaching or exhorting someone?

3) Are any special words or grammatical forms (such as special particles) used to indicate when a question is rhetorical?

Even a first-language speaker of the receptor language needs to make this study. If you are aware of the differences between the source language and your own language, this will help you to notice places where adjustments are necessary.

Remember

Every translator needs to study questions in the receptor language. Observe when and how rhetorical questions are used in the language, and for what purposes. You need to know what words or grammatical forms show that a rhetorical question is being used.

Be alert to recognise when a question form in the source text is rhetorical.

For each rhetorical question, consider what the author's purpose was in using that form.

Then consider how that meaning can best be expressed *accurately*, *clearly*, *naturally*, and *acceptably* in the receptor language.

35.6 Exercises in identifying and analysing rhetorical questions

Exercise 4

For each of the passages below, do the following:

(1) State the purpose or function of each of the following questions. Check the context whenever necessary.

(2) Imagine you are translating into a language that never uses rhetorical questions. Re-express each example (in English) in a form that expresses the correct implied meaning, but without using question form. Try to keep the same emphasis and emotional feelings.

a. When the disciples saw it, they marvelled, saying, "How did the fig tree wither at once?" (Matthew 21:20)

b. Can a blind man lead a blind man? Will they not both fall into a pit? (Luke 6:39)

c. And she (Martha) went up to him and said, "Lord, do you not care that my sister has left me to serve alone? Tell her then to help me." (Luke 10:40)

d. Are not five sparrows sold for two pennies? (Luke 12:6)

e. And the Lord said, "Who then is the faithful and wise manager, whom the master will set over his household, to give them their portion of food at the proper time?" (Luke 12:42)

f. The Samaritan woman said to him, "How is it that you, a Jew, ask a drink from me, a woman of Samaria?" (John 4:9)

g. When he had washed their feet...he said to them, "Do you understand what I have done to you? You call me Teacher and Lord, and you are right." (John 13:12–13)

h. Pilate answered, "Am I a Jew? Your own nation and the chief priests have delivered you over to me; what have you done?" (John 18:35)

i. But Peter said, "Ananias, why has Satan filled your heart to lie to the Holy Spirit and to keep back part of the proceeds of the land? While it remained unsold, did it not remain your own? And after it was sold, was it not at your disposal? Why is it that you have contrived this deed in your heart? You have not lied to men but to God." When Ananias heard these words, he fell down and breathed his last. And great fear came upon all who heard of it. (Acts 5:3–5)

j. What shall we say then? Are we to continue in sin that grace may abound? By no means! How can we who died to sin still live in it? (Romans 6:1–2)

Exercise 5

For each of the following passages, compare the version quoted below with at least two other English versions, or versions in another language. For each passage, do the following:

(1) State the function of the rhetorical question. If there is more than one function, state all the functions.

(2) Re-express the passage (in English) in a way that expresses the correct implied meaning, but which avoids the question form.

Example from Hebrews 2:3	**Function**
How shall we escape if we neglect such a great salvation?	To emphasise a fact

⇒ There is (certainly) no way (at all) that we shall escape if we neglect such a great salvation.

Passage	**Function**
a. But to what shall I compare this generation? It is like children sitting in the marketplaces. (Matthew 11:16)	
b. Jesus answered, "O faithless and twisted generation, how long am I to be with you and bear with you? Bring your son here." (Luke 9:41)	
c. Has not Moses given you the law? Yet none of you keeps the law. Why do you seek to kill me? (John 7:19)	
d. Are you greater than our father Abraham, who died? (John 8:53)	
e. (Simon Peter) said to him, "Lord, do you wash my feet?" (John 13:6)	
f. What then shall we say to these things? If God is for us, who can be against us? (Romans 8:31)	
g. Would you have no fear of the one who is in authority? Then do what is good, and you will receive his approval. (Romans 13:3–4)	

h. Was anyone at the time of his call already circumcised? Let him not seek to remove the marks of circumcision. (1 Corinthians 7:18)

i. If the whole body were an eye, where would be the hearing? If the whole body were an ear, where would be the sense of smell? (1 Corinthians 12:17)

j. You were running well! Who hindered you from obeying the truth? (Galatians 5:7)

Exercise 6

Study Luke 11:5–13. Translate this passage into your language, paying attention to the translation of rhetorical questions.

35.7 Concerning the translation of real questions

(1) Like rhetorical questions, *real questions* often have implications, shown by the form of the questions.

  a) Where on earth have you been?

  This question might be used by a parent to a child who returns home very late. It is a real question, it does expect an answer, but the form of the question also indicates the attitude of surprise and irritation on the part of the speaker.

  b) You won't be back by Tuesday, will you?

  This is also a real question, but the form of the question indicates that the speaker thinks that the person he is addressing will not be back by Tuesday, and is expecting him to confirm this.

(2) The attitude that someone has when he asks a question is part of the meaning. A good translation will express this attitude. Translators need to keep alert to recognise the attitude behind a question, and any other implications it might have.

(3) The answers to questions also need to be translated with care. Many languages have different ways of replying to a question, depending on the form of the questions. This is particularly true when the question is a "negative" question.

Compare the possible answers to the negative question, "Aren't you coming?"

- If the person who is addressed is <u>not</u> coming,

  then the "English" answer is:

  "No." (meaning, "No, I am not coming.")

  But many languages would answer:

  "Yes." (meaning, "You are right, I am not coming.")

  Arden Sanders (personal communication) reports that this would be the correct response in Tok Pisin of Papua New Guinea.

- If the person who is addressed <u>is</u> coming,

  then the "English" answer is:

  "Yes." (meaning, "Yes, I am coming.")

  But many languages would answer:

  "No." (meaning, "No, you are not right, I am coming.")

Care is needed to avoid misunderstanding!

There are different ways of responding to a statement too, in different languages.

> Genesis 18:15   But Sarah denied, saying, "I did not laugh"; for she was afraid. He said, "No, but you did laugh." (*ESV*, literal translation from Hebrew)

In modern English, it would be more natural to say, "Yes, you did."

> NIV   Sarah was afraid, so she lied and said, "I did not laugh." But he said, "Yes, you did laugh."
>
> GNT   Because Sarah was afraid, she denied it. "I didn't laugh," she said. "Yes, you did," he replied. "You laughed."

The form of the response will depend on the relationship of those who are interacting, as well as the situation.

Additional resources on "Rhetorical Questions"

BT4 online materials

35_Rhetorical_questions_1-Two_kinds_of_questions.pptx
35_Rhetorical_questions_2-Bible_examples.pptx
35_Rhetorical_questions_3-How_to_translate.pptx
35_Rhetorical_questions_in_the_JESUS_Film.pptx

For further reading

Estes, Douglas. 2017. *Questions and rhetoric in the Greek New Testament: An essential reference resource for exegesis*. Grand Rapids: Zondervan.

Notes on Translation 44, June 1972.
(The whole issue relates to rhetorical questions, including the following articles:)

Beekman, John. Analyzing and translating the questions of the New Testament, 3–21.
Elkins, Richard E. Supposition rules for rhetorical questions in English and Western Bukidnon Manobo, 21–24.
Andrews, Henrietta. Rhetorical questions in Otomí of the State of Mexico (San Felipe Santiago), 25–28.
Kirkpatrick, Lilla. Rhetorical questions in Korku of Central India, 28–32.
Crouch, Marjorie. Rhetorical questions in Vagla of Ghana, W. Africa, 32–36.
Levinsohn, Stephen H. Questions in Inga, and their use in Mark's Gospel, 36–39.
Longacre, Robert E. Rhetorical questions in Trique, 39–40.
Rountree, S. Catherine. Questions-invitations, 40.
Sayers, Barbara J. What is it that I don't know? 40.

Chapter 36

Translation Challenges – A Review

Below is a list of translation challenges that have been discussed in this manual. Read it through to remind yourself of points for which you need to be alert as you translate.

(1) Meanings that do not match (chapter 21)   Words in the receptor language often do not match one-to-one with the meaning of words in the source language.

> Solution: Translate a word according to its meaning in the context. One word in the source language may be translated by different words in the receptor language, according to context.

(2) Words that have different senses (chapter 21)   One word may have several different meanings, depending on the context.

> Solution: Translate a word according to its sense in the context in which it occurs.

(3) Words that go together (chapter 21)   In any language, words occur together with certain other words in natural collocations. The natural collocations are different in different languages.

> Solution: When translating, use words with their natural partners in the receptor language.

(4) Unknown ideas (chapters 22 and 23)   The biblical text may include reference to an object or concept that is unknown to the audience of the translation.

> Possible solutions include the following:
> 1) Use a descriptive phrase.
> 2) Substitute something similar.
> 3) Use a foreign word from another language.
> 4) Use a more general word.
> 5) Use more specific words.

(5) Key biblical terms (chapter 24)   Key biblical terms refer to Jewish and Christian religious customs and beliefs, concepts that may be unknown to the audience of the translation.

Solution: To translate special biblical words, follow these four steps:
1) Study the meaning of the original word.
2) Compare the word with other words of similar meaning.
3) Think of possible ways to translate the term. Choose one tentatively.
4) Test the term you have tentatively chosen by observing how it is understood by representative speakers of the receptor language. Also observe whether it gives the correct meaning in different passages of Scripture in which it occurs.

(6) Cultural differences (chapter 25)   There are many differences between the biblical culture and the receptor language culture. The biblical author wrote for people living many hundreds or thousands of years ago.

Solution: Be faithful to the historical facts; do not change these. But translate in such a way that the author's original intended meaning will be understood by the new audience.

(7) Ways of providing background information (chapters 14 and 15)   The reader of the translation may need some background information in order to understand the original message.

Solution: Additional background information can be supplied to the reader with the following types of information:

Pictures/illustrations, glossary, footnotes

Introductions to Bible books

Bible background booklets

(8) Event ideas (chapter 26)   In English, event ideas are sometimes expressed by abstract nouns. The relationship between the event and the participants in the event may not be clear.

Solution: To discover the meaning more plainly, try re-expressing event ideas as verbs.

(9) "Of" phrases (chapter 27)   "Of" phrases or other genitive constructions in the English source text express many different relationships.

Solution: Keep alert to recognise "of" phrases in the source text. Study the relationship between the words carefully.

(10) Passive verbs (chapter 28)   Many languages do not have a passive form, but have other ways of expressing the same differences of meaning.

Solution: Study natural texts in the receptor language to discover equivalent ways to express the same meaning.

(11) Shortcuts (chapter 29)   The source language text may have a grammatical shortcut, leaving out some words because the meaning would have been understood by his original audience.

Solution: It may be necessary to make the missing part explicit. It is important to make the full meaning clear.

(12) Complex passages (chapter 30)   Sometimes the meaning of a passage is hard to understand.

Solution: It may help to analyse the passage following three steps:
1) Find event ideas and re-express them as verbs.
2) Fill in the participants in these events.
3) Re-write the passage to show the relationships clearly.

(13) Order of events (chapter 31) In the biblical text, events are not always told in the order in which they happened. This may be confusing.

> Solution: Make sure that there are clear grammatical signals to make the facts clear. If necessary, re-order the information, so that the events are told in the order in which they happened.

(14) Long sentences (chapter 32) A sentence in the source text may be long and complicated.

> Solution: Consider breaking long complex sentences into shorter sentences. Also take time to study the natural sentence structures of the receptor language and follow these natural structures as you translate. See chapters 38 and 40 for further information.

(15) Comparisons – simile and metaphor (chapter 33) A topic may be compared with something else. The *point of similarity* between the topic and the illustration is not always clear.

> Solution: Before translating, find out
> 1) what the topic is – what is being talked about;
> 2) what the illustration is – what the topic is compared to; and
> 3) what the point of similarity is – what characteristic is shared.
>
> Translate in a way that makes the full meaning clear.

(16) Other figures of speech (chapter 34) Sometimes the actual meaning of a phrase is different from the surface meaning of the words.

> Solution: First find the real meaning. Then re-express that meaning in a way that will be clearly understood, while keeping the same impact and effect.

(17) Rhetorical questions (chapter 35) Some questions do not expect an answer, but are used for some other purpose.

> Solution: For every question in the source text, first ask, "Is it a real question or a rhetorical question?" If it is a rhetorical question, then ask, "What is its purpose in this context?" Translate in a way that achieves the same purpose.

Part 6

Discovering Your Language

Introduction to part 6

Every language has its own unique patterns. It is fascinating to discover the patterns of a language, and to become aware of its unique patterns and variety.

Through studying his own language, a translator comes to appreciate its wealth and potential, and is more able to use its richness in his translation.

He also becomes more alert to places where his language differs from English, or whatever source language he is translating from. Because of this, he is better able to avoid the danger of following the form of the source language too closely in his translation.

In this manual, it is only possible to give some beginning guidelines on how to discover the richness of your language. But this is an important beginning, which lays a foundation for further research. Discuss this with your translation consultant, who will be able to give you further materials to guide you in studying your language.

Chapter 37

Principles of Consistent Spelling

The purpose of this chapter is to help translators in situations where a system for writing the language has only recently been developed.

It is important that translators can write the receptor language accurately, before beginning extensive translation work. If they have not acquired this skill, this will distract their attention from thinking about the content of the translation.

Time spent at the beginning of the project on training translators and other team members to write the language accurately will save much more time later. If good habits are formed at the beginning, fewer mistakes will slip in, and less editing work will be needed.

> If an agreed system for writing the receptor language has not yet been developed, discuss with your advisor or consultant what practical steps can be taken towards developing a spelling system. This will take time, hard work, interaction, and cooperation with others. The help of someone trained in linguistics will be needed.

There are many different writing systems used in different parts of the world. The consultants in your language area will guide you to find the system most appropriate for your language. They will consider the features of the language family to which this language belongs.

We are focusing here on languages that use the symbols of the English alphabet, technically known as the Latin (or Roman) alphabet, possibly with some additional letters or accent marks.

A question: What publications are already available in your language?

Make a list of the books and other materials that have been published in your language or about your language. If you do not have copies, explore to find out how you can get copies.

Is there a book that describes how to write the language? Be sure to get a copy and to study it well.

37.1 Qualities of a consistent spelling system

In a consistent spelling system, three points are true:

- Each symbol always represents the same sound.
- Each sound is always represented by the same symbol.
- There are no unnecessary silent letters.[1]

Once you have learnt to recognise the sounds of your language, and know the way to write each sound, you will be able to write every word correctly. You will not need to learn the spelling of hundreds of words.

New readers will learn to read easily because, once they have learnt the letters of the alphabet, they will be able to sound out new words.

37.2 The English language writing system

Unfortunately, English does not have a consistent writing system.

37.2.1 In English, one symbol can stand for several different sounds.

Read the words in each column aloud and listen to the sound represented by the bolded letters.

List 1	List 2	List 3	List 4	List 5
c**ough**	**c**ane	**ch**air	**g**o	**h**ot
t**ough**	**c**ap	**ch**oir	**g**irl	**h**our
al**though**	**c**ircle	ma**ch**ine	**g**entleman	
thr**ough**	**c**inema			
b**ough**				

37.2.2 In English, the same sound can be spelt in different ways.

c**i**nema, s**i**ck
sh**ee**p, pa**ss**ion, na**ti**on
s**ea**, b**ee**, b**e**, k**ey**, rec**ei**ve, bel**ie**ve
thr**ew**, thr**ough**, bl**ue**, d**o**
r**ai**n, r**eig**n, l**a**ne, br**ea**k

37.2.3 English has many "silent" or "extra" letters that do not represent any sound at all.

Can you hear the "k" in the following words?

know, **k**nife, **k**nee

---

[1] These points give a simple summary statement. In deciding on a consistent spelling system for a given language, other factors need to be considered, such as use of capital letters – where the capital letter and the equivalent small letter stand for the same sound. Or consistent spelling of certain grammatical features. This will depend on the phonological and grammatical analysis of the language concerned.

What "silent letters" can you find in the following words?

>hour, honour (compare with "house")
>
>psalm, Sarah, sword
>
>pepper (compare with "paper")
>
>fuss (compare with "bus")

It is clear from these examples that neither the vowels nor the consonants of English are written consistently.

Remember

A consistent writing system follows these principles:
- Each symbol always represents the same sound.
- Each sound is always represented by the same symbol.
- There are no unnecessary silent letters.

In some languages there may be certain letters that are used to mark special features of the language. For example, *h* is sometimes used to mark a tone or vowel difference. In that case, even though the letter is not pronounced, it has an important purpose.

37.3 Focus on vowel sounds

Every language has a fixed set of sounds. For example, one language may have 7 vowel sounds and 25 consonants. Another language may have 12 vowels and 19 consonants.

The English language has been analysed as having 12 distinctive vowel sounds and 8 diphthongs (gliding vowel sounds). In the English alphabet, however, there are only five vowel symbols: a e i o u. If the English alphabet is being used to write the vowels of a language that has more than five vowel sounds, one of the following methods may be used to distinguish the different sounds:

- Use a diacritic mark under or over one or more of the vowel letters. For example, Jur Mödö uses *ï, ë,* and *ö* as vowel letters in addition to *i, e,* and *o,* as do several languages in South Sudan. See also *o̧* and *ȩ,* as in the Mbembe example below.
- Alternatively, use an extra symbol, such as ɛ or ɔ.
- Possibly use a combination of two vowel symbols. One of the first two options is usually preferred to a combination of symbols.

Some additional features to learn

There may be some nasalised vowel sounds, sometimes written with a mark over the letter.

There may be differences in vowel length. For example, in the Mbembe language, *ȩbanga,* with short [a], means "dirtiness," while *ȩbaanga,* with long [aa], means "a nail."

The Dinka language of South Sudan difference in vowel length sometimes signals the difference between singular and plural, as in *dit* "bird" but *diit* "birds."

Example

The following words are from the Mbembe language, spoken in Cross River State, Nigeria, belonging to the Benue-Congo language family.

The marks under the vowels represent different vowel sounds:

e and *ẹ* represent two different sounds. In phonetic writing, *ẹ* is transcribed as [ɛ].

o and *ọ* represent two different sounds. In phonetic writing, *ọ* is transcribed as [ɔ].

This chart illustrates that the Mbembe language has seven contrastive vowels, *a e ẹ i o ọ u*.

a	abarada	'bigness'	i	icho	'year'
	aduk	'island'		idima	'calabash'
e	echi	'tree, stick'	o	obo	'death'
	eso	'head'		ose	'story'
	ebe	'early farm'		obe	'maggot in palm'
ẹ	ẹfa	'dog'	ọ	ọwọmọ	'plantain'
	ẹjọ	'water pot'		ọgbọ	'age group'
			u	evu	'goat'
				otum	'common lizard'

(*u* does not occur at the beginning of a word.)

Vowel sounds in your language

How many vowel sounds are there in the language you are writing? How is each one written? List them, with a "guide word" for each vowel sound.

37.4 Focus on consonant sounds

The English language has been analysed as having 24 consonant sounds. Some of these sounds are written with "double consonants," for example, *ch, sh, th, ng*. Overall English consonants are written more consistently than English vowels, but still with many inconsistencies.

Consonant sounds in your language

(1) How many consonant sounds are there in the language you are writing? Are there any sounds written with double consonants? List them, with a "guide word" for each one. The "guide word" will remind you of how to spell that sound. For example,

Consonant	Guide word	Meaning of the guide word
bh	ẹbhaam	'cow'
kp	ẹkpa	'bag'
ng	egbong	'war'

(2) Are there any other consonant sounds that need special attention? List these also, with a "guide word" for each one.

(3) Do you observe any restrictions on the position in which certain consonants occur? For example, in some languages only certain consonants can occur at the end of a word.

37.5 Focus on tone in your language

Does the language you are writing have contrastive tone? Are there words that have the same consonant and vowel sounds but are different by the pitch of the voice?

In the following examples, vowels pronounced with low pitch are unmarked, while those pronounced with high pitch are marked with an accent mark:

(1) For example,

ǫkka	'mother'
ǫkká	'crab'
gwo	'to shave the head'
gwó	'to drink'

Sometimes tone may signal an important grammatical difference.

(2) For example,

mǫ́tá with high-high tone	'he will go' (positive)
mǫtá with low-high tone	'he will not go' (negative)

If the language you are writing has contrastive tone, do the following:

(1) Make a list of some words that differ from each other only by tone. If the spelling system of the language has a system for marking tone, write the correct tone marks.

(2) Are there any grammatical features that are signalled by tone difference and marked in a special way? If so, list them and describe how each is written, giving examples.

37.6 Focus on word separation in your language

(1) Write down any special rules that need to be remembered concerning the separation of words in your language. This may include rules concerning writing compound words.

(2) Look back at one of the texts you have written in your language – for example, the writing exercises in chapter 6. Note any points that need to be remembered concerning separating words.

37.7 Focus on punctuation in your language

(1) List the punctuation marks that are used in the language you are writing and describe how each one is used. Note any ways in which a punctuation mark is used differently from the way it is used in English.

For example, is the punctuation mark *apostrophe* (') used in writing the language?

> In English the *apostrophe* punctuation mark is used in two different ways:
> 1) It indicates possession on nouns, as in "the child's mother," "the dog's tail"
> 2) It indicates the omission of one or more letters, as in the following:
>
>   "He isn't coming."   for   "He is not coming."
>   "Don't do that!"   for   "Do not do that!"
>   "It's time to go."   for   "It is time to go."

If the apostrophe mark is used in writing your language, write a statement to describe how it is used, with examples.

(2) Review the texts you have written so far in the language, making any necessary corrections for punctuation. Note any special rules that need to be observed about punctuation.

37.8 Unresolved issues

If the writing system for your language is fairly new, there may be some points that need further research and study. Note any issues that need further investigation.

Is there already a book for your language that explains how the sounds of the language are written? If not, consider how one can be prepared. Who should be responsible for this?

Points to check when editing a manuscript

1. *Spelling*
   Is each vowel and consonant sound correctly written?
   Has tone been marked where necessary?

2. *Capital letters*
   Are all proper names written with a capital letter?
   Have all sentences been started with a capital letter?

3. *Word separation*
   Have words been separated in the correct places?
   Have any words been joined together that should have been separated?
   Have any words been separated when they should have been joined?

4. *Sentence and paragraph division*
   Have sentence breaks been made in the correct places?
   Have all the sentence breaks been marked by punctuation?
   Have paragraph divisions been made in the correct places?

5. *Punctuation*
   Have all questions been marked with a question mark?
   Have all direct speech quotations been opened and closed?

Additional resources on "Principles of Consistent Spelling"

BT4 online materials

37_Examples_of_orthography_issues.pptx
37_Principles_of_a_good_writing_system.pptx
37_Principles_of_a_good_writing_system.pdf
37_Principles_of_a_good_writing_system-Quiz.pdf

Chapter 38

Different Kinds of Texts – Speech Genres

38.1 Different kinds of discourse

Language is used for different purposes. We use language to inform people of new facts, to tell a story or preach a sermon, to exhort or urge people to do certain things, to explain to people how to do something, and for many other purposes. The form of language used varies according to the purpose. For example, a sermon or political speech has features that are very different from those of a traditional story or a recipe for making bread. In studying the overall structure of a text, we need to consider what kind of communication it is.

The technical terms used to refer to different kinds of texts are *genres* or *speech genres*.

Speech genres can be discussed with reference to languages in general. For example, most language communities have songs or poetry. Most have a way of making commandments or laws, so that when you see a certain format, you know that this is an authoritative document. Most, perhaps all, language groups have traditional stories as well as other kinds of narrative texts.

Each of these kinds of speech has its own features, which will vary from language to language. For example, traditional stories usually have a special way of opening and closing the story, and a typical pattern in the story, often ending with something like "and that is why…" When those listening hear the opening form of a story, they know that they should expect a fictional story. The speaker would not have used that form if he intended to give an account of an event that had happened in real life.

38.2 Comparing different speech genres

38.2.1 Contrasting prose and poetry

Speech genres have been grouped in different ways, with different labels. In most languages, there is a clear distinction between "prose" and "poetry." But the purpose for which poetry is used varies. Thinking of the Psalms and other parts of the Old Testament, poetic form is often used in the Bible to praise God, and for prophecies (messages from God to human beings). In modern English, poetry is often used for humour!

The form of poetry differs from language to language, but often involves

- a special format, perhaps lines with similar lengths, or a pattern of long and short lines;
- a pattern to the sounds of the words, with alliteration (repetition of the same sounds) or rhyme;
- a repetition of some kind – sometimes repeating the same thought in more than one way, sometimes repeating the same phrase or line several times;
- a concentration of figures of speech, including metaphors and other comparative allusions;
- a special rhythm. Poetry may also be related to music and song.

In the Bible, poetry is often used to express strong emotions or attitudes. The translator must consider how to communicate the same effects in his own language.

38.2.2 Different kinds of prose

The following speech genres are found in most languages, although they are often very different in form from one language to another.

Narrative discourse

Telling events that happened in sequence, usually told in the past tense. A narrative may be a record of something that happened, or it may be an untrue or fictional story. There are different kinds of narrative:

- Historical narrative – a chronological account or report of events that have happened
- Personal experience – an account of events witnessed by the author, or told as first-hand evidence
- A story with characters (participants) who are interacting with each other. There may be quotations of their conversation together. Stories could include:
    - a true account of events that have happened;
    - parables, with a teaching point;
    - traditional stories – often with a special opening (e.g., "once upon a time"), arousing certain expectations in the hearer or reader; and
    - other kinds of fictional stories for entertainment.

Hortatory discourse

Aiming to persuade people to think or behave in a certain way; sometimes to rebuke. These can take different forms, such as the following:

- Instructions to servants or others on how something is to be done
- Formal speeches by a king or political leader
- A sermon
    Example: the speech of Stephen in Acts 7 (which also contains narrative text)
- Teaching passages
    Example: Jesus' teaching in the Gospels
- Advice from a father to his son
- Letters
    Example: Paul's letters in the New Testament, giving advice to believers, also involving encouragement or rebuke, teaching, and exhortation.

Laws and commandments; instructions

- Direct laws, applying under all circumstances
    Example: the Ten Commandments in Exodus 20:1–17
- Laws that depend on certain conditions, instructions on what to do if a certain circumstance arises
    Example: Luke 6:30 *and from one who takes away your goods, do not demand them back.*

Procedural discourse

- Instructions on how to do something
    Example: instructions on how to build the ark in Genesis 6:14–16
- Information on how something used to be done in the past

Conversation

- Two or more participants interacting with each other, quoting what they say
- A dramatic play

Prayer, intercession

Example: The Lord's Prayer in Luke 11:2–4 or Matthew 6:9–13

38.3 Studying speech genres in your language

A translator needs to be aware of the features of different genres that are found in the Bible and compare these with the forms of language used under comparable circumstances in the receptor language today. This will involve two kinds of study:

- Study of the Bible texts, observing the features of the different biblical speech genres
- Study of natural texts of different kinds in the receptor language

Chapter 39 presents a method for collecting and arranging sample texts in the receptor language in a way that helps you observe the structure and patterns of the language. Chapters 40 and 41 give examples and suggestions for studying specific discourse-related topics.

This will be a progressive study, over many years. In this training module, we focus on narrative text. A large part of the Bible, both Old and New Testaments, is in narrative form.

It should be noted that a Bible book may be of one genre in general but may include text of different genres. The Gospels, for example, are basically narrative texts, but include teaching passages, parables, conversations, Old Testament quotations, and other kinds of text.

38.4 Ethnoarts

In recent years attention has been given to exploring special oral and art genres that a language group may have developed within their own traditional culture. These are art forms that have been used and appreciated by members of the group over many years. They may include songs and spoken genres, kinds of music or dance, and painting or other visual art forms.

A book by Brian Schrag, for which the details are given below, and the websites cited below, provide information on how to explore such traditional and always unique art forms, and how to encourage each people group to use these traditional forms in effective communication of a message. More and more communities are drawing on their traditional genres as they translate the Bible, and in Scripture engagement, literacy, and transformational development activities.

Additional resources on "Different Kinds of Texts – Speech Genres"

BT4 online materials

38_Recognizing_different_kinds_of_texts.pptx
38_Testing_6-Genre_questions.pptx

Websites

The following websites share experience, examples and opportunities relating to the study of traditional art forms, demonstrating their value in effective communication:

ethnoarts.sil.org/.

www.ArtsForABetterFuture.org/.
    (Information about a training program designed to help language communities recognise and develop their indigenous art forms for Bible translation, Scripture engagement, and language development.)

For further reading

Schrag, Brian, and James Krabill. 2013. *Creating local arts together: A manual to help communities reach their kingdom goals*. Pasadena: William Carey Library.
Stahl, Janet. 2017. Bible storytelling and healing communities. *Global Arts and Christian Faith* 5(1). http://artsandchristianfaith.org/index.php/journal/article/download/30/32.
Wendland, Ernst R., 2002. A literary-rhetorical approach to biblical text analysis and translation. In Timothy Wilt (ed.), *Bible translation: Frames of reference*, 179–230. Manchester: St. Jerome Publishing.
Wendland, Ernst R. 2004. *Translating the literature of Scripture: A literary-rhetorical approach to Bible translation*. Publications in Translation and Textlinguistics 1. Dallas: SIL International.

Wendland, Ernst R. 2018. "Literary Functional Equivalence" (LiFE) Translation—A brief description. For those who have registered with Academia.edu, this is accessible at: https://www.academia.edu/3168198/_Literary_Functional_Equivalence_LiFE_Translation--A_Brief_Description.

Chapter 39

Discovering Your Language – How to Chart a Text

39.1 Collecting the data

In this chapter, we will discuss how to study a text in your language to discover the unique patterns of the language. Texts for study must be texts that are freely and naturally told in the language. Ask someone who is known as a good speaker of the language to tell a story, record it as he speaks, and then write the text down from the recording. (This is called "transcribing" a text.)

Texts that have been translated from another language, or which are spoken by someone who does not speak this language as his first language, are not suitable.

Over time, collect a variety of different kinds of texts. These should include different text genres, like narrative of personal experiences, reports of historical events, traditional stories, conversations, speeches, teaching or exhortation, discussions and explanations, proverbs, letters, songs, and poetry. For detailed study, we suggest you begin by studying narrative texts.

Some other suggestions include the following:

- Ask older people to tell what they know about the history of their people, or about events they remember from the past.
- Ask for a description and explanation of a special festival or ceremony.
- Ask an older person to tell you some traditional stories.
- Ask a woman to describe how she makes soup, cleans house, or does other work.
- Ask a man to describe how to build a house, or another activity.
- Record a speech made by a chief or other important person on a special occasion.
- Look for opportunities to record conversations between two or more people.

39.2 Write down and edit the texts

Transcribe the texts you have recorded, using the normal spelling system of the language. If you feel it is necessary, you can make small changes to correct any places where you feel the speaker made a mistake. But do not make any large changes. If you feel there are major errors in a text, then leave that one aside and choose another text to study.

Why collect and write texts in your language?

- To keep the traditional stories, history, and customs of your people, preserving them for future generations.
- To produce useful and interesting easy reading material, to motivate people to read their language and so that they can practise reading.
- To have natural material in the language so that you can study and describe the natural, unique patterns of the language.
- To help translators become aware of the beauty and richness of the language so that they can use these resources to the full as they translate.

Definition of some grammatical terms

A *clause* is usually a verb together with other parts that relate to that verb, such as a subject, object, or prepositional phrase. A clause may be *finite*, that is, it can stand as a sentence by itself. Or it may be *dependent*, that is, being related to a finite clause, forming part of a sentence. Another term meaning the same as dependent in this context is *subordinate*.

A *sentence* may consist of a single finite clause or a combination of clauses that relate to one another.

A *preposition* is a word that shows the relationship between a noun or pronoun and other words in a sentence. Prepositions are words like *in* and *out*, *above* and *below*, and *to* and *from*.

39.3 How to chart a text – an example

The following short chart shows a way of displaying a text so that you can see the structure of each clause. The text has been written out continuously just as it was related. Nothing has been rearranged or changed. (The part of the text numbered between sentences 9 and 10 is an interruption to the story and is therefore not counted as part of the story.)

Look at the headings of the columns. As you look at the display you can see already that, in English, connecting words and time words often come at the beginning of a sentence.

From this display you can also see how sentences and paragraphs are connected together, and other features of the grammar.

This sample English text is the first part of the story told in *Things Fall Apart*, by Chinua Achebe, pages 87–88 of the edition published by Heinemann. This display provides a model for charting the text. It also provides an English text, which you can use in studying how English handles certain discourse features, comparing the English pattern with the pattern of your own language. A new paragraph is marked by the symbol " ¶ ".

To view a longer portion of this text in charted form, see the file 39_Achebe_Tortoise_text_charted.pdf. This is accessible on the **BT4 online materials** website.

	What comes before the subject	Subject	Verb	What comes after the verb
1	Once upon a time	all the birds	were invited	to a feast in the sky.
2a		They	were	very happy
2b	and		began to prepare	themselves for the great day.
3a		They	painted	their bodies with red cam wood
3b	and		drew	beautiful patterns on them with "uli."
4a¶		Tortoise	saw	all these preparations
4b	and soon		discovered	[what it all meant].
5a		Nothing [that happened in the world of the animals]	ever escaped	his notice;
5b		he	was	full of cunning.
6a	As soon as	he	heard	of the great feast in the sky,
6b		his throat	began to itch	at the very thought.
7a		There	was	a famine in those days
7b	and	Tortoise	had not eaten	a good meal for two moons.
8		His body	rattled	like a piece of dry stick in his empty shell.
9	So	he	began to plan	[how he would go to the sky]."

"But he had no wings," said Ezinma. "Be patient," replied her mother. "That is the story…"	(Note: This exchange interrupts the story. Ezinma's mother then continues with her story.)

10a	…	Tortoise	had	no wings
10b	but	he	went	to the birds
10c	and		asked	[to be allowed to go with them].

39.4 Chart a text in your language

Take a text in your language and display it in a similar way. We suggest a narrative text for this first exercise.

You may need to adjust the order of the columns. In English, the object of the verb, and other things that depend on the verb, usually follow the verb. In some languages, however, the verb usually comes at the end of the clause, with the grammatical object before the verb. Discuss this with your consultant or advisor.

Discuss with your consultant how to chart your texts. Some people prefer to write the text out by hand. Others prefer to work on a computer. At the end of this chapter there is the reference for a template that you can copy onto your computer, adjusting the columns as needed, and then key the text into it, keeping the natural order of the text.

39.5 Choose topics to study

Some topics for study include the following:

- Connecting words and phrases – what words indicate the relationship between clauses and between sentences?
- Time words or phrases – how is the time of an event indicated?
- Paragraph divisions – does the text seem to divide into units that focus on a certain subject? What indicates that a new paragraph is beginning? Are there certain connecting words that seem to mark the beginning of a new paragraph?
- Participant identification – what are different ways in which participants in a story are identified? How are they introduced into the story? Once introduced, how are they referred to? Most languages have a way to use *pronouns* to refer to the participants.

Chapter 40 focuses on the topic of pronoun reference and gives some guidance on how to explore the pronoun system in your language.

Other discourse-related topics for research are listed in chapter 41. Discuss with your consultant what topics are the best to start with in your situation.

Begin your study focusing on the texts you have charted. Go through these texts and mark each example of the topic you have chosen to study. For example, if the topic you are studying is *rhetorical questions*, mark each example of a rhetorical question you find in the texts.

39.6 List questions and observations

Your aim is to discover the characteristics of the feature you are studying. For rhetorical questions, you would be asking questions like the following:

- For what purposes are rhetorical questions used?
- How often are they used?
- Is there anything that shows that a question is rhetorical? How did you know it was a rhetorical question and not a real question?
- Do rhetorical questions have any typical grammatical structures?
- In what speech genres do rhetorical questions occur?
  Your advisor or consultant will suggest points to investigate.

Use the same method to study other topics. Chapter 41 gives suggestions on questions to research for different topics.

39.7 Keep a record of your discoveries

A notebook or loose-leaf file is good for this purpose. Or keep a folder on your computer for such notes on different topics. A written record of what you have discovered is useful in the following ways:

- It helps you to check your conclusions. Sometimes early conclusions must be modified as you observe more examples.
- It is good to refer back from time to time, to remind yourself of patterns you have observed. As you translate, you can examine portions of your translation, to see whether you have followed these natural patterns in the translation.

- Reading what you have discovered will help others who are interested in the language, or who are interested in studying related languages.
- A further step will be to study how the patterns of your language are different from the patterns of English — or of other languages with which you are familiar.
- Begin to study the same feature in biblical texts. Note what is the same and what is different. Think about translation adjustments that will need to be made.

There are suggestions for topics that might be studied in chapter 41 of this manual. You will not be able to study all of them. Discuss with your advisor or consultant which will be most relevant and interesting for your language.

39.8 Ongoing study

As you start to translate different kinds of discourse, take time to look at the features of that kind of discourse in biblical texts. Then study texts of a similar kind in your own language.

For example, before beginning to translate poetry in the Bible such as Psalms or Mary's song of praise in Luke 1:46–55, study the songs and poetry of your own language. Find out the characteristic features of poetry in the language. Or, before beginning to translate hortatory or teaching texts, such as the letters of Paul, or other New Testament letters, study texts in your language that teach or explain. Find out the features of this kind of text.

Additional resources on "How to Chart a Text"

BT4 online materials

39_Charting_texts_1-Clauses_and_phrases.pptx
39_Charting_texts_2-Example.pptx
39_Introducing_features_of_narrative_discourse.pptx
39_Achebe_Tortoise_text_for_charting.pdf
39_Achebe_Tortoise_text_charted.pdf
39_How_to_record_and_transcribe_texts.pdf
39_How_to_chart_a_narrative_text.pdf
39_Template_for_charting_texts.pdf
39_Template_for_charting_texts-Example.pdf

For further reading

Dooley, Robert, and Stephen Levinsohn. 2001. *Analyzing discourse: A manual of basic concepts.* Dallas: SIL International.
Levinsohn, Stephen. 2015. *Self-instruction materials on non-narrative discourse analysis.* Dallas: SIL International. See https://www.sil.org/system/files/reapdata/12/09/77/12097783140226278345967129899177220760/NonNarr2015.pdf. (For advanced study.)
Levinsohn, Stephen. 2000. *Discourse features of New Testament Greek: A coursebook on the information structure of New Testament Greek.* Second edition. Dallas: SIL International.
Nicolle, Stephen. 2017. *Narrative discourse analysis and Bible translation: Training materials based on Acts 16:16–40.* SIL Forum for Language Fieldwork 2017-001. Dallas: SIL International. See https://www.sil.org/resources/publications/entry/69386. This is also on Translator's Workplace. (For advanced study.)

Runge, Steven E. 2010. *Discourse grammar of the Greek New Testament: A practical introduction for teaching and exegesis.* Bellingham, WA: Lexham Press.

Chapter 40

Pronoun Reference

This chapter guides translators in studying how pronouns are used in the receptor language. It also alerts translators to challenges that may arise in translation when pronouns are used in the source text.

40.1 Review: What is a pronoun?

A *pronoun* is a word that refers to, or takes the place of, a noun or a noun phrase. It may refer to someone or something mentioned previously in the text – for example, in English: "he," "she," "it," "they," or to the person or persons speaking – "I," "we."

Pronouns can usually function in all the positions where a noun can function. For example, a pronoun can function as subject or object in a clause, or as a possessive – "his book," "your hand." Or it can function in a prepositional phrase: "to him," "among us." See further examples from English below.

Exercise

For practice in recognising pronouns, identify the pronouns in the following text, Luke 5:4–8:

> ⁴ And when he had finished speaking, he said to Simon, "Put out into the deep and let down your nets for a catch." ⁵ And Simon answered, "Master, we toiled all night and took nothing! But at your word I will let down the nets." ⁶ And when they had done this, they enclosed many fish, and their nets were breaking. ⁷ They signaled to their partners in the other boat to come and help them. And they came and filled both the boats, so that they began to sink. ⁸ But when Simon Peter saw it, he fell down at Jesus' knees, saying, "Depart from me, for I am a sinful man, O Lord."

40.2 The English pronoun system

Pronouns in English		
	Singular subject/object/possessive	**Plural** subject/object/possessive
1st person	I/me/my/mine	we/us/our
2nd person	you/you/your	you/you/your
3rd person masculine	he/him/his	they/them/their
3rd person feminine	she/her/her	
3rd person neuter	it/it/its	

2nd person singular and plural ("you") in English

At the time when the *King James Version* was translated, "ye," "you," and "your" were the forms for the second person plural, and "thou," "thee," and "thy" for the second person singular. In modern English, however, the pronoun "you" may refer either to one person or to many people. There is no difference between the singular and the plural form, or between the subject and object form.

For this reason, it may sometimes be unclear in the English text whether singular or plural is meant.

Examples:

Mark 14:37–38   "Simon, are <u>you</u> [singular] asleep? Could <u>you</u> [singular] not watch one hour? <u>Watch</u> [plural] and <u>pray</u> [plural] that <u>you</u> [plural] may not enter into temptation."

The Hebrew and Greek languages make a distinction between the singular and the plural 2nd person pronoun, while English does not. When translating from English, be careful to use the correct form. Usually it is clear from the context, but there are some passages where the context does not make it plain, and you need to check the form in the original language. In the following example, the change of pronoun makes a significant difference in the meaning.

Luke 22:31–32a   "Simon, Simon, behold Satan demanded to have <u>you</u> [plural], that he might sift <u>you</u> [plural] like wheat, but I have prayed for <u>you</u> [singular] that <u>your</u> [singular] faith may not fail."

1 Timothy 6:21
- *RSV*   Grace be with you.
- *GNT*   God's grace be with you all.

The pronoun in 1 Timothy 6:21 is plural in the original Greek text. The greeting is addressed not only to Timothy personally, but to the whole church where he is. The GNT translation makes this clear.

40.3 Some differences in pronoun systems

Languages have different pronoun systems, marking different qualities. Here are some examples of differences that are made in some languages.

40.3.1 Alternative forms of the 1st person plural pronouns

Some languages have two forms of the 1st person plural pronoun.

(1) One form is used when the speaker is talking about himself together with the people to whom he is speaking. This is called the "inclusive" form.

(2) The other form is used if the speaker is talking about himself with other people, but not including the people to whom he is speaking. This is called the "exclusive" form.

Some languages have a dual form, used when "we" refers to the speaker and one other person. The Mambila language of Gongola State, Nigeria, has the following three different forms for the 1st person plural:

	Singular "I"	Exclusive dual "we" – I (the speaker), and one other person, excluding the person addressed	Exclusive plural "we" – I (the speaker), and other people, excluding the person addressed	Inclusive plural "we" – I (the speaker), and other people, including the person addressed
1st person	meh	behle	behl	vu

40.3.2 Other grammatical differences that may be reflected in the pronoun system

(1) Languages with noun class systems are likely to have different pronoun forms depending on the class of the noun referred to.

(2) Some languages have different forms of the pronoun with different tenses or other forms of the verb.

40.4 Explore the pronoun system in your language

(1) Study the texts in your language, especially the text of which you have made a display. Mark all the pronouns in the text. Discuss with your consultant anything you observe about pronouns in your language. Are there ways in which pronouns seem to be used differently from the way that English uses pronouns?

(2) Make a chart of the subject pronouns in your own language. You may find that there is more than one set of subject pronouns, depending on the tense of the verb or other factors.

40.5 When translating, make sure it is clear to whom or to what each pronoun refers

As noted at the beginning of this chapter, pronouns are words that stand in the place of a noun or a noun phrase. They usually refer back to something that has already been mentioned.

Confusion can arise if it is not clear to whom or what a pronoun refers. Compare the following translations of Mark 9:20–21:

> KJV   And they brought him unto him: and when he saw him, straightway the spirit tare him; and he fell on the ground, and wallowed foaming. And he asked his father, How long is it ago since this came unto him? And he said, Of a child.
>
> NIV   So they brought him. When the spirit saw Jesus, it immediately threw the boy into a convulsion. He fell to the ground and rolled around, foaming at the mouth. Jesus asked the boy's father, "How long has he been like this?" "From childhood," he answered.
>
> NLT   So they brought the boy. But when the evil spirit saw Jesus, it threw the child into a violent convulsion, and he fell to the ground, writhing and foaming at the mouth. "How long has this been happening?" Jesus asked the boy's father. He replied, "Since he was a little boy."

Remember

Always check carefully that it is clear to whom or what each pronoun refers.

Each language has its own pattern of pronoun reference. For clarity, you may sometimes need to use a noun in the translation where the source text has a pronoun.

But beware of going to the opposite extreme by using nouns and noun phrases where it would be more natural to use a pronoun. Consider the following example:

> 2 Samuel 5:17–19   When the Philistines heard that David had been anointed king over Israel, all the Philistines went up to search for David. But David heard of it and went down to the stronghold. ¹⁸ Now the Philistines had come and spread out in the Valley of Rephaim. ¹⁹ And David inquired of the LORD, "Shall I go up against the Philistines? Will you give them into my hand?" And the LORD said to David, "Go up, for I will certainly give the Philistines into your hand."

Which nouns could be replaced by pronouns to make this translation more natural in English?

40.6 Some points to watch

40.6.1 Clarify who is speaking, or to whom the words are addressed

> Mark 1:2   As it is written in Isaiah the prophet, "Behold, I send my messenger before thy face." (RSV)
>
> *A reader might suppose that "I" refers to Isaiah. The GNT translation makes the correct reference clear:*
>
> GNT   It began as the prophet Isaiah had written: "God said, 'I will send my messenger ahead of you.'"
>
> Hebrews 10:5   Wherefore when he cometh into the world, he saith, Sacrifice and offering thou wouldst not. (KJV)
>
> GNT   For this reason, when Christ was about to come into this world, he said to God: "You do not want sacrifices and offerings…"

40.6.2 A 3rd person reference to the 1st person

In some languages, a person may refer to himself as if he were talking about someone else:

> Genesis 19:2 [Lot] said, "My lords, turn aside, I pray you, to <u>your servant's house</u>." (*RSV*)
>
> *Lot was inviting them to come into his own house. A translation that makes it appear that he was talking about the house of someone else would be inaccurate. In this context, the form used expresses special respect to those who are addressed. The translation should be clear concerning who is referred to, and should also express the same degree of respect. In languages where third person reference to oneself is not natural, it might be necessary to say something like this: "My lords, turn aside, I pray you, to my house, for I am your servant."*

A detailed discussion of the use of 3rd person pronoun to refer to the 1st person may be found in *Translating the Word of God*, by J. Beekman and J. C. Callow, pages 106–116.

In the New Testament, Jesus sometimes refers to himself in the third person, especially when using the title "Son of Man."

40.6.3 Confusion may arise because of speech quotations

> Mark 13:6 [Jesus said,] "Many will come in my name saying, 'I am he.'"
>
> *In one language a serious misunderstanding arose when this verse was translated literally. To the readers it seemed that "I" referred to the speaker, that is, Jesus. They could not understand why the Lord Jesus seemed to be saying that these people should not say that he, Jesus, is the Christ. So the verse had to be re-translated as follows:*
>
> Jesus said, "Many will come claiming that they speak in my name and saying that they are the Christ."
>
> *In some languages a quotation inside another quotation is always in the indirect form.*

40.6.4 At the beginning of a new section, make explicit who is being referred to

This is helpful because people may start to read at the beginning of the section. If only a pronoun is used, they do not know to whom or what it refers.

> Mark 3:1–2 Again he entered the synagogue, and a man was there who had a withered hand. ² And they watched him, to see whether he would heal him on the sabbath, so that they might accuse him. (*RSV*)

40.6.5 Be careful when dealing with English pronouns, which are marked for gender

In English, different pronouns are used for masculine, feminine, and neuter forms: "he/him," "she/her," and "it." Some languages do not distinguish between masculine, feminine, and neuter in the pronoun. So, when translating from English care is needed.

> John 11:36 So the Jews said, "See how he loved him."
>
> *In a language in which there is no difference between "him" and "her," it could seem in the context that the pronoun referred to Mary, rather than to Lazarus. In such a case it would be better to translate explicitly, "See how he [Jesus] loved Lazarus."*

40.7 Exercises

Exercise 1

Study each of the following passages carefully in its context. In each passage there is a possible problem of pronoun reference. Compare with other English translations. Rewrite each passage, in English, making the correct meaning clear.

Mark 14:27	And Jesus said to them, "You will all fall away, for it is written, 'I will strike the shepherd, and the sheep will be scattered.'"
Luke 8:22–23	One day he got into a boat with his disciples, and he said to them, "Let us go across to the other side of the lake." So they set out, ²³ and as they sailed he fell asleep. And a windstorm came down on the lake, and they were filling with water and were in danger.
Luke 12:5	But I will warn you whom to fear: fear him who, after he has killed, has authority to cast into hell. Yes, I tell you, fear him!
Galatians 5:8	This persuasion is not from him who calls you.
Ephesians 1:11–14	¹¹ In him we have obtained an inheritance, having been predestined according to the purpose of him who works all things according to the counsel of his will, ¹² so that we who were the first to hope in Christ might be to the praise of his glory. ¹³ In him you also, when you heard the word of truth, the gospel of your salvation, and believed in him, were sealed with the promised Holy Spirit, ¹⁴ who is the guarantee of our inheritance until we acquire possession of it, to the praise of his glory.
Hebrews 11:27–28	By faith he left Egypt, not being afraid of the anger of the king, for he endured as seeing him who is invisible. ²⁸ By faith he kept the Passover and sprinkled the blood, so that the Destroyer of the firstborn might not touch them.
1 Kings 3:24–25	And the king said, "Bring me a sword." So a sword was brought before the king. ²⁵ And the king said, "Divide the living child in two, and give half to the one and half to the other."

Exercise 2

(1) Below are some passages from Mark chapter 2 in the *ESV* and *GNT* translations, printed side by side. Compare the two versions carefully. Underline in the *GNT* version those places where a noun phrase or name has been used where a pronoun is used in the *ESV*.

(2) Make notes to explain why in each place you think the translator of the *GNT* used a noun phrase or noun instead of a pronoun.

40.7 Exercises

ESV	GNT
¹ And when he returned to Capernaum after some days, it was reported that he was at home. ² And many were gathered together, so that there was no more room, not even at the door. And he was preaching the word to them. ³ And they came, bringing to him a paralytic carried by four men. ⁴ And when they could not get near him because of the crowd, they removed the roof above him, and when they had made an opening, they let down the bed on which the paralytic lay.	¹ A few days later Jesus went back to Capernaum, and the news spread that he was at home. ² So many people came together that there was no room left, not even out in front of the door. Jesus was preaching the message to them ³ when four men arrived, carrying a paralyzed man to Jesus. ⁴ Because of the crowd, however, they could not get the man to him. So they made a hole in the roof right above the place where Jesus was. When they had made the opening, they let the man down, lying on his mat.
¹³ He went out again beside the sea, and all the crowd was coming to him, and he was teaching them. ¹⁴ And as he passed by, he saw Levi the son of Alphaeus sitting at the tax booth, and he said to him, "Follow me." And he rose and followed him.	¹³ Jesus went back again to the shore of Lake Galilee. A crowd came to him, and he started teaching them. ¹⁴ As he walked along, he saw a tax collector, Levi son of Alphaeus, sitting in his office. Jesus said to him, "Follow me." Levi got up and followed him.
¹⁵ And as he reclined at table in his house, many tax collectors and sinners were reclining with Jesus and his disciples, for there were many who followed him.	¹⁵ Later on Jesus was having a meal in Levi's house. A large number of tax collectors and other outcasts were following Jesus, and many of them joined him and his disciples at the table.
¹⁸ Now John's disciples and the Pharisees were fasting. And people came and said to him, "Why do John's disciples and the disciples of the Pharisees fast, but your disciples do not fast?"	¹⁸ On one occasion the followers of John the Baptist and the Pharisees were fasting. Some people came to Jesus and asked him, "Why is it that the disciples of John the Baptist and the disciples of the Pharisees fast, but yours do not?"
²³ One Sabbath he was going through the grainfields, and as they made their way, his disciples began to pluck heads of grain. ²⁴ And the Pharisees were saying to him, "Look, why are they doing what is not lawful on the Sabbath?" ²⁵ And he said to them, "Have you never read what David did, when he was in need and was hungry, he and those who were with him: ²⁶ how he entered the house of God, in the time of Abiathar the high priest, and ate the bread of the Presence, which it is not lawful for any but the priests to eat, and also gave it to those who were with him?"	²³ Jesus was walking through some wheat fields on a Sabbath. As his disciples walked along with him, they began to pick the ears of wheat. ²⁴ So the Pharisees said to Jesus, "Look, it is against our Law for your disciples to do that on the Sabbath!" ²⁵ Jesus answered, "Have you never read what David did that time when he needed something to eat? He and his men were hungry, ²⁶ so he went into the house of God and ate the bread offered to God. This happened when Abiathar was the High Priest. According to our Law only the priests may eat this bread—but David ate it and even gave it to his men."

Exercise 3

Discuss possible problems concerning pronoun reference in the following examples. Look up each passage in its context and compare with translations in different Bible versions.

Matthew 4:7   Jesus said to him, "Again it is written, 'You shall not put the Lord your God to the test.'"

Luke 1:41–43   And when Elizabeth heard the greeting of Mary, the baby leaped in her womb. And Elizabeth was filled with the Holy Spirit, ⁴² and

	she exclaimed with a loud cry, "Blessed are you among women, and blessed is the fruit of your womb! [43] And why is this granted to me that the mother of my Lord should come to me?"
Luke 9:26	For whoever is ashamed of me and of my words, of him will the Son of Man be ashamed when he comes in his glory and the glory of the Father and of the holy angels.
Ephesians 1:1–2	Paul, an apostle of Christ Jesus by the will of God, To the saints who are in Ephesus, and are faithful in Christ Jesus: [2] Grace to you and peace from God our Father and the Lord Jesus Christ.

Additional resource on "Pronoun Reference"

BT4 online materials

40_Exploring_pronouns.pdf

Chapter 41

Looking at the Big Picture – Discourse Perspective

This chapter suggests specific topics for study in the receptor language. It is suggested that a prospective translator begin by studying two or three topics, choosing those that seem to be most relevant for his language, and keeping notes of his observations. As time continues, he will keep observing both spoken and written forms of his language to see whether or not those initial observations are confirmed by further examples. He will also continue to study further topics, as issues come up in the translation project that send him back to do further research on his language. Exploring one's own language is an ongoing task!

The material for study will be the texts in the receptor language that have been charted, and other texts in which to look for further examples of the topic under study. It is also helpful to compare the forms used in the receptor language with the forms used in English, observing where they are similar and where they are different. The English text of Achebe's Tortoise Story, charted in section 39.3, provides some limited data for observation. Participants should also listen to spoken conversation and observe other written texts, of different speech genres.

Topics for study

What follows is a list of topics from which to select what is most relevant for your language and translation situation. The topics can be taken in any order. Certain issues may come up while checking translations and this may lead you to prioritise the study of that issue.

Prospective translators should discuss with their consultant or facilitator which topic(s) they should choose for their initial discourse study.

1. **Sentence connections**

    (1) In the display that you have made of a text in your language, study the column headed "Connecting words." Make a list of connecting words or phrases that are used more than once, with notes on how they are used.

    a) Are there any connecting words that seem to be very frequently used in your language? Make notes on how these words are used.

b) For any common connecting words, count how many times this occurs in a sample text. Then take a translated passage of similar length and type, and count how many times this occurs in the translation. Discuss the result with your consultant or advisor.

(2) Are there examples of "overlap constructions" in your language, where the last clause of one sentence is repeated at the beginning of the next sentence? (This is sometimes called a "tail-head construction.") How frequently does this occur? A point to watch as you study other kinds of texts will be whether it occurs more frequently in certain kinds of text (for example, narrative stories) than in others. For example,

> All the chiefs gathered together and discussed the matter. As they discussed the matter...
> After walking for many hours, he reached the market. When he reached the market...

(3) In some languages, new information is usually introduced in a main clause, rather than in a subordinate clause.

For example, in Mark 11:27 the information that Jesus went to the temple and walked there is new information, not previously known to the reader. In some languages, this new information is best introduced in a main clause.

> Mark 11:27   And they came to Jerusalem. And as he was walking in the temple, the chief priests and the scribes and elders came to him.
>
> ⇒   And they came to Jerusalem. <u>Jesus went into the temple and was walking there</u>. As he was walking there, the chief priests and the scribes and elders came to him.

(4) In what other ways are connections between sentences indicated?
   a) Are there any connecting particles that come in other positions, apart from at the beginning of the sentence?
   b) Is there anything in the verb phrase that indicates the relationship between sentences? For example, a change in the tense of the verb.

(5) Make summary notes on what you have observed about sentence connections. Note particularly any differences you have noticed between your language and English. Consider what implications this may have for translation.

2. Frequency of verbs

(1) Take the English or other source language text you are comparing. Mark every verb.
(2) Now take the text you are studying in your own language. Mark every verb.
(3) Compare the two texts. Answer the following questions:
   a) Count the number of verbs in two pages of text in your own language. Count the number of verbs in a similar amount of text in English. Which language uses the most verbs, English or your own language?
   b) Are there any verbs that seem to occur particularly frequently in your language? If so, list them. Observe how they are used.
   c) Does your language sometimes use several verbs one after the other? If so, write down examples. (These are called "serial verbs.")
   d) Give examples of any places in the texts where it seems that your language would use a verb, but English would use some other form.

(4) Now examine a portion of translation you have made in your language. If possible, this should be a kind of text similar to those you are studying in English and your language. For example, if you are studying stories, then a translated parable would be suitable. Mark all the verbs in the translation. Count them. Compare the number with the number you counted in a similar quantity of text in your language. Discuss the result with your consultant or advisor.

(5) Make summary notes on what you have observed.

3. Verbal nouns and event ideas

A "verbal noun" is a noun that refers to an event. It refers to something that happens rather than to a thing. Examples in English are: "singing," "disobedience," "death," "observation."

(1) Circle any examples of verbal nouns that you can find in the English or other source language text you are studying.

(2) In the English text in section 39.3, compare with line 42, "he was a great orator," and line 59 "his speech was very eloquent." Although both references involve the same event idea, "speak," the first puts the focus on the person: "he was a person who could speak very well," while the second puts the focus on the act of speaking. This is an important difference. In translating, the same difference of focus should be maintained, although this may be indicated by a different grammatical form.

(3) Circle any examples of verbal nouns that you can find in the text in your own language.

(4) In which language do verbal nouns seem to be more frequent, in your own language or in the other language with which you are comparing?

(5) If you do not at first find any verbal nouns in the text of your own language, it does not necessarily mean that they do not occur at all. Look at other texts in your language to see if you find examples. Observe in what kinds of texts they are used, and for what purpose.

(6) Make summary notes on what you have observed about how verbal nouns are used in your language.

4. Active-passive constructions

The difference between active and passive forms in English was discussed in chapter 28. In the active form, the subject of the sentence is the person doing the action. In the passive form, the subject is the person or thing to which the action is being done.

(1) Mark all the passive forms you can find in the verbs of the English or other language text you are studying.

(2) Mark all the passive forms you can find in the verbs of the text in your own language. (Remember that in the display you made of the text, you have listed the verbs in one column. This will make your task easier.)

  a) Write down examples of any passive forms that you find in the text in your language.

  b) Did you find any passive forms in your text? If you found examples, does the passive form in your language seem to be more frequent or less frequent than in English? For what purposes is it used?

  c) Are there any examples of clauses where the subject is indefinite ("one" did something) or impersonal ("they" did something, not referring to anyone specific)?

(3) Write summary notes on what you have discovered about passive forms in your language.

5. Time and tense

(1) In the text you are studying in your language, mark everything that tells anything about the time when an action took place.
- a) List examples of any words or phrases that indicate time in your language. Do time words and phrases usually come at the beginning of a sentence? In what other positions can they occur?
- b) Is the same verb tense used throughout the text? Mark any places where there seems to be a change of tense. Discuss these with your consultant or advisor.
- c) List examples of different verb tenses that you have observed in the text. Begin to make a chart of the different verb tenses that occur, noting how each one is signalled in the language.

(2) Make summary notes about anything interesting you have observed about time words and verb tenses in your language.

6. Paragraphs

A paragraph is a unit of text, consisting of one or more sentences, which deals with a single theme or idea. A new paragraph usually signals that a new idea is being introduced into a discourse.

(1) Paragraph breaks have been marked in the English story in section 39.3. In what different ways is the beginning of a new paragraph indicated?

(2) Study the text(s) you have charted in your own language. Have you already indicated paragraph breaks? Looking at both the content of the text and the connective phrases or words in the text, what signals are there that help you to know where paragraph divisions should be made in texts in your language?

7. Speech quotations

A "direct quotation" is a quotation where the exact words are quoted exactly as the original speaker spoke them. For example,

She said, "Come."

He said, "I will come."

An "indirect" or "non-direct quotation" is a quotation where the words are quoted in a modified form. Often there are changes of tense or pronouns. For example,

She told him to come.

He said that he would come.

In English grammar, the term "indirect" is used. However, the term "non-direct" is used here, since the form in some languages may be different from the English indirect form. In some languages, there is more than one kind of non-direct quotation.

To study

(1) Take a clean copy of the English or other language you are studying.
- a) Mark all direct quotations in one colour.
- b) Mark all quotations that are not direct in another colour.

c) Using a third colour, mark all "speech introductory" clauses. A speech introductory clause is one that introduces a quotation. For example, <u>He said</u> that he would come. <u>She asked</u>, "Are you there?"

(2) Do the same thing in the text in your own language. It may help if you use the same colours in the same way.

   a) Count the number of direct quotations and the number of non-direct quotations in your text. Which is more frequent?

   b) If both direct and non-direct quotations are used, under what conditions are each used? Look for these points:
   - Sometimes direct quotations are used more at the climax of a story, non-direct quotations elsewhere.
   - Sometimes direct quotations are used when the main character of the story is speaking, while the speech of minor characters may be quoted in non-direct form.

(3) Does there seem to be more than one type of non-direct quotation?

(4) Does anything interesting happen in the way that pronouns are used in quotations? Are there any pronouns that occur only in quotations?

(5) Are there any examples of quotations inside another quotation? If so, in what form is the inner quotation? In some languages, quotations inside another quotation are always non-direct. This can have important implications for translation.

(6) Look at the speech introductory clauses in your text.

   a) Where does the speech introductory clause come? Is it always before the quotation? Are there any examples in your texts where it comes after the quotation or in the middle of a quotation?

   b) List the verbs that may occur ("said," "asked," "exclaimed"). Some languages have a wide variety of speech introductory verbs, others use very few.

   c) What is the usual pattern for a speech introductory clause? Does it usually (or always) include a certain speech introductory particle? Is the person to whom the speech is being made always explicitly mentioned ("The chief said to them that . . .")?

   d) Is the form of the speech introductory clause sometimes shortened? If so, when does this happen? (In some languages, it happens when there is a series of quotations, "he said . . . she said . . . he said . . .")

8. Commands

Look for examples of commands or instructions in your texts. How are commands and exhortations expressed? Are different verbs used, depending on the status and attitude of the person who is speaking and those of the person he is addressing?

9. Questions

The difference between real and rhetorical questions is explained in chapter 35.

(1) Mark all the questions in the text you are studying in English. Mark them as either real or rhetorical.

(2) Mark all the questions in the text you are studying in your own language. Mark them as either real or rhetorical. Look for further examples in other texts.

   a) Does your language use rhetorical questions at all?

   b) If so, for what purposes are they used?

(3) Compare the way that rhetorical questions are used in your language with the way that they are used in the Bible. Some ways in which they are used in the Bible are described in section 35.3.

   a) Are there any purposes for which rhetorical questions are used in the Bible for which there seems to be no parallel in your language?

   b) Are there any purposes for which rhetorical questions are used in your language for which they do not seem to be used in the Bible?

(4) Make summary notes on what you have observed.

10. Negative

(1) Make a list of different ways in which negative meaning can be expressed in your language.

(2) Are different negative forms used depending on whether the sentence is a statement, a command, or a question?

(3) In what ways can the negative be emphasised?

(4) When a positive statement and a negative statement occur together in a sentence, in what order do they usually come? Does a negative clause usually come at the end of a sentence?

11. Participant reference

The "participants" in an event are the people or things that take part in that event.

(1) List the main participants in the English text you are studying. Then choose the most important participant in the story. Using a coloured pencil or font, circle every reference to that participant (whether by a noun, or a pronoun, or in any other way.) Using a different colour, do the same thing for at least one other participant.

(2) Do the same thing for participants in the text you are studying in your own language.

   a) In what ways is a new participant introduced into the story in your language?

   b) When a participant has already been introduced, in what ways is he referred to again?

   c) When is a participant referred to by a noun?

   d) Are there any ways of bringing one participant into special focus? Or of emphasising one of the participants?

   e) Does the same pattern apply for the main participant as for other participants? Or are there differences?

(3) Summarise what you have observed, noting differences from English.

12. Relative clauses

Relative clauses in English are usually introduced by "who" or "which." There are two kinds of relative clauses:

- *Defining relative clauses*: A defining relative clause specifies who is referred to:

    The boys who stole the apples were seen by the farmer.

    The relative clause, "who stole the apples," defines which boys were seen by the farmer. (Defining relative clauses are also sometimes called "restrictive clauses.")

- *Descriptive relative clauses*: A descriptive relative clause gives additional information about the thing or person it describes, but does not define it.

    The boys, who had all studied hard, passed their exams brilliantly.

Some languages have only defining relative clauses, not descriptive ones. It is important to know whether this is the case in your language.

(1) Mark all the relative clauses in the English or other language text you are studying.

(2) Mark all the relative clauses in the text you are studying in your own language.

   a) Count the number of relative clauses in the English or other language text, and in a similar amount of similar text in your own language. Which language seems to use more relative clauses?

   b) Study the relative clauses you have marked in your own language. Mark them as either *defining* or *descriptive*. Are there examples of both types in your texts, or of only one type? Discuss what you discover with your consultant or advisor.

   c) Is information that has not already been mentioned earlier in the text ever mentioned for the first time in a relative clause?

   d) Does more than one relative clause ever occur one after the other? Does more than one relative clause ever occur in the same sentence? Are there examples where a relative clause can occur inside another relative clause ("embedded relative clauses")?

   e) Do relative clauses ever qualify anything other than the subject of a sentence? If so, give examples.

(3) Make summary notes on what you have observed about relative clauses in your language. If you have discovered that your language only uses defining clauses, not descriptive clauses, then you will need to take special care when translating relative clauses in the source text. Some restructuring will be necessary in your translation.

13. Logical relations

This chart shows different logical relations that can occur within a sentence, or between larger units of text.

Reason	The clothes are clean because Mary washed them. I came to see you this evening because I was hungry.
Result *(not necessarily intentional)*	Mary washed the clothes and now they are clean. Mary washed the clothes and the colours have spoiled.
Purpose *(intentional)*	Mary washed the clothes in order to get them clean.
Condition *(the condition may be either possible or untrue)*	If it rains tomorrow, I will go to market. If I were a rich man, I would buy this house.
Concession-Contra-expectation	Even though Mary washed the clothes, they are not clean.
Means-Result	Mary got the clothes clean by washing them.

| Grounds-Conclusion | The clothes are clean, so Mary must have washed them. |
| Grounds-Exhortation | Mary, the clothes are not clean, so wash them. |

Exercise 1

(1) Find examples of these logical relationships in texts in your language. Note examples of different ways in which each may be expressed.

(2) Make notes on the relative position of the components. For example, does a reason usually come before or after a result?

Exercise 2

Identify the relationship between the clauses in each of the following verses.

a. She wrapped him in cloths and placed him in a manger, because there was no room for them in the inn. (Luke 2:7)

b. So if you worship me, it will all be yours. (Luke 4:7)

c. They ... took him to the brow of the hill on which the town was built, in order to throw him down the cliff. (Luke 4:29)

d. They came and filled both boats so full that they began to sink. (Luke 5:7)

e. Yet the news about him spread all the more, so that crowds of people came to hear him and to be healed of their sicknesses. (Luke 5:15)

f. He puts it on its stand, so that those who come in may see the light. (Luke 11:33)

g. If it bears fruit next year, fine! If not, then cut it down. (Luke 15:39)

For further discussion and examples of logical relations, see Barnwell, *Introduction to Semantics and Translation*, chapters 14–21.

14. Genitive constructions

Genitive constructions are discussed in chapter 27.

Review

A genitive construction is one in which two nouns (or a noun and a pronoun) are closely related together. Genitive constructions are also known as "noun-noun" constructions. In English, a very common type of noun-noun construction is the "of" construction.
In English there are three different types of genitive construction:

- NOUN "of" NOUN   For example, "the house of the boy"
- NOUN's NOUN   For example, "the boy's house"
- POSSESSIVE PRONOUN-NOUN For example, "his house"

(1) Choose a sample English text, a text that has been told or written by someone who speaks English as his first language, not translated. Mark examples of all three types of genitive construction.

(2) Re-express the meaning of each noun-noun phrase in a way that makes the relationship between the parts clear. Do not change the meaning in any way. All event ideas should be expressed by verbs.

(3) Then take the text you have prepared in your own language. Mark all the noun-noun constructions that you can find. Compare these with those you have marked in the English text.

   a) Which language seems to use more noun-noun constructions? Your own language or English?
   b) Do any of the noun-noun constructions in your own language include nouns that express event ideas?
   c) List the different kinds of relationships that may be expressed by noun-noun constructions in your language. Do they all express possession? Or are there other relationships?
   d) Are there any examples in the texts in your own language of "verbal nouns" as part of a noun-noun construction?
   e) Compare what you have observed in your own language with what you observe about noun-noun constructions in English. Discuss this with your consultant or instructor.

(4) Make summary notes on what you have discovered.

15. Singular and plural

Different languages show the difference between singular and plural nouns in different ways. In addition to observing how the singular and plural are indicated on the noun itself, you need to observe (1) whether, how, and when the verb also changes, depending on whether the subject is singular or plural; and (2) what other grammatical forms also change to match with the class of the noun they refer to, for example, pronouns.

Some languages have multiple classes of nouns.

(1) The following example shows how the plural is formed in the Mbembe language. Study the words and the summary statement below.

(2) Then study how plural nouns are formed in your own language. Make a summary statement to describe this. If your language is a noun-class language, discuss with your consultant who will be able to give you information about the systems in related languages.

Example from Mbembe (Cross River State, Nigeria) – limited data

	Singular		Plural	
1.	ǫraanga	river	araanga	rivers
2.	ǫnǫng	person	anǫng	people
3.	ogǫgǫ	white ant	agǫgǫ	white ants
4.	ǫwǫmǫ	plantain	awǫmǫ	plantains
5.	echi	tree	nchi	trees
6.	eten	animal	nten	animals
7.	eso	head	nso	heads
8.	ete	fishing basket	nte	fishing baskets
9.	ikpo	cap	okpo	caps
10.	iyin	feather	oyin	feathers
11.	iphe	kind of dish	ophe	dishes

Sample summary statement (for this limited data)

In the Mbembe language, the singular and plural of nouns are shown by changing the vowel or the syllabic sound "n" at the beginning of the word.

- Nouns that begin with o or ọ in the singular, begin with *a* in the plural.
  For example, *ọraanga/araanga* "river/rivers."
- Nouns that begin with e or ẹ in the singular, begin with *n* in the plural.
  For example, *eten/nten* "animal/animals."
- Nouns that begin with *i* in the singular, begin with *o* in the plural.
  For example, *ikpo/okpo* "cap/caps"

16. Qualifiers (also called "attributes")

(1) Mark all qualifying words, such as adjectives and adverbs in the English or other language text.

(2) Mark all qualifying words in the text in your own language.

  a) Does your language seem to use more or less adjectives than English or the other language with which you are comparing?

  b) In what other ways does your language express ideas that English or another language may express by adjectives and adverbs?

  c) How does your language express size ("big," "little"), quantity ("many," "few," "plenty"), quality ("good," "bad," "well"), and other attributes?

17. Numbers

(1) What is the basic unit in the counting system in your language? Is it five? or ten? or twenty?

  In English, the basic unit is 10. For example, 80 is 8 times 10.
  In some languages, the basic unit is 20. 80 would be expressed as 4 times 20.

(2) What is the largest number for which there is a single word? Is it 100? or 400? or 1000?

  In English, large numbers are counted in multiples of 100 or 1000. In some languages, large numbers are counted in multiples of 400.

(3) Write the following numbers in your language:
  a) 5000   – as in Mark 6:44
  b) 72   – as in Luke 10:1
  c) 153   – as in John 21:11
  d) 276   – as in Acts 27:37
  e) 144,000 and 12,000 – as in Revelation 7:4–8

18. Onomatopoeia, exclamatory words, and ideophones

The term *onomatopoeia* refers to words that in some way represent the sound of the thing to which they refer. English examples include "hiss," "bang," "buzz." Be alert for examples of this feature in the receptor language and observe how it is used.

Exclamatory words, also called "exclamations" or "interjections," are sometimes onomatopoeic. A biblical example: Revelation 18:16 "Woe, woe, O great city" (*NET* version, Greek οὐαί). In most languages, however, exclamatory words occur mainly in spoken conversation, except when quoting conversations, seldom in written texts. Again, observe what is natural in the receptor language.

Ideophones are expressive words or phrases where the sound of the word reflects the quality to which it refers. In languages that have this feature, ideophones should be used in the translation wherever they effectively express the meaning of the original text, provided this is appropriate for the style of the passage. They may not be suitable in all contexts as they may sometimes have a humorous effect. Examples of Scripture texts where an ideophone might be appropriate include the following:

Genesis 7:12	And rain fell upon the earth forty days and forty nights.	
	⇒ *Rain rained for forty days tchrrr.* (Baka, South Sudan)	
Luke 6:49	It fell, and the ruin of the house was great.	
	⇒ *The house fell begmm.* (Mbembe, Nigeria)	
Luke 9:29	And his raiment became dazzling white.	
	⇒ *His clothes shone, they were white benwangggg.* (Mbembe)	

Are ideophones used in your language?

(1) Mark any examples of ideophones in the text in your language. Look for further examples in other texts.

   a) Does your language have ideophones? Note down examples.

   b) In what kinds of texts are ideophones used? For what purpose are they used?

   c) Think of some places in the Bible where ideophones might be appropriately used in your translation.

(2) Mark any examples of exclamatory words in your texts.

   a) In what kinds of texts are they used? Are they used frequently in conversation?

   b) Think of places in the translation of the Bible where exclamatory words might be used in your translation to express emotional feeling.

(3) Make summary notes on what you have observed.

19. Figures of speech

(1) Underline all examples of figures of speech in the text in your language. Look for further examples in other texts.

(2) Study the figures of speech you have observed. For what purposes are they used?

(3) Compare the figures of speech you have observed in your language with the different kinds of figures of speech that occur in the Bible. Some figures of speech that occur in the Bible are discussed in chapters 33 and 34.

   a) Give examples of metaphors or other comparisons from your texts.

   b) Are there any kinds of figures of speech in your language that seem to be different from those that occur in the Bible?

   c) Are there any kinds of figures of speech that occur in the Bible that do not seem to occur in your language?

20. Focus and emphasis

(1) In the text you are studying in your language, mark any places where a concept or idea is brought into special focus. How is this indicated?

(2) What special ways are there for emphasising an idea?

(3) What ways are there for contrasting ideas?

21. Background and parenthesis

(1) When there is an explanation about background facts, where in the text does this usually come? How does one know when this background information ends and the main line of the text begins again? In what other grammatical ways is it indicated that this is background information?

(2) When a parenthesis occurs in a text, how is this indicated? Are there any grammatical signals? (A "parenthesis" is an interruption in the main line of the text. It may be a side comment or explanation, for example.)

(3) When the author doubles back to describe something that happened at an earlier point in the story, how is this indicated?

22. Beginnings and endings

The ending of a discourse often relates to the beginning, especially in certain speech genres – for example, stories.

(1) Is there a particular pattern for beginning and ending a traditional story in your language? If so, give an example. For what kinds of stories is this pattern used?

(2) As you go on to study other kinds of texts, watch for any forms that typically occur at the beginning or end of a text.

(3) Look at the beginning and end of each Bible book, to see whether the end picks up an intention stated by the author at the beginning of the book.

23. Climax

The "climax" is the most intense point in the development of an event or of a text. In a dramatic or literary work, the climax is a major turning point, the point for which the preceding text has been preparing the way.

In the stories or other texts that you have collected in your language, can you recognise certain points that can be identified as the climax of the story?

24. Vocative phrases

A "vocative phrase" is a phrase used to address someone directly. For example,

They said to him, "Sir, we wish to see Jesus." (John 12:21)

He cried out with a loud voice, "Lazarus, come out." (John 11:43)

Stephen said, "Brothers and fathers, hear me." (Acts 7:2)

Consider each context carefully and use the form of address that is appropriate for (a) the person addressed, (b) the person speaking, and (c) the attitude and emotions of the person speaking.

(1) Underline any examples of vocative phrases that occur in the text in your language. Look for more examples in other texts.

(2) Are vocative phrases used frequently in your language either in everyday speech or in certain speech genres? Or are they used only very occasionally?

(3) Make a list of the vocative phrases that are used most frequently in your language. Note down how each one would be used, to whom it would be addressed, and what attitude it would show on the part of the speaker. For example, it might be that the term "father" would be used to address any respected older man.

25. Attitude

(1) If a speaker is showing special respect to the person or people he is addressing, how is this indicated? Are certain forms used when a younger person is addressing an older person? The term *honorific* is often used for special words used in this way.

(2) If the speaker is showing contempt to the person or people he is addressing, how is this indicated? What about other attitudes?

26. Repetition and reduplication

Underline any places in the texts in your language where repetition or reduplication is used. For what purposes is it used? Is it used for emphasis? For what other purposes is it used?

27. Particles

(1) There may be certain words or particles that occur frequently in a language but are difficult to translate. They may indicate emphasis or focus. List any particles of this kind that occur in your language.

(2) For each of the particles you have listed, go through some texts marking every example of this particle. Study these texts and try to make a summary statement about how the particle is used.

> **Remember**
>
> Keep studying texts in your own language. Your first observations will be tentative. Keep observing (and listening to) other texts to see if your first observations are confirmed by further examples.
>
> Ongoing study of your language will include the study of different kinds of texts, such as
>
> - narratives – for example, accounts of historical events, personal accounts, traditional stories, stories that teach;
> - conversations;
> - speeches and exhortations;
> - teaching and explanations;
> - descriptions;
> - proverbs and riddles;
> - prayers;
> - letters;
> - poetry and songs (of praise or lamentation).

Part 7

Planning and Organising a Bible Translation Project

At the beginning of every translation project, it is important that there is an overall plan for the project, including agreement on how representatives of the language community will be responsibly involved. In short, this preparation phase includes

- involving the churches and community in the receptor language area, informing them about the proposed Bible translation project, and inviting their cooperation;
- setting up an organising committee and together preparing a vision statement (a "brief") for the project;
- interacting with a national or regional Bible translation organisation to develop a partnership;
- preparing and processing a financial budget;
- doing basic linguistic analysis and developing a writing system for the language, if this is not already in place; and
- selecting and providing initial training of the translators.

In training translators, the first translation goals should be chosen with the agreed long-term goals of the project in mind. See the suggestions at the end of chapter 9 in the section "Translation Practice."

Chapter 42

The Role of the Churches and Community in a Translation Project – Translation Is Teamwork!

Translation projects vary greatly and there is no standard pattern. Each translation project must be planned according to the local situation. The aim in this chapter is to cover the general principles, and to help those who are involved in planning to gain a good understanding of the different aspects of the work that need to be considered.

In this discussion, it is assumed that the translators are first-language speakers of the receptor language concerned.

A booklet is available with the title *Planning a Bible Translation Project*. This can be adapted and reproduced for use in areas where a Bible translation project is starting or is already in progress. The purpose of the booklet is to inform local leaders and others about what is involved in a Bible translation project and about the responsibilities of all involved. It is designed for situations in which there are already some churches in the area. The text of this booklet is accessible as listed in the **BT4 online materials** at the end of this chapter.

Those initiating a translation project should be careful to avoid duplication of work that is already in progress.

42.1 Ownership of the project

Bible translation projects are taking place in many different situations. In some areas, there may be a strong church, perhaps with several church denominations represented. In other areas, there may be very little local support. A goal in every situation will be to keep good relationships with all involved.

Wherever there are churches in the area, the churches should have a leading role in the project and take responsibility in the following ways:

- Interact and decide together on the goals of the project.
- Contribute funds to meet the expenses of the project.

- Identify people from the leadership and membership of the churches who have potential to become translators, and free them from some of their church responsibilities if they are selected to become translators, so that they have time to serve on the translation team.
- Appoint representatives to be "reviewers." Reviewers will read through the translation as it is produced and send feedback to the translation team.
- Use the translation in church services and meetings as it becomes available, through lectionary and other Bible readings, Bible studies, and in other ways.
- Pray regularly for the translation team and for all aspects of the work.

It is good to consider possibilities for registering the project legally as a non-profit non-government organisation (NGO). This gives the project a legal status and demonstrates commitment to a well-organised system for recording finances and for making financial reports.

> As noted in the introduction to this manual, women have had a leading role in many translation projects, along with men. In the text below, wherever the pronoun "he" is mentioned, please read "he or she."

42.2 Translation project committee

It is recommended that a representative local leadership committee be formed for every Bible translation project. This committee does not do the translation but is responsible for the major decisions concerning the project. The committee is often named "The *Kalaba* Language and Translation Committee" (where "Kalaba" represents the name of the language concerned). The committee may deal with issues related to the writing of the language, to literacy and Scripture use activities, as well as Bible translation. If the project is legally registered as a non-governmental organisation (NGO), the committee may be referred to as "The Kalaba Language and Translation Board."

The translation committee will include representatives appointed by the different church denominations in the area. Any other groups in the area should also be represented. For example, if there are different dialects, these should be represented on the committee.

If a significant proportion of the speakers of the language belong to another religion, there may need to be two committees: one focusing on the development and use of the language, made up of representatives of the whole community, and another focusing on the Bible translation work, comprising representatives of the churches.

Qualifications

In situations where Bible translation is a primary focus, members of the committee will be committed Christians who are themselves convinced of the need for the Scriptures in the intended receptor language. They must be ready to give time to carry out the responsibilities listed below.

Responsibilities

- Represent the churches and community in matters concerning the project.
- Represent the project to the churches and community, keeping them informed of the progress and concerns of the project, and promoting the project.

- Identify the primary audience for the translation and also secondary audiences who will have access to the translation.
- Interact with all concerned to decide on the goals for the project and the time frame;
- Coordinate with all concerned to draw up a vision statement (memorandum of understanding) that records the major decisions made concerning the project – see chapter 43.
- Help select and appoint the translators, the reviewers, and others involved in the work of the project; monitor them, encourage them, and help facilitate their work.
- Encourage people to pray for the translators and for all aspects of the project.
- Raise money to meet the expenses of the project and ensure that accounts of income and expenditure are carefully kept and reported. The local churches should support the project financially to the full extent of their ability.
- Encourage the distribution and use of the translated Scriptures, both during the time when the translation is being tested, and when it has been published.
- Be involved in decisions relating to publication, such as the format of printed and audio products and the choice of publisher.

42.3 Pastors, evangelists, and other church leaders

Church leaders have an important part in the translation program.

Responsibilities

- Recognise the value of the local language in effective communication and encourage a positive attitude toward use of the language.
- Read portions of the translated Scriptures regularly in church services, prayer meetings, and other gatherings, and use these in preaching and teaching.
- Encourage people to use the translated Scriptures; for example, in Bible study groups, in family devotions, in song and with music, and in personal study.
- Encourage people to listen to audio recordings of the translated Scriptures.
- Encourage people to learn to read their own language and provide opportunities for this.
- Keep people informed about the translation project.
- Be involved in discussion on the translation of key biblical terms and other translation-related issues.
- Review and test the translation.
- Gather comments and suggestions on draft translations and give feedback to the translators and others on the translation team. The translators can then correct any faults that are discovered before the printed version is published.

42.4 Teamwork – members of the translation team

The task of translating the Bible into any language is something that no one person can do alone. That task belongs to the whole church in the language area. There must be a team of people sharing in the work.

Every Bible translation project is different. The gifts and abilities of the people involved are different. Sometimes one person may fill two or more of the roles. Sometimes the work may be divided out in a way that is different from what is described here. But this description will help to give an idea of the total work that is involved.

Situations are different too. In some areas there are strong churches, with many active Christians. In other areas the churches are still small, or there may not be any church at all yet. So the planning of the project needs to be adjusted to fit the situation.

Such a great task can only be completed successfully if the whole team works together. Each member of the team must know his part in the task and must do it faithfully. Each member of the team must be ready to give time and to work hard.

Figure 6 illustrates the typical composition of a translation project.

The qualifications and responsibilities of these team members have been described elsewhere in this manual. They are also presented in detail in the booklet *Planning a Bible translation project*, accessible in **BT4 online materials**.

42.5 Relationship to a Bible translation organisation

Most Bible translation projects relate to a national or regional Bible translation organisation. In forming a partnership, the project commits to follow agreed principles and procedures in Bible translation while the translation organisation agrees to support the project, typically in the following ways:

- By providing national or regional training courses and workshops to train translators and other team members, in linguistics, translation principles, literacy, and computer skills;
- By visiting the project occasionally to review progress and encourage the team;
- By providing linguistic and translation consultant assistance;
- By providing technical computer assistance;
- By facilitating the purchase of computers and other equipment;
- By facilitating publication of both audio and printed publications, helping the project leaders relate to a Bible translation publishing agency.

Figure 6. Local Bible translation project.
© 2018 by Seed Company.
Used by permission.

Where some financial assistance is needed, the national or regional organisation may be able to help identify a source of financial help, usually through an international Bible translation agency, and assist in the development of an agreement.

> Translation is teamwork. Those serving as translators will have different strengths. One may be a strong exegete, having a good knowledge of other languages and of the Bible. Another may be gifted in expressing the meaning creatively and in good style in the receptor language. Another may have the ability to notice details and to edit carefully and well.
>
> The team needs to work together, using the gifts and knowledge God has distributed among them to the full.

Additional resources on "The Role of the Churches and Community in a Translation Project"

BT4 online materials

42_Finances_and_other_aspects_of_planning_a_translation_project.pptx
42_Planning_a_translation_project-Roles_and_responsibilities.pptx
42_Planning_a_Bible_translation_project-Booklet.pdf
  (This text is designed to be printed as a booklet. Settings need to be adjusted to facilitate (a) printing on the appropriate size of paper (A4 or Letter) with portrait orientation, and (b) to print double-sided. See illustration.

  If your printer can automatically print on both sides (duplex printing), then use this option. If not, follow the on-screen prompt in Microsoft Word to re-load the paper, when the first sides have finished printing. Tip for manual double-sided printers: If the pages come out in the wrong order when the booklet is laid out, you may find your printer settings have an option you can use to switch the page ordering for the second side, or you can re-arrange the page order by hand before re-loading the paper.)

For further reading

Marmor, Thomas, and Eric Bartels. Forthcoming. *Managing language programs: Perspectives, processes and practices*. Dallas: SIL International Pike Center for Integrative Scholarship. E-book, accessible at the website link: www.leanpub.com/PLPM/.

Chapter 43

Preparing a Translation Brief

A *translation brief* can also be described as a "vision statement" or a "memorandum of understanding" for the translation project.

43.1 The purpose of a translation brief[1]

It is widely recommended that, at the beginning of a translation project, a document is drawn up that records the goals, purpose, and procedures that have been agreed for the project. This statement results from extensive interaction and discussion by those involved. It records their joint agreement and their commitments. The intention is to help all involved, especially local partners, keep focused on the agreed goals, track progress, and avoid misunderstandings.

In the past, Bible translation agencies have often been responsible for initiating and defining translation projects. Currently, wherever possible, the local community and especially churches in the area concerned are the "owners" of the project. The translation brief reflects their goals and decisions. The Language and Translation Committee for the project is often the body responsible for composing this document and for processing it with all partners, to ensure that it does indeed represent the decisions that have been agreed. The initial brief is then reviewed and updated periodically, and is followed up by regular reports on the progress of the project.

43.2 How to prepare a project brief

Situations vary, and the information that will be included in a project brief will vary, depending on what is relevant for this specific project. The following kinds of information are likely to be included:

---

[1] The idea of making a translation brief originated from *Skopos* theory as developed by the German linguists Hans Vermeer and Katharina Reiss, and applied to Bible translation by Dr Christiane Nord (1997) of Germany and others. *Skopos* means "intended purpose and use." In order to achieve a satisfactory translation, translators should keep in focus (a) the situation in which the translation will be used, (b) the specific audience for whom it is intended, and (c) the purpose it is intended to achieve. Therefore, at the beginning of a translation project, it is important to have a clear statement of the values and goals that have been discussed and agreed for this project.

1) Who are the partners cooperating in the project?
   - partners within the community, such as church denominations
   - partners outside the community, such as regional, national, or international Bible translation organisations
2) Is there a locally appointed Language and/or Translation Committee who are steering the project? Include details of how committee members were chosen and appointed, length of office, and agreed method for re-appointment or election.
3) Who is the intended audience of the translation? Is it mainly for older people or younger people? For educated people or less educated? For people in the churches or for those who have no knowledge of Christianity?
4) What are the translation goals? For example, a single Gospel, a New Testament, a full Bible? What will be translated first? Include short-term and long-term goals, with some indication on target dates for completion of specific goals.
5) In what form(s) will the translation be published? Will it be printed? Or in audio form? Or both print and audio?
6) What will be the source texts? Is it clearly agreed that the original Hebrew, Aramaic, and Greek texts are the final authority? What major language Bible version(s) will be used as source texts? If appropriate, mention other versions that will be consulted.
7) How will the translation be distributed and used?

The following information may also be included, but this will depend on the local situation and on other partnerships. Alternatively, some of this information may be included in a separate memorandum of understanding that is agreed upon with a regional, national, or international Bible translation organisation (see also chapter 42, section 42.5), or with a local education department.

8) Are there any other translation projects in the area with whom it may be possible to partner by sharing training programs or other activities?
9) Is there an agreed budget for the project? How will funds be raised? Who on the translation team will receive a salary? What reports of income and expenditure do the funding agencies and donors expect from the project? Who is responsible for financial reporting?
10) Are there local authorities who should be informed and involved, perhaps in issues concerning the system used for writing the language or the teaching of the reading of the language?

43.3 An example of a project brief[2]

Project Brief for the Kalaba Language and Translation Project

This document records the goals and plans of the Kalaba Language and Translation Project (KLTP), as discussed and agreed by church and community leaders in the area where Kalaba is spoken, following a series of community meetings.

Goals: The goal of the project is to translate the New Testament and selected Old Testament portions into the Kalaba language. We aim to complete this translation by (date 8 years from the date of writing) as God enables us, following a proposed plan.

Cooperation and partnership: We seek to promote and facilitate the active participation of the whole Christian community and also the wider community, to the greatest extent possible. Draft versions of translations will be available to the churches and others, encouraging their use and inviting feedback.

The project has also formed a partnership with the Regional Bible Translation Organisation, and representatives of the KLTP have signed a memorandum of agreement to confirm this.

Governance: The project is registered with (give details, for example, the Corporate Affairs Commission) as a non-governmental, non-profit making organisation. The body responsible for the administration of the project is the Kalaba Language and Translation Committee, consisting of Chairman, Vice-chairman, Secretary, Treasurer, and 3 members. The committee members were elected at a community meeting in date, and will serve for a three-year term. See the more detailed statement on the roles and responsibilities of the Committee.

Project Coordinator: Mr A will serve as the Coordinator for the project. Mr A has completed training for this role and holds a degree in Bible translation. He will be responsible for guiding the selection, training, and supervision of the translators and other team members and will be the main liaison with the Technical Director of the Regional Bible Translation Organisation. He will report regularly to the chairman of the Kalaba Language and Translation Project Committee.

Translation team: Five speakers of Kalaba (list names) have been appointed to serve as translators. In addition, up to twenty speakers of the language will be appointed as reviewers. These will include representatives of all the church denominations in the area, and of all the dialect areas.

The members of the translation team have each signed a statement of commitment to service to the translation project and have agreed to the conditions of service prepared by the Kalaba Language and Translation Committee.

Finances: The committee is committed to raise funding to meet the budgeted expenses of the project, to keep assets in good order, and to present a yearly account of both income and expenditure to an annual general meeting in October each year, at which time the budget for the following year will also be reviewed. Mr XX will serve as Treasurer and will be responsible for keeping accounts and presenting reports. The Project Coordinator and the listed translators will serve full-time, and will receive an agreed salary. Others will serve on a volunteer basis.

A copy of the budget is available on request.

---

[2] Choose a title that will be clear and understandable to the receptor community, whether "Project Brief" or "Vision Statement" or "Memorandum of Understanding."

Writing of the language: The translation will use the orthography (spelling system) developed over the last two years and officially recognised by the National Language Centre, also by Educational Authorities in the Kalaba area.

Variations of the language: The primary dialect used for the translation will be Bakala. After careful research, this dialect has been chosen as being the form of the language that is most widely used and understood. Other dialects will also be considered with the goal that the translation will use forms of the language that are widely understood. In the dictionary that is being prepared, variant forms in all dialects will be recorded.

Audience of the translation: Our aim and desire is that the translation will communicate clearly to the majority of Kalaba speakers, including those of other backgrounds as well as Christians. Starting from early in the translation process, and as the translation progresses, draft editions of translated selections and whole Bible books will be produced and circulated, inviting feedback. In this way, all speakers of the language will have opportunity to give suggestions for the improvement of the translation. Suggestions will be processed by the translation team and consultant with the goal that the translation will be as accurate, clear, and natural as possible.

Literacy: The Committee is cooperating with local educational authorities concerning the introduction of classes for teaching reading and writing of the language in schools. There are also plans to work with churches and other community groups to provide opportunities for adults and young people to learn to read and write in the language.

Media: The translation will be published in printed form and in various audio formats. The Jesus Film will also be prepared in the language.

Affiliation and partnership: We acknowledge the Memorandum of Understanding signed with the Regional Bible Translation Organisation and are committed to do our part as described in that document. This includes submitting quarterly reports, due on the following dates: December 31, March 31, June 30, and September 30. Members of the Kalaba translation team will participate in courses and workshops offered from time to time by the regional organisation, as relevant for the project.

The Kalaba Project is also a member of the Regional Bible Translation Fellowship, which includes projects in this area in which Scripture translation is in progress.

Commitment: We, the undersigned, representing the churches and community of the Kalaba language area, confirm our commitment to work together to complete these goals, under the direction and enabling of God. We ask all partners to pray with us that these goals may be completed in a way that glorifies God.

Affirmed this day (*date*) by the Kalaba Language and Translation Committee, comprising representatives of participating churches and organisations...

Here follows a list of names with a space for signatures – an occasion for formal signing is recommended, wherever possible, in order to promote good understanding, unity, and commitment among all those involved.

43.4 A detailed statement for the translation team

It may also be helpful to prepare a separate document or template, which is intended for the translators and other members of the team actively involved in the translation task. This may overlap to some extent with the translation brief but is addressed specifically to the translators. This records agreement on issues on which translators need to coordinate, such as formatting, consistent use of spelling of names, and consistent use of agreed key terms. It may also record agreement on the responsibilities of different members of the team (including which books are assigned to each translator to draft) and projected time goals. This document may develop as the project proceeds and as more decisions are made and need to be recorded and shared.

Early agreement will save much later editing work to achieve consistency. Here are some issues that need to be considered:

> **Issues to be agreed, for the guidance of the translators, aiming to achieve consistency**
>
> **Translation Principles (summarising information already agreed in the translation brief)**
>
> 1. What style of translation are we aiming for?
> 2. Who do we think of as the primary audience?
> 3. Which source language version will be our primary source text? What other versions will be used for reference?
> 4. Will the translation be produced in printed form or in audio form? Or both print and audio?
> 5. Will all books be published in draft form as they become ready?
>
> **Text and Exegesis**
>
> 6. Which text do we follow when there are textual alternatives?
> 7. Which source language version is the usual model for formatting? (This may apply to following section divisions, paragraphing, indentations, and use of quotation marks.)
> 8. Which exegetical resources do we use? For example, *UBS Translator's Handbooks*, *Translator's Notes*.
>
> **Cross-cultural issues**
>
> 9. What are the guidelines for translating measurements, weights, money amounts? Do we usually follow a specific English or other language of wider communication version (while recognising that this will depend on the context)?
>
> **Language and writing**
>
> 10. Where there are different dialect alternatives, which dialect is to be used?
> 11. What are the guidelines for spelling names? For example, places, Bible characters? How can we make sure that team members are being consistent with each other in spelling names?
> 12. Can borrowed words ever be used? Under what circumstances?
> 13. Guidelines for use of punctuation marks (such as hyphens, colons, semicolons, brackets, commas, quotation marks).

Supplementary helps

14. Those drafting translations should include (a) a book introduction for the book, (b) section headings, (c) notes on pictures/illustrations needed, and (d) draft footnotes. These supplementary helps will be reviewed during the team check and discussed with the consultant.
15. A glossary will be included at the back of the volume. Those drafting translations should mark words to be included in the glossary.

Other issues will come up as the translation progresses. When new decisions are made, these can be added to this summary statement. If the translators working on different books follow agreed guidelines on these issues, this will save a lot of editing work in the later stages of the project.

43.5 Statement on agreed Bible translation principles and procedures

The statement of the Forum of Bible Agencies International on "Basic Principles and Procedures for Bible Translation" can be viewed at https://forum-intl.org/resources/translation-standards/. This statement was developed cooperatively by the major international Bible translation agencies worldwide and is widely accepted.

In many situations, it may be sufficient to provide the link to this statement in the general project brief, stating that the translators are following these recommended principles and procedures.

In some situations, however, it may be helpful to have a specific statement of agreement on translation principles and procedures. For example, where concerns have been expressed on the translation of certain key biblical terms, a commitment to follow what has been agreed can be included in the statement. An alternative to having a separate statement would be to include a note on specific, relevant points, in the general project brief.

The sample statement below is based on the statement of the Forum of Bible Agencies International on "Basic Principles and Procedures for Bible Translation" referred to above. It is offered as a possible base for adaptation to meet the needs of a specific situation, in situations where a statement is requested.

Sample
Statement of Translation Principles and Procedures

Partners in the Kalaba Language and Translation Project have agreed that the following translation principles and procedures will be followed:

Faithfulness in translation: The goal of the project is to translate the Scriptures accurately, without loss, change, distortion or embellishment of the meaning of the original text. Accuracy in Bible translation is the faithful communication, as exactly as possible, of the meaning of the original text, as determined using sound principles of exegesis.

Original source texts: The translation of books of the Old Testament will be based on the Masoretic Hebrew text. For the New Testament, translations will follow the UBS 5th edition of the Greek New Testament (Nestle-Aland 28th edition), being the version followed by most major versions in English and other languages of wider communication.

Intermediary source texts and reference versions: Reliable Bible translations in other languages will be referred to as intermediary source texts. It is agreed that the primary English source text will be the *NIV*. Translators will also refer to the *ESV*, *NET*, *GNT*, and *NLT*, also to regional language translations and to reliable commentaries and lexicons.

Additional supplementary material: Book introductions, footnotes, glossary, illustrations, and maps will be included as necessary to provide essential background information that is needed to help the readers of the Scriptures understand the historical biblical context. These supplementary materials will be checked with a translation consultant along with the translated text.

Translation style: The translators will aim to communicate the message of the biblical author in a way that speakers of the language can readily understand. The emotions and attitudes, the flavour and impact of the original will be communicated in forms consistent with normal usage in the receptor language.

The translators will also aim to preserve the variety of the original. The literary forms employed in the original text, such as poetry, prophecy, narrative, and exhortation, will be represented by corresponding forms with similar communicative functions in the receptor language. The verbal beauty, impact, and implicatures of the original will be retained to the greatest extent possible.

Key biblical terms: The meaning of key biblical terms (for example, "prophet," "priest," "temple," "synagogue," "Christ," "Son of God," "kingdom of God") will be studied carefully and every effort will be made to identify terms in the language that express the true meaning accurately. These terms will be discussed and tested widely to ensure agreement and consistent use of the terms.

Historical accuracy: The translators are committed to represent faithfully the original historical and cultural context in a way that will be meaningful to the receptor audience. Historical facts and events will be expressed without distortion.

Freedom from personal bias: The translators are committed to make every effort to ensure that no political, ideological, social, cultural, or theological agenda can distort the translation.

The following translation procedures will be followed:

Translation procedure: The project will follow the ten-step procedure for translation as described in the document, "Ten Translation Steps." This includes (a) careful study of the source text, (b) drafting, keeping both written and audio production in mind, and (c) keyboarding by a translator or team member trained in the use of the appropriate software.

Checking and reviewing of the translation: The process also includes checking of the whole translation with a qualified translation consultant who will be able to help verify the accuracy to the original source text.

Translation drafts will be shared extensively with representative members of the community of speakers of the receptor language, to give plenty of opportunity to gather feedback for the translation team. The aim is to find out whether the translation communicates accurately, clearly, and naturally, keeping in mind the sensitivities and experience of the receptor audience. Different methods of testing will be used.

Final approval: Before publication of the translation, appointed representatives of the participating churches and organisations will meet to read and listen to freely chosen portions of the translation and give their final approval for publication in both printed and audio forms.

Additional resources on "Preparing a Translation Brief"

BT4 online materials

43_Preparing_a_translation_brief.pptx
43_Translation_procedure_10_steps.pptx
43_Ten_translation_steps.pdf

Websites

Forum of Bible Agencies International statement: "Basic principles and procedures for Bible translation." See https://forum-intl.org/resources/translation-standards/.
Skopos theory. See https://en.wikipedia.org/wiki/Skopos_theory.

For further reading

Nida, Eugene A. 1982. Establishing translation principles and procedures. *The Bible Translator* 33(2):208–213. http://www.ubs-translations.org/tbt/1982/02/TBT198202.html?num=208&x=0&y=0&num1=.
Nord, Christiane. 1997. *Translating as a purposeful activity: Functionalist approaches explained.* Translation Theories Explored 1. Manchester: St. Jerome Publishing. Routledge edition 2015. Second edition 2018.
Vermeer, Hans Josef. 2000. Skopos and commission in translation action. In Lawrence Venuti (ed.), *The Translation Studies Reader*, 221–232. London & New York: Routledge.

Chapter 44

Planning and Organising a Translation Project – Discussion Topics

> The topics suggested below are for discussion by the Language and Translation Committee and the Project Coordinator for the project concerned. The outcome of these discussions will contribute to the development of the translation brief or memorandum of understanding.

These topics can also be discussed usefully in the context of a training course or workshop for translators. The points are intended to stimulate understanding, creative thinking, and interaction, sharing ideas and thinking through how to apply them to the translation projects involved. Select discussion topics that seem most relevant for the projects represented.

In situations when prospective translators from several projects are together, participants can be invited to speak about the project in their own languages – sharing what has already been done, what they know they still need to do, and any challenges or problems they face. Participants in the discussion will learn from each other, and from more experienced personnel who are also involved in the discussion.

Course participants can also be asked to write notes on selected topics, with application to the project in which they are involved. They are encouraged to share these thoughts with their consultant or mentor for further interaction.

For reference: See the booklet *Planning a Bible Translation Project* (filename 42_Planning_a_Bible_ translation_project-Booklet.pdf). This can be viewed in **BT4 Online Materials**.

Discussion 1: What are the reasons that a translation project is being planned for this language?

What is the intended outcome of the project, the outcome that is hoped for?

Who is the main audience for whom the translation is being prepared? Who will use the translation? Is the translation for adults or children? For educated people or uneducated? For church goers or non-church goers?

Discussion 2: Who will be the partners in the project?

Will all local churches participate? How can we encourage all churches to participate? Are there other local organisations who can be invited to participate?

Will the project relate to any regional, national, or international Bible translation organisations?

Can the project cooperate with education authorities on the development of the language and on literacy training activities? Who will be responsible for exploring this possibility?

Discussion 3: Who will be responsible for organising and leading the translation project?

How can a Project Committee be formed? How will the members of the committee be chosen and appointed? What are the responsibilities of the committee?

How can a Translation Project Brief be prepared, recording the agreed goals of the project and the commitments of those involved? (See chapter 43.)

Who will report on the progress of the project and distribute reports to partners?

Discussion 4: What further preparatory work needs to be done?

For example, (1) development of a writing system, if this is not already in place, and development of literacy materials, and (2) initial training of translators and other team members.

Discussion 5: Translation is teamwork. Who will be the members of the team?

How many translators will be needed? What qualifications do Bible translators need to have?

How can translators be selected and trained? What other full-time team members are needed in addition to translators?

What sort of remuneration should members of the team receive to enable them to work full time on the translation?

Discussion 6: Financing a translation project

(Refer to the booklet *Planning a Bible Translation Project* for a list of expenses that may be involved.)

- What will be the expenses of the project?
- Who is responsible for raising finances for the project?
- What opportunities are there for raising funds locally?
- What possibilities are there for other financial help?

Discussion 7: Translation goals

List all the publications that you would like to see completed in your project eventually. Will publications be in print, audio, or both?

What do you plan as the first Scripture publication for the project? Consider (a) any Scripture publications already available in the language and (b) any planned lectionary reading system used by churches in the area.

Narrative passages from the Gospels or from the Old Testament are often most suitable for the first Scripture translation work.

Discussion 8: Scripture publication

Who will be responsible for publishing draft editions and the first publications? Where possible, it is good for Scripture to be published within the country, with a national copyright or ISBN (= International Standard Book Number).

Looking ahead, what about publishing a whole New Testament or a whole Bible?

Discussion 9: What must be done to encourage the use of the translated Scriptures?

How can we encourage and help pastors, evangelists, and other Christian leaders to set an example by using the translated Scriptures?

What other books can be published to encourage the use of the Scriptures? For example, Scripture selections for use in evangelism or teaching, easy-to-read Scripture portions for new readers, and helps for Bible study groups.

How can we develop a system for arranging the revision, printing, and publication of further editions when copies of the first edition have been sold out?

How can we develop an efficient system for distributing the books and for collecting the money from sales? The money from sales must be properly accounted for so that it is available for further reprints.

Discussion 10: What plans are there for teaching speakers of the language to read in their language?

How could the teaching of reading in the language be introduced in the local educational system? Can churches organise literacy classes for their members? Consider the needs of both (1) those who can read in another language but have not yet learned to read and write in their own first language, and (2) those who are not yet able to read in any language.

Appendix: The Cultural and Geographical Background of the Bible

Bible translators are attempting to communicate to readers and hearers of today messages that were given two thousand or more years ago to a very different audience, in a very different living situation. It is important for translators to have a good knowledge of the cultures and living situations of those who received the original Scripture texts, covering the period from the time of Abraham to New Testament times. This includes geographical conditions, customs, animal life, plants, and other items that are mentioned in the Bible, but which may be unfamiliar to many who are reading the Bible today.

See resources in Paratext to help translators access the cultural and geographical knowledge that they need. This information can be easily accessed through jump links from the "Source Language Text" view and "Enhanced Resources" in Paratext.

The following materials are also available to view to help translators acquire this Bible background knowledge that they need:

A. *Fauna and Flora of the Bible*. 1980. Second edition. Prepared in cooperation with the Committee on Translations of the United Bible Societies. Helps for Translators. New York: United Bible Societies. Available for viewing in *Translator's Workplace*.

B. "The Story of the Grapevine – according to the Bible" – "A series of 6 PowerPoint presentations on the grapevine and its products by Anne Garber Kompaore," comprises:

1. The story of the grapevine and its fruit
2. Planting and growing the grape vine
3. Grape harvest and winepress
4. The fruit of the vine
5. Drinking wine
6. Summary, conclusion, and bibliography

These can be viewed or downloaded at the following website: https://map.bloomfire.com/posts/1431549-the-story-of-the-grapevine-according-to-the-bible/.

C. "Bible_background_survey-Prof_Don_Fairbairn.pptx" – A presentation prepared by Professor Don Fairbairn, formerly on the staff of Erskine Theological Seminary, now teaching at Gordon-Conwell Theological Seminary. His permission to make this material available is much appreciated. Available to view on the **BT4 online materials** website.

D. "Bible Backgrounds Sample Videos" – Available at the following site: https://www.youtube.com/channel/UChHCmkrvI5CCdYii5SWBuXA/. These are also accessible from SIL International Media Services at https://www.internationalmediaservices.org/bible-backgrounds/. These sites include videos on the following topics:

- Agriculture Part 1
- Agriculture Part 2
- Fishing
- Writing scrolls and instruments
- Water sources
- Eating customs
- Burial and mourning customs
- The temple in Jerusalem

E. A 2-DVD set, "Bible Lands as Classroom," describes the historical, cultural, and geographical context of the Bible. This is available for purchase from the United Bible Societies. For further details see https://thebibletranslator.org/product/bible-lands-as-classroom-2-dvd-set/.

F. "Photo companion to the Bible" – "More than 10,000 images illustrating Matthew, Mark, Luke, and John with modern and historic photographs of ancient sites, museum artifacts, and cultural scenes." Available for purchase from the following site: https://www.bibleplaces.com/gospels/.

References

Barnwell, Katharine. 1991. *Manuel de traduction biblique. Cours d'introduction aux principes de traduction*. Epinay-sur-Seine: SIL International. Adaptation de la 3éme édition anglaise du manuel *Bible Translation*, destiné aux traducteurs en langue maternelle. Available to view in *Translator's Workplace*.

Beekman, John, and John Callow. 1974. *Translating the Word of God: With Scripture and topical indexes*. Grand Rapids: Zondervan. Also accessible *on Translator's Workplace*.

Carson, D. A. 1987. The limits of dynamic equivalence in Bible translation. *Notes on Translation* 121:1–15.

Debrunner, Hans. 1967. *A history of Christianity in Ghana*. Accra: Waterville Publishing House.

Fox, David G. 1959. How intelligible is a literal translation? *The Bible Translator* 10(4):174–176. http://www.ubs-translations.org/tbt/1984/02/TBT198402.html.

Nida, Eugene A., and Charles R. Taber. 1969. *The theory and practice of translation*. Leiden: E. J. Brill, for the United Bible Societies. Originally published in the series, Helps for Translators 8. Reprinted 1974 and 1982. Fourth impression 2003.

Nord, Christiane. (1997) 2018. *Translating as a purposeful activity: Functionalist approaches explained*. Translation Theories Explored 1. Manchester: St. Jerome Publishing. Routledge edition 2015. Second edition 2018.

Noss, Philip A., and Charles S. Houser, eds. 2019. *A guide to Bible translation: People, languages and topics*. Swindon, England: United Bible Societies.

SIL International. 2019. *Translator's Workplace* (TW) collection. Access online at https://www.sil.org/resources/publications/tw. (*Translator's Workplace* [TW] is an extensive library of reference materials selected for the work of Bible translation. This extraordinary collection has been designed to meet the varying needs of translators worldwide and includes Bibles, Greek and Hebrew texts, dictionaries, commentaries, translation handbooks, articles, and other reference materials. Notable publishers have graciously permitted the use of resources within the TW collection to be distributed to those specifically assigned the work of Bible translation. *Translator's Workplace* is published by SIL International on Faithlife Corporation's Logos Bible Software platform. A license is required to download TW. See https://www.sil.org/ resources/publications/tw and read the FAQs for more information on content and licensing.)

Wendland, Ernst R. 2004. *Translating the literature of Scripture: A literary-rhetorical approach to Bible translation*. Publications in Translation and Textlinguistics 1. Dallas: SIL International.
Wendland, Ernst R. 2013. *Orality and the Scriptures: Composition, translation, and transmission*. Publications in Translation and Textlinguistics 6. Dallas: SIL International.

Dr Katharine "Katy" Barnwell has been involved in Bible translation since 1963, initially as a facilitator for the Mbembe translation project in Nigeria, then more widely involved as an International Translation Consultant, focusing on training other translation consultants. From 1989–1999 she was International Translation Coordinator for SIL International®, and then Director of Training and Consulting for Seed Company, developing the *Luke Partnership* program in cooperation with the Jesus Film Project®. She currently serves as a Senior Translation Consultant.

Katy completed her PhD (*A grammatical description of Mbembe: A Cross-River language*) at the School of Oriental and African Studies, University of London, in 1969 and is the author of many books, textbooks, and papers in the field of Bible translation.

Selected publications

- *Introduction to Semantics and Translation with Special Reference to Bible Translation.* 1980. Second edition. High Wycombe, UK: Summer Institute of Linguistics.
- *A Handbook for Translation Consultants.* 2002. Dallas, TX: International Translation Department, SIL International.
- *Linguistics and New Testament Interpretation: Essays on Discourse Analysis,* edited by David Alan Black, Katharine Barnwell, and Stephen Levinsohn. 1992. Nashville, TN: Broadman.

Further publications

- www.sil.org/biography/katharine-barnwell

CPSIA information can be obtained
at www.ICGtesting.com
Printed in the USA
BVHW021619110123
656011BV00007B/65

9 781556 714078